How to Meditate on the Stages of the Path

How to Meditate on the Stages of the Path

A GUIDE TO THE LAMRIM

by Kathleen McDonald
(Sangye Khadro)

Wisdom

Wisdom Publications
132 Perry Street
New York, NY 10014 USA
wisdom.org

Library of Congress Cataloging-in-Publication Data
Names: McDonald, Kathleen, 1952– author.
Title: How to meditate on the stages of the path: a guide to the Lamrim /
    by Kathleen McDonald (Sangye Khadro).
Description: First edition. | New York: Wisdom Publications, 2024. | Includes index.
Identifiers: LCCN 2024008414 (print) | LCCN 2024008415 (ebook) |
    ISBN 9781614298939 (paperback) | ISBN 9781614299066 (ebook)
Subjects: LCSH: Meditation—Buddhism. | Lam-rim. | Enlightenment (Buddhism) |
    Spiritual life—Buddhism.
Classification: LCC BQ5612 .M336 2024 (print) | LCC BQ5612 (ebook) |
    DDC 294.3/4435—dc23/eng/20240511
LC record available at https://lccn.loc.gov/2024008414
LC ebook record available at https://lccn.loc.gov/2024008415

ISBN 978-1-61429-893-9   ebook ISBN 978-1-61429-906-6

28 27 26 25 24
5 4 3 2 1

Buddha image on page 36 © Andy Weber. Cover art and design by Phil Pascuzzo. Interior
design by Gopa & Ted2, Inc.

Printed in Canada.

Please visit fscus.org.

Contents

Preface

MORE THAN 2,500 years ago, a young man named Siddhartha sat down under a tree in northern India and began to meditate. Although born into a wealthy royal family, he came to recognize that life's pleasures were fleeting and unreliable and that the world was full of painful experiences—sickness, aging, death, disappointment, and grief. He decided to leave home and meditate in the forest, seeking a state beyond suffering and confusion. After six years of intense striving, he was in the final phase of his spiritual journey. He had learned from spiritual teachers, fellow meditators, and his own trials and errors, and was now determined to succeed. That night, sitting beneath what came to be known as the bodhi tree, with the full moon shining upon him, he at last reached his goal and became a buddha, one whom we know as Buddha Shakyamuni.

What exactly is the state he attained, variously called enlightenment, awakening, or buddhahood? You pretty much have to be there yourself to really understand it. But simply speaking, enlightenment means being free forever from every type of afflictive experience; thus, buddhas have no suffering, physical or mental. On top of that, they have perfected every positive, beneficial quality such as love, compassion, ethical conduct, patience, and wisdom, and in turn they continuously experience only joy and tranquility. Enlightenment doesn't happen all at once in a flash, but is the culmination of a long process of gradual transformation that occurs mainly due to seeing things as they really are, which is quite different from the way we normally see them.

Many beings have already attained buddhahood, and all of us have the potential—known as buddha nature—to attain it as well. It's not easy or quick, but if we are willing to begin learning and practicing now, we can take our first steps toward enlightenment in this lifetime.

Some might think enlightenment sounds boring, as if buddhas just sit around all day feeling peaceful and blissful. That's a misunderstanding. Although their minds are always peaceful, they are continuously aware of others and ready to assist them. Long before reaching enlightenment, they cultivated love and compassion for every living being in the universe and committed themselves to freeing everyone from suffering and helping them attain genuine happiness. With that motivation, they practiced the path to enlightenment over many lifetimes. The path itself involves benefiting others, as we will see later, and once they reach enlightenment, buddhas continue working for others every minute and second. There's no time to be bored! They are totally delighted to help others until everyone else has attained enlightenment as well, no matter how long it takes.

So, enlightenment is possible for each and every one of us. It's actually the best thing we can do for ourselves, because it means being free from all misery, pain, depression, dissatisfaction, and negative emotions, and abiding forever in peace, joy, love, and compassion. What could be more wonderful than that? It's also the best thing we can do for others because once we reach that state, we have unlimited knowledge and ability to help all other beings according to their needs and wishes.

How do we become a buddha? Is it enough to just sit like Buddha Shakyamuni with our legs crossed, eyes closed, smiling peacefully, and hope that our mind will somehow transform into enlightened mind? No. Becoming enlightened is the result of many causes and conditions and something that is cultivated over a long period of time.

The Buddha spent numerous lifetimes creating those causes before his birth as Siddhartha. Fortunately for us, after attaining enlightenment, he spent the remaining forty-five years of his life teaching, explaining the path to enlightenment and guiding his followers. His teachings have been passed down continuously since then, from realized masters to their disciples, and remain a living tradition to this day.

Some of those past masters compiled the teachings into a step-by-step guide that explains what we need to do to get from our present unenlightened state all the way to the enlightened state of a buddha. That is what is known as *lamrim* in Tibetan—the gradual path, or stages of the path, to enlightenment, where *lam* means path and *rim* means stages. The lamrim consists of a series of topics we engage in by way of three steps: First, we listen to explanations by qualified teachers and study reliable books. Second, we think about what we have learned to gain a more accurate understanding. Third, we meditate on the understanding we attained in the first two steps to make ourselves thoroughly familiar with it and bring about a transformation of our mind and way of living. More details about these three steps will be given later.

Numerous books on lamrim, translated from Tibetan, are available in English—a list of recommended titles can be found at the end of this book. There are also lamrim courses offered by Tibetan Buddhist centers around the world, as well as online. The focus of this book is, as the title indicates, how to meditate on the lamrim. It contains a brief introduction to each topic, then presents suggested ways of meditating on them. So if you are new to lamrim, you will need to supplement the material provided here with other resources. If you are new to meditation, I suggest that you start with my first book, *How to Meditate,* or another basic meditation guide, so that you have the background training that is needed to engage in these practices.

OVERVIEW OF THIS BOOK

Part 1 is an introductory section that provides such information as a brief history of the lamrim, meditation basics, how to use the book, how to set up a session of lamrim meditation, and so on. Part 2 contains several preliminary practices that can be done prior to meditation on the lamrim to make your meditation session more effective. Parts 3, 4, 5, and 6 contain the actual lamrim meditations, arranged according to the level of a practitioner's spiritual capacity. An appendix provides several additional meditations for more advanced students and other supplementary material. At the end of the book you will find a glossary of Buddhist terms and a list of suggested further resources.

As mentioned earlier, lamrim topics are meant to be thought about and meditated upon rather than simply read about, and I have tried my best to explain how to do that. However, if you are not yet ready to engage with the material in this book at that level, it's fine to read through it, but try to do so in a leisurely and reflective way, pausing to contemplate as many of the points as possible. I think you will find that more meaningful and satisfying than rushing through the book so you can move on to the next one on your list. It's my heartfelt wish that you will gain as much benefit as I have from learning about these topics and allowing them to sink deeply within you.

ACKNOWLEDGMENTS

I wish to express my heartfelt appreciation to the precious teachers from whom I have learned the lamrim and other aspects of Buddhist philosophy and practice. I first encountered the lamrim in 1973 while attending classes at the Library of Tibetan Works and Archives in Dharamsala, India, taught by my first teacher, Geshe Ngawang Dhargyey. I continued learning lamrim while staying at Kopan Monastery in Nepal from 1974–77. During that time, I was fortunate to attend four consecutive month-long lamrim courses taught by Lama Thubten Yeshe and Lama Zopa Rinpoche and engaged in several group meditation retreats that deepened my understanding of the path to enlightenment. Since then I have attended lamrim teachings offered by other masters, including the Dalai Lama, Ribur Rinpoche, and Khensur Jampa Tegchok. I have done several personal lamrim retreats and, on the advice of my teachers, have also taught courses on it—an excellent way to expand and deepen one's own understanding.

I also wish to thank my friend Tiziana Losa, from whom the idea of the book initially arose. We were classmates in the second FPMT (Foundation for the Preservation of the Mahayana Tradition) Masters Program held at Istituto Lama Tzong Khapa in Italy from 2008 to 2013. Throughout the first year of the program, I led weekly lamrim meditations for the other students. Tiziana was the Italian interpreter for those sessions, and she later used a translation of my notes to lead lamrim meditations for Italian students in other times and venues. Several years ago, she requested that I edit the notes and develop them into a book—as there was no such book in Italian, she felt it would be very beneficial for Italian-speaking students. While working on the book—polishing the English, making changes and additions—it occurred to me that it might be useful for English-speaking students as well, so I approached Wisdom Publications, who replied that they would be happy to publish it. My first book, *How to Meditate*, continues to be popular (it's now in its ninth printing), and we thought that the present volume would be a sequel to that for those who wish to explore the Buddha's teachings in greater depth and learn how to meditate on them.

I am also very grateful to Ven. Thubten Lamsel and Tiziana Losa for proofreading the entire manuscript and offering valuable suggestions, and to Geshe Dadul Namgyal and Ven. Thubten Chodron for their comments and corrections to chapter 23, on the perfection of wisdom. Many thanks as well to Brianna Quick for her skillful editing, to Ben Gleason for ushering the manuscript from design to print, and to everyone else at Wisdom Publications who helped bring this book to its final edition.

PART 1

FIRST STEPS

These teachings offer the means to free oneself from delusion—a path that eventually leads to freedom from all suffering and to the bliss of enlightenment. The more one comes to understand the Dharma, or Buddhist teachings, the weaker will be the grip of pride, hatred, greed, and other negative emotions that cause so much suffering. Applying this understanding in daily life over a period of months and years will gradually transform the mind . . .

THE DALAI LAMA, *The Way to Freedom*

Introduction to the Lamrim

What Is the Lamrim?

LAMRIM, or stages of the path, is a genre of texts and teachings that developed in Tibet starting in the eleventh century. Somewhat like the way Google Maps instructs us on how to reach a certain destination, the lamrim lays out the main points of the Buddha's teachings in a step-by-step manner that shows us how to transform ourselves from an ordinary, unenlightened being into an enlightened being, a buddha. Buddhas are those who have overcome all disturbing, incorrect thoughts and emotions and have perfected all positive, virtuous qualities. They are free of problems and are able to help all other beings reach the same state. Mahayana Buddhism says that every living being has buddha nature—the potential to become a buddha—and the way to accomplish this is found in the lamrim.

The intended audience of traditional lamrim texts and teachings are people who already have a fairly good understanding of Buddhism and the path to enlightenment as well as a strong determination to follow this path. But those who are new to Buddhism can also benefit from studying and meditating on the lamrim. In addition to increasing our knowledge of Buddhist ideas and practice, lamrim meditations can help us develop more realistic and constructive ways of thinking that counteract attitudes harmful to ourselves and others, such as depression, hatred, and greed.

A few examples will help illustrate these benefits. For instance, one of the first meditations in the series is on the preciousness of human life. Here we contemplate the positive qualities and opportunities of our present life in order to generate enthusiasm to use it well and wisely, for the benefit of ourselves and others. This meditation is an excellent way to lift ourselves out of depression and despair.

The meditations on the breath, the nature of mind, and impermanence provide insight into the transitory nature of thoughts and emotions—how they come and go in our mind like clouds in the sky. This understanding is an effective antidote to any mental state that is disturbing and potentially harmful.

In the chapter on the origins of suffering in part 4, you will learn a number of antidotes to anger and attachment, or greed, that involve different ways of looking at people and objects that trigger those mental states. Additional tools for overcoming anger can be found in parts 5 and 6, within the meditations for developing bodhichitta and patience. You may not agree with every perspective or find every antidote in this book effective for your mind, but hopefully you will find at least a few that will help you adopt more positive ways of viewing yourself, others, and the world and its troubles.

The root cause of all disturbing emotions, according to Buddhism, is ignorance—not knowing how things really exist, but seeing them in a mistaken, hallucinated way. This starts with the way we see ourselves—thinking there's a real, solid, independent self or "I" existing somewhere inside of us, when in fact such a self does not exist. This topic, known as selflessness or emptiness, is one of the most difficult to comprehend but is also highly fascinating, challenging, and crucial— understanding it is the key to freedom from suffering and to enlightenment. Meditations on this topic are included in the last chapter of part 6, on the perfection of wisdom.

HOW DID THE LAMRIM DEVELOP?

The Buddha, who lived in India in the fifth and sixth centuries BCE, taught for forty-five years after he attained enlightenment. The collection of his teachings, known as sutras, is vast—the Tibetan canon comprises 108 hefty volumes. Among the Buddha's teachings is a group of sutras called the Perfection of Wisdom (Prajnaparamita) Sutras. Although their main subject matter is the cultivation of the wisdom that understands the true nature of reality, they also explain other aspects of the path—such as compassion and generosity—that a person needs to practice to attain enlightenment. These sutras are the main source of the teachings included in the lamrim.

Over the centuries after the Buddha passed away, as his teachings spread throughout Asia, they were studied, meditated on, and transmitted from accomplished teachers to their disciples. Many masters also composed commentaries to elucidate the difficult points in the sutras. One of these commentaries in particular, Maitreya's *Ornament for Clear Realization* (*Abhisamayalamkara*), occupies a special place in the development of the lamrim because it clarifies the "hidden meaning" of the Perfection of Wisdom Sutras: the stages and paths whereby a bodhisattva proceeds to enlightenment.

Buddhism was introduced in Tibet in the seventh century CE, mainly from India. Later, the Indian master Atisha (982–1054 CE)—a renowned scholar and practitioner—was invited to Tibet by a religious king who was concerned about the somewhat degenerate state of Buddhism in his country. Atisha traveled to Tibet when he was around sixty years of age and spent the remainder of his life there, teaching and composing texts. He wrote the first lamrim text, *A Lamp for the Path to Enlightenment* (*Bodhipathapradipa*), which distills the essence of the Buddhist scriptures into a practical, easily comprehensible guide to the path. Over the next millennium, other lamrim texts of varying lengths were composed by Tibetan masters, such as Lama Tsongkhapa and several of the Dalai Lamas (see the suggested further reading list at the end of this book to learn more).

Lamrim texts contain a series of topics to be learned, contemplated, and meditated on to bring about a gradual transformation of our mind from negative to positive, from confused to clear, from unenlightened to enlightened. Since the traditional lamrim texts were written in Tibet, where most people were exposed to Buddhist beliefs and practices from childhood, these texts assume a high level of familiarity with and acceptance of the Buddhist worldview, particularly that of Mahayana Buddhism. Right from the beginning they mention such topics as rebirth, karma, cyclic existence (with its different realms of sentient beings), the possibility of attaining nirvana and enlightenment, and so forth, as if these are common knowledge. Thus, they are quite different from basic Buddhist books written by contemporary authors or textbooks used in a Buddhism 101 class at your local college. If you are new to Buddhism and find topics like rebirth and karma challenging, it might be best to start with more basic books (you can find some on the suggested further reading list).

The Dalai Lama's recommendation is that newcomers to Buddhism should be taught the two truths and the four truths, as these topics form the foundation of Buddhist thought and practice. The topic of the *two truths* is complex and profound—entire volumes have been written about it.[1] Basically it means there are two levels of reality: the *conventional* or *relative*—our everyday experiences of people, places, activities, and our own self, body, and mind—and the *ultimate*—a deeper level of reality underlying the conventional. Usually known as *emptiness* or voidness, it means that things don't exist as they appear— they are not inherently or independently existent. Everything is "empty" of that way of existing. Failure to recognize this lies at the root of our suffering, so genuine freedom and enlightenment depend on identifying this false mode of existence and seeing things as they are. More will be said about emptiness later in the book, especially in the chapter on the perfection of wisdom in part 6.

The four truths (the *four noble truths*, or four truths of the aryas) are suffering, its causes, its cessation, and the path to that cessation. Explanations and meditations on these four are contained in part 4 of this book. The last two are somewhat difficult to fathom but the first two are easy to recognize—they happen to us many times each day.

If you are unfamiliar with the two truths, the four truths, and other basic Buddhist teachings, you're still welcome to try out the meditations in this book; there may be some you will immediately feel comfortable with, but others you might find difficult. Nevertheless, keep an open mind and investigate both the Buddhist ideas you find challenging as well as your own preconceptions and assumptions. The Buddha said that we should investigate his teachings the way a goldsmith checks gold to determine whether it's genuine or not. He also said that correct spiritual teachings or practices are those that bring benefit and happiness, while incorrect ones lead to harm and suffering. In this light, you can experiment with the practices and ideas to see if they are helpful or not; you do not have to believe or practice everything.

THREE LEVELS

Most of the material contained in the lamrim is divided into three sections. Some lamrim books refer to these as the three scopes—small scope, medium scope, and great scope—while others call them three levels—initial level, intermediate level, and advanced level. Here I will mainly use the latter system. These three levels contain practices meant for three types of practitioners with different levels of capacity.

1. The practices of the *initial level* are designed for those of initial capacity, who are concerned about avoiding unfortunate rebirths and obtaining fortunate ones in their future lives.

2. The practices of the *intermediate level* are for those of medium capacity, who recognize the faults of unenlightened existence—known as *samsara*, or cyclic existence—and understand there's no genuine, lasting happiness anywhere in samsara. They wish to attain liberation, or nirvana, and be free forever from samsaric rebirth.

3. The practices of the *advanced level* are for those of great capacity, who wish to help all beings become free of samsara with its myriad sufferings. Their goal is to become fully enlightened buddhas to be of benefit to all sentient beings.[2]

The lamrim is actually designed for the third type of person, those aspiring to attain enlightenment for the benefit of all other beings. However, that aspiration (known as *bodhichitta*, or "mind of enlightenment") can only be developed on the basis of the first two levels, the initial and intermediate. This means that if we wish to become a buddha, we must start by becoming concerned about our future lives and learn how to avoid unfortunate rebirths and obtain fortunate ones. One reason for this is that becoming a buddha usually takes numerous lifetimes; we therefore need to ensure we will have the proper conditions in future lives to continue following the path. We also need to know how to guide other beings away from unfortunate rebirths. Thus, we need to learn about and meditate on the topics included in the initial level.

On top of that, we need to recognize the faults of samsara and develop the determination to free ourselves from it. The reason for this is that to cultivate bodhichitta—the wish to free all sentient beings from every type of suffering—we must understand those sufferings and realize that samsara is a thoroughly disagreeable situation, like a prison. That realization will empower our compassion and loving-kindness and enable us to generate bodhichitta. Therefore, we need to learn and meditate on the topics included in the intermediate level.

Thus, only by learning and meditating on the topics in the first two levels will we be able to correctly engage in the topics of the third, the advanced level. However, this does not mean we cannot start learning and meditating on the advanced-level topics before we have accomplished those of the earlier levels. It simply means that we cannot skip the earlier topics, thinking we don't need them because we are aiming for buddhahood. The traditional approach is to study and meditate on the entire lamrim, right from the beginning. This is similar to studying a map before making a journey and continuing to rely on it while traveling.

THE ACTUAL TOPICS

The first topic in traditional lamrim texts is how to rely on a spiritual teacher. This is relevant for those who have gained a thorough understanding of the entire path to enlightenment and sincerely wish to follow it. Such people need to rely on the guidance of qualified spiritual teachers and relate to them in a healthy way. Since this book is geared more for those who are still learning about the path and investigating whether it's something they wish to follow, the meditations on this topic have been included in an appendix. Depending on your level of understanding and interest, you can practice those meditations from the beginning or leave them for a later time.

The second topic, precious human life, is usually presented as a foundation for all three levels—although some texts include it within the initial level. Realizing that our human birth provides the ideal situation for spiritual practice, but is also rare and difficult to acquire, inspires us to use it wisely by following a spiritual path. For the sake of convenience, this topic has been included in part 3, along with meditations for the initial level. An additional meditation, on the nature of mind, is also included at the beginning of part 3. This topic is not usually found in lamrim texts but is helpful for those coming newly to Buddhism from different backgrounds and with diverse worldviews.

Following the section on the precious human life you will find the practices, or meditations, included in each of the three levels, as follows.

1. Practices for Persons of Initial Capacity (Initial Level)
At this level of the path, we first need to become concerned about our
future lives in the sense of wanting to avoid unfortunate rebirths and
obtain fortunate ones. To generate this concern, we meditate on
- impermanence and death, to realize our life will definitely
  come to an end, and
- the sufferings of the three unfortunate realms, to become convinced that we must avoid being born in them.

Second, we need to learn *how* to avoid unfortunate rebirths and obtain
fortunate ones. The means for accomplishing this are
- taking refuge in the Three Jewels—the Buddha, Dharma, and
  Sangha—which provide the necessary guidance regarding our
  future lives, and
- learning about karma—specifically, how to refrain from nonvirtue and create virtue—since that is what actually determines
  our future rebirths.

2. Practices for Persons of Medium Capacity (Intermediate Level)
First, we develop the determination to be free of samsara, the cycle of
death and rebirth, by meditating on
- the general sufferings of samsara, and
- the sufferings of the upper realms (humans and gods).

Second, we learn the method to become free of samsara by meditating on
- the causes of samsara—karma and delusions (mental afflictions)—
  with the aim of eliminating these, and
- the three higher trainings—ethics, concentration, and wisdom,
  which are the means to eliminate the causes of samsara.

3. Practices for Persons of Great Capacity (Advanced Level)
- First, we contemplate the benefits of bodhichitta in order to
  become enthusiastic about developing that attitude.
- Second, we meditate on the actual methods for generating
  bodhichitta: the sevenfold cause-and-effect instruction and the
  method of equalizing and exchanging oneself for others.

- Third, we train in the six perfections of a bodhisattva—generosity, ethics, patience, joyous effort, concentration, and wisdom—the main causes for becoming a buddha.

THREE STEPS

As you can see, the lamrim contains a multitude of different topics. We are advised to approach these using a threefold process:

1. *Listen and learn.* It's best to learn the lamrim directly from qualified teachers, but we can also expand our knowledge and understanding by listening to online talks and reading books.
2. *Contemplate.* While listening to and reading about the explanations of each topic, we reflect on the ideas presented so that we may understand them better.
3. *Meditate.* Once we reach a firm understanding of a topic from listening and contemplating, we focus on it with single-pointed concentration for as long as possible so that the insight suffuses our mind, bringing about lasting transformation.

This process is carried out gradually over our life—or even multiple lives—and all three steps need to be repeated numerous times. The first time we *listen* to lamrim teachings or read a lamrim book, the understanding we gain will probably be superficial and sketchy. By continuing to listen, read, and study, our knowledge and comprehension will gradually become more complete, clear, and refined.

We also need to *contemplate* what we hear and read to attain a broader and deeper understanding. If we have doubts or questions, we can ask our teachers or more experienced students. Try to avoid getting stuck in your doubts like a car stuck in the mud, its wheels spinning but going nowhere.

As for the third step, one of my teachers, Khensur Jampa Tegchok, explained that in the context of this threefold process, *meditation* "refers to putting the mind on a subject that has been clearly ascertained through contemplation."[3] In other words, after spending some time working on the first two steps, we reach a correct, stable understanding of that topic and are ready to meditate on it with single-pointed concentration. He says that if our ability to concentrate is still limited, we do our best to keep our mind focused on the topic and bring it back when it wanders away.

The whole purpose of meditation is to transform our mind in a constructive way, and for this to happen, we need to become so thoroughly familiar with the lamrim topics that they become our natural way of thinking and living our life. By relying on this threefold process, our minds gradually change and we develop the realizations that constitute the path to enlightenment.

Meditating on the Lamrim

2

WHAT IS MEDITATION?

THE TIBETAN term for meditation is *gom*, meaning "to familiarize." The attitudes and behaviors we are most familiar with are the ones that will occur in our experience most easily and frequently. This is similar to the notion of neuroplasticity: that repeated experience changes and shapes the brain, creating new neural pathways. For example, if we develop the habit of getting angry at even small mishaps and expressing our anger verbally and physically, we will find ourselves getting angry and acting it out with increasing frequency and ease. On the other hand, cultivating concern for others and doing our best to avoid hurting or upsetting them will lead to an increase in those attitudes and ways of acting.

Buddhist meditation is practiced in order to familiarize our mind with virtuous, constructive thoughts and feelings because those are the source of genuine happiness and peace, both for ourselves and others; they are also the cause of all realizations, up to enlightenment. In addition, meditation is used to counteract and overcome negative states of mind, such as anger and greed, which are the source of all suffering and problems—both individual and collective. It should be easy to recognize that social and global troubles—war, terrorism, violent crime, substance abuse, injustice, corruption—arise from afflictive mental states. Learning to manage and overcome these in ourselves is an effective contribution we can make to others and society, as exemplified by a popular saying: "Be the change you want to see in the world."

There are different kinds of meditation found in Buddhism, some of which are used when we meditate on the lamrim. One way of dividing meditative practices is into *analytical* and *stabilizing*.

Analytical meditation

Also known as "checking meditation," this involves contemplating, or thinking about, a topic such as the preciousness of our human life, karma, impermanence, or the four truths, in order to have a deeper understanding of it. The ultimate purpose of analytical meditation is to develop special insight (Sanskrit: *vipashyana*; Pali: *vipassana*) into the actual way things exist: that they do not exist inherently, independently, from their own side. This is known as "emptiness of inherent existence" and is the ultimate nature of all things. There are other topics we must understand prior to realizing emptiness, and analytical meditation is used to gain insight into those as well.

How is analytical meditation done? Ideally, we would have listened to teachings on, read about, and studied the topic we plan to meditate on, so that we have a fairly good idea of the points we need to contemplate. During our meditation session, we can have a book (such as this one) or notes in front of us to remind us of those points in case we don't know them by heart. Then we go through the points one by one, bringing in what we have heard and read about each one, exploring any doubts we might have, and using reasons—rational thinking—to arrive at certainty about the topic. One way of doing this kind of meditation is to imagine we are explaining the topic to someone, in writing or conversation. Another technique is to imagine having an internal dialogue, asking ourselves questions such as "The Buddha said such and such; do I agree with that or not? If not, what are my reasons? Are those good, solid reasons or flimsy ones?" It is also helpful to bring to mind our own experiences or the experiences of others we have heard about to illustrate the various points of the topic.

The purpose of analytical meditation is to gain insight, or deeper understanding, of the lamrim topics. This might or might not happen in every session, so keep your mind free of rigid expectations and open to whatever occurs. Sometimes the mind will enthusiastically engage with the topic, but at other times you might notice resistance. In that case it could be helpful to explore the resistance: Why does my mind feel that way? What preconceptions are being challenged? This should be done gently and with compassion for yourself rather than trying to force your mind to accept something it isn't ready to.

Do your best to keep your mind focused on the various points of the topic to understand them better. Be content with whatever insights arise and avoid grasping at specific results. With time and regular practice, your understanding and insight will grow and deepen. It is also useful to be mindful of your meditation topic during your other daily activities and not completely forget it when you get up from your cushion. For example, you might meditate on karma in the morning and understand the importance of refraining from unwholesome behavior, but later at work your mind gets hijacked by anger or craving and you act unskillfully. This is not ideal! Of course, it takes time to change our mind and our behavior—we can't transform in one day or even one year. Still, we should try our best to allow our meditative insights to percolate through our daily actions.

Khensur Tegchok explained that in general, analytical meditation *is* meditation, but within the threefold process explained earlier, it is included in the second step, contemplation—that is, when we think about a topic to "decisively ascertain its meaning and how to practice it." In this scheme, he says the third step, meditation, "refers to putting the mind on a subject that has been clearly ascertained through contemplation. It is best to put the mind on the object single-pointedly, but that is not necessary."[4]

To illustrate the threefold process with an example, let's say you attend a course or retreat where you hear an explanation of the preciousness of human life; you also read about it in lamrim books. That is the first step in the process, listening and learning. During the course, the teacher or a senior student leads a guided analytical meditation on the preciousness of human life, explaining how to meditate on the various points and giving you time to contemplate each one. Later at home, you may try doing the meditation on your own. All these meditations constitute step two, contemplation. If, in any of your meditation sessions, you reach a clear understanding of what it means to have a precious human life and how very fortunate you are to have one, you should pause the thinking process and concentrate your mind single-pointedly on that insight as long as you can until it fades. That concentration is what actually constitutes the third step, meditation.

By practicing the three steps consistently over a period of months and years, we will gradually become so familiar with the topic that we need just a small amount of analysis to bring the insight to mind, and we can then focus on it single-pointedly. In other words, when we sit down to meditate, we may need to spend only a few minutes on the second step, contemplation or analysis, and can move quickly to the third step, meditation.

Based on Khensur Tegchok's explanation—and given that this book is intended for newcomers to lamrim meditation—the term *analytical meditation* is used here for the second step in the threefold process, *contemplation*. But there is a way to combine analytical meditation with stabilizing (single-pointed) meditation in one session; this will be explained below.

Stabilizing meditation

In general, stabilizing meditation is used to develop concentration and eventually to attain calm abiding (Sanskrit: *shamatha*). This is a special kind of concentration that enables one to remain focused on a chosen object for as long as one wishes, while experiencing physical and mental bliss and pliancy. Concentration and calm abiding are necessary for any real, lasting insight and mental transformation. By engaging in stabilizing meditation, we are training our mind to stay focused on a single object—the breath, an image of the Buddha, loving-kindness, and so on—without interruption. A simple way of practicing stabilizing meditation on the breath is found below, and additional instructions on this type of meditation will be given in part 6, under the perfection of concentration.

Analytical and stabilizing meditations are complementary and can be used together in one session. For example, when doing a meditation on death, we contemplate the different points of that topic—that death is definite, the time of death is uncertain, and so on. We bring to mind what we have heard and read about this topic as well as our own experiences and those of others. At a certain point we might get a feeling, like an *aha* moment, related to what we've been meditating on— for example, "I am definitely going to die!" or "Death could happen anytime!" When such an insight arises, we should stop thinking and focus our attention single-pointedly on this awareness for as long as possible—even a few seconds—in order to soak our mind in that experience. In other words, we switch from analytical to stabilizing meditation. When the feeling fades, we can either return to contemplating or conclude the session.

This method of combining the two kinds of meditation enables our insights to be more deeply integrated into our mind and way of being. The stronger our concentration, the deeper the insight will penetrate. We need to repeat this process again and again with anything we want to understand so that it transforms into actual experience. In his book, *Buddha's Brain*, neuropsychologist Rick Hanson explains a similar method of staying focused on a positive experience for five seconds or more to create positive explicit memories and improve our overall physical and mental health.[5]

Stabilizing meditations to train our concentration will also be more successful if some skillful analysis is used. For example, at the start of our meditation session we generate a positive motivation, which involves analytical thought. While meditating, obstacles such as irritation or craving might arise. If we are unable to let go of these, we can use analysis to understand the underlying problem and apply an antidote, then refocus our mind on our meditation object.

Another way to divide meditations is into the following two types:

1. *Meditation on an object to understand it.* This involves meditating on a topic such as precious human life, impermanence, or emptiness in order to gain a better understanding of it and to familiarize our mind with it.

2. *Meditation to transform our mind into the object.* With certain topics, such as compassion and loving-kindness, the aim is not simply to gain an intellectual understanding—"compassion means such and such; its causes are this and that." Instead, the aim is to *generate* those states of mind; to transform our mind so that it *experiences* compassion—wishing sentient beings to be free of their suffering—and loving-kindness—wishing them to be happy.

Another meditation technique frequently used in Tibetan Buddhism is visualization, which involves creating and focusing on images in our mind. For example, when doing preparatory practices before lamrim meditation we are advised to visualize figures such as the Buddha, our spiritual teachers, bodhisattvas, and so on, and request their inspiration so that the lamrim understandings will take root and grow in our mind.

We can also incorporate visualization in certain analytical meditations, such as those on loving-kindness or compassion. Our meditation will be more powerful if we imagine specific people and beings and contemplate how they wish to be happy and free from their suffering.

Further advice about meditation, how to deal with various problems that arise when we meditate, and other basic information can be found in my earlier book, *How to Meditate*.[6]

How to Conduct a Session of Lamrim Meditation

To be most effective, lamrim meditation is done within a practice session that includes visualization of the Buddha or other enlightened figures and recitation of prayers. This puts our mind in the most conducive state to gain the insights and experiences we need to transform ourselves and make progress on the path. The "Practice for Lamrim Meditation" on page 35 is one such practice; it includes the main *preparatory practices* for nurturing the positive potential of our mind. An explanation of these is found below on page 22. If you are short of time or prefer a simpler practice, you can visualize the Buddha—or another Buddha figure you feel affinity with, such as Tara or Chenrezig—in the space in front of you, spend a few minutes mentally taking refuge and generating a positive motivation, and then begin the meditation.

Before sitting down to meditate, make sure your meditation space is clean and tidy and that you will not be interrupted during your session (for example, turn your phone off or put it on airplane mode). Sit on your cushion or chair in the recommended posture, then take a few minutes to relax and settle your body and mind. You might want to do meditation on the breath (page 31) for several minutes to calm your mind.

Then begin the practice for lamrim meditation, which starts with generating a positive motivation. Tibetan lamas strongly emphasize the importance of having a good motivation for spiritual practice because it is one of the chief factors determining the outcome of anything we do. We can see this in our everyday experience; for example, giving a donation or helping someone in need can turn out badly if we have a hidden agenda, such as expecting something in return. When it comes to Buddhist practice such as meditation, it is particularly crucial that our motivation is in line with the Dharma. That means we should at least aim for favorable future lives rather than pleasure, fame, and material gain in this life.

The ideal motivation for lamrim practice is bodhichitta, the altruistic intention to become fully enlightened for the benefit of all beings. Having such a motivation may be difficult, however, if you are still in the process of learning and familiarizing yourself with the lamrim. You might not be convinced that there is such a thing as enlightenment or that you are capable of attaining it. In that case, try at least to have a motivation that considers the well-being of others, for example, "I am doing this meditation in order to work on myself so I can be more helpful to other people and beings, as much as possible." That is just a suggestion; feel free to compose your own motivation using words and phrases that come from your heart, expressing your most sincere altruistic wishes.

That is followed by visualizing the Buddha and reciting several verses: taking refuge, the four immeasurables, the seven limbs, the mandala offering, the request prayer, and the mantra of the Buddha. These are optional, depending on your understanding of and inclination for such practices. After reciting the Buddha's mantra, begin the meditation on the lamrim topic of your choice using the instructions above on how to do analytical meditation.

When it comes to choosing a topic, one recommended way is to meditate on one lamrim topic per session, starting with the first and working your way through them in order. There are over sixty meditations included in this book, so doing one session per day will take you around two months to meditate on all of them. After completing one round, you then start again with the first topic.

Another way is to meditate on the same topic for a few days (or more) in a row, until you feel you have gained a good, solid understanding of it. Then move on to the next topic and spend as much time as needed on that one. It's also a good idea to occasionally do a retreat, for a weekend or longer, with several sessions of lamrim meditation each day. If you have a spiritual teacher, you can request that he or she provide you with personal advice on how to meditate on the lamrim topics.

It is not necessary to always meditate on the topics in the prescribed order. If some topics are too difficult to understand or relate to, you can skip over them and focus on those you do find helpful and relevant. You can also choose topics that meet your needs at specific times. For example, the meditations on impermanence and death could be useful at a time when you are facing the death of a loved one; those on love, compassion, or patience might be just what you need when going through relationship problems. Nevertheless, it's beneficial to gradually acquire an understanding of the entire range of topics and how they fit together, even if at first you may not understand their meaning or relevance.

As for the length of your sessions, that depends on your ability to stay focused, your daily routine, and so on. Try to spend at least ten minutes meditating on your chosen lamrim topic, but feel free to meditate longer. Some of the meditations contain many points, but you are not obliged to meditate on all of them in one session, especially a short one. Instead, you can divide the points—meditating on some of them in one session and continuing where you left off in the following session.

When you finish the lamrim meditation, conclude your session by dissolving the image of the Buddha and dedicating the merit, as explained on page 26. Spend a few moments allowing whatever insights and positive feelings you experienced during the meditation to absorb deeply into you before getting up to begin your next activity. Reading "The Three Principal Aspects of the Path" is optional, depending on how much time you have, but don't skip the dissolution of the Buddha and the dedication of merit—those are valuable.

THERE'S MORE THAN ONE WAY TO MEDITATE ON THE LAMRIM

Be aware that there isn't one single way to meditate on the lamrim topics that everyone must follow strictly and cannot deviate from. The explanations in this book indicate *one* way of meditating on the topics—based on what I have learned and found to be effective—but these are only suggestions; understand that there are other ways. Feel free to explore different ways of doing the meditations, based on teachings you have heard, books you have read, advice you have received from your teachers or experienced meditators, and so on. As your knowledge and understanding of the lamrim increases, your meditations on the topics will gradually broaden and develop.

The point of doing these meditations is to bring about a positive transformation in our minds: decreasing incorrect ideas and disturbing emotions, and increasing correct, realistic conceptions and positive mental states. There are numerous ways to transform our minds, and each of us needs to discover what works best for us.

Lama Thubten Yeshe, the wonderful teacher and founder of the Foundation for the Preservation of the Mahayana Tradition (FPMT), was once asked by a student how we can know if we are meditating correctly. He replied that if we notice an increase in our kindness, patience, and ability to get along with others, that means our practice is going well. On the other hand, if we are becoming more unkind, impatient, and selfish, and our relationships with others are fraught with problems, something isn't right with our practice. Lama Yeshe's response clearly indicates that the purpose of meditation is to become a better person; we should keep that as our focus rather than attaining visions, psychic powers, or out-of-body experiences.

While meditating on the lamrim, do not simply read what is written in the book, but pause and really contemplate as many of the points as you have time for. If you are unable to complete all the points in one session, you can pick up where you left off in the next one.

Each meditation ends with a conclusion. These describe the ideal understandings, thoughts, or feelings you should reach after contemplating that topic. You may or may not have arrived at this conclusion in your meditation session. If you haven't, do not worry; you might need multiple sessions on the topic before you reach that conclusion. You can also create your own conclusion based on what you understood during the session. This might include deciding to do more study or research, seek help from your teachers or fellow meditators, or simply spend more time contemplating that topic.

THE ORDER OF THE TOPICS

This book mainly follows the traditional order found in lamrim texts. An exception is the topic of relying on a spiritual teacher, which is usually placed at the beginning but here is included in the appendix. This is because traditionally, the intended audience of the lamrim are people who already have a good understanding of Buddhist teachings in general and the path to enlightenment in particular and are ready to start following this path. Such people would have already connected with one or more spiritual teachers from whom they received instructions and whose guidance they are following, and it makes sense for them to meditate on the correct way to relate to those teachers straightaway.

However, I have found that these days, not everyone who begins learning and meditating on the lamrim has established a relationship with a spiritual teacher. Some may have met and studied with one or more teachers but are still in the process of getting to know them and deciding which one(s) they wish to establish a teacher-disciple relationship with. If you fall into that category, you might still like to do the meditations on the topic of relying on a spiritual teacher, to get more familiar with that topic and prepare for the time when you *will* be in a teacher-disciple relationship. But it's also fine to start with the first topics presented here, the nature of mind and the precious human life, and try the meditations on spiritual teachers later—for example, after completing all the topics of the three levels. At that point, you will have a better understanding of the entire path to enlightenment and thus will be better able to appreciate the importance of relying on a spiritual teacher.

PREPARATORY PRACTICES

It is recommended that when we meditate on the lamrim, we combine it with a set of preparatory practices. These practices put us in a more conducive state of mind for meditation by clearing away unhelpful thoughts and generating positive, helpful ones. This is similar to gardening. To grow delicious vegetables and beautiful flowers in our garden, we need to prepare the soil by removing stones and old roots and enriching it with fertilizer. Similarly, the purpose of meditation is to cultivate positive states of mind such as wisdom, compassion, patience, and so on, and to overcome negative attitudes like anger, attachment, and ignorance. Doing preparatory practices prior to meditation and ending with a dedication of the positive energy of our practice are important points for success in meditation.

Traditionally, there are six preparatory practices to be done before lamrim meditation.

1. Cleaning the room and setting up an altar
Meditating in a clean, tidy place will put our mind in a more clear and positive state. Having an altar also helps us feel inspired during the meditation session. The altar can be simple: on a table or shelf in front of the place where you sit, place images of the Buddha, your teachers, and other enlightened figures that inspire you, such as Chenrezig and Tara.

2. Making offerings on the altar
These can include flowers, candles or electric lights, foods such as fruits and cookies, water or other drinks, and so on. The offerings should be clean and fresh. Making offerings is an excellent way to accumulate merit, or positive energy, to help our mind make progress on the path. It is customary in the Tibetan tradition to offer seven bowls of water representing seven types of delightful offerings.[7]

3. Sitting in a good posture and generating a positive motivation
The recommended posture consists of seven points:

  i. Have your legs crossed in the full-lotus position—where each foot is placed on the thigh of the opposite leg—or in whatever way is most comfortable for you. If you have difficulty sitting cross-legged, it is fine to meditate in a chair with your feet flat on the floor.

  ii. Let your hands rest in your lap, with the right on top of the left and the palms facing upward. Touch the tips of your thumbs together, forming a triangle above your hands. Relax your shoulders and keep your arms slightly away from your sides.

  iii. Keep your back straight. If you meditate in a chair with a slanted back, it's better to sit with a straight back toward the front of the chair rather than lean back. You can use a pillow to provide support for your lower back.

  iv. It's best to keep your eyes slightly open, to prevent sleepiness, with your gaze directed downward. If this is too difficult, you can close your eyes, but don't fall asleep!

  v. Keep your mouth and jaw relaxed, teeth slightly apart, and lips together.

  vi. Place the tip of your tongue on the roof of your mouth behind the upper teeth. This reduces the flow of saliva and the need to swallow.

vii. Have your head inclined downward a little bit. Holding it too high may increase mental agitation and holding it too low may cause dullness or sleepiness.

If it's difficult to adopt all seven points, do your best to find a position that is comfortable but still conducive for meditation.

As for the motivation for doing meditation, the best is bodhichitta: wishing to attain full enlightenment in order to benefit all beings. But if you do not feel ready for such a vast aspiration, try at least to have the altruistic intention to benefit others as much as you can. For example, you might think, "May this meditation be as beneficial as possible to as many beings as possible." Then recite the verses of taking refuge and generating bodhichitta. The verse of the four immeasurable thoughts can also be recited. (These prayers can be found in the practice for lamrim meditation.)

4. Visualizing the merit field
This can be elaborate, as described in traditional lamrim texts, or simple: for example, visualizing a single figure such as Shakyamuni Buddha and thinking that he embodies all objects of refuge.

5. Accumulating merit and purifying negativities
A condensed way to do this is by reciting the seven-limb prayer and short mandala offering. The seven-limb prayer includes seven practices for the purpose of accumulating positive energy, or merit, and purifying negative energy. Here is a brief explanation of these seven:

i. *Prostration:* Prostrating is a means of showing appreciation and respect for the objects of refuge—the Buddha, Dharma, and Sangha, as well as our spiritual teachers. It is an excellent way to overcome arrogance and purify our negative karma. The simplest way to prostrate is placing one's hands together in front of the heart in a gesture of respect; we can do this during our session, sitting on our meditation seat.

ii. *Offering:* Making offerings is a powerful antidote to selfishness and attachment and an important way to accumulate the merit we need to progress on the path to enlightenment. The verse mentions two kinds of offerings, actual and imagined. Actual offerings are those we physically offer—the flowers, fruits, candles, and so forth we place on our altar. Imagined offerings are those we visualize—imagining beautiful flowers, lights, foods, and so on in the space around us and mentally offering them to the Buddha. We can also mentally offer whatever beautiful and pleasing objects we observe during the day and dedicate the merit of doing so to our attainment of enlightenment for the benefit of all beings.

iii. Confession: Here we confess, or declare, any negative actions we have done with our body, speech, and mind, like killing, lying, malicious thoughts, and so on. If we do not purify these, they will cause us suffering in this and future lives and hinder our attainment of spiritual goals such as liberation and enlightenment.

Purification involves four steps, known as the four opponent powers: regret, reliance, remedy, and resolve. (1) We acknowledge with *regret* the negative actions we have done. (2) Since most negative actions are done in relation to either the Three Jewels or sentient beings, *reliance* involves renewing our refuge in the Three Jewels and commitment to act compassionately, helping sentient beings and not harming them. (3) *Remedy* means doing something positive to counteract our negative actions. Examples of such positive actions are making offerings, doing prostrations, reciting mantras, and practicing meditation with a positive motivation. (4) *Resolve* refers to making the promise to avoid doing the same negative actions again. If we are confident that we can completely refrain from certain heavy nonvirtues, such as killing, we can promise to never do them again. But with other actions, such as lying or getting angry, making such a promise would be unrealistic and impossible to keep. Instead, we could promise to avoid those actions for a limited amount of time, even five minutes or one hour. As we become more accustomed to refraining from these actions, we can gradually increase that amount of time to one day, one week, and so on. In this way we learn to manage our mind and our behavior more skillfully.[8]

iv. Rejoicing: This involves feeling happy about the positive, virtuous actions done by oneself and others, understanding that such actions are the cause of the happiness that we all seek. Rejoicing is the opposite of jealousy and resentment, states of mind that are unhappy, tight, and negative. The attitude of rejoicing, on the other hand, is joyful, relaxed, and positive—a loving response that enables us to share in the goodness and happiness of others and inspires us to create more virtue.

v. Requesting the buddhas not to pass away:[9] The buddhas are completely dedicated to helping all sentient beings until the end of samsara. Nevertheless, we need to create the causes to meet and receive teachings from them; this is the purpose of requesting them to remain in the world. Doing this purifies negative actions we may have done in the past toward spiritual teachers and buddhas and keeps our mind open and appreciative of their help and guidance. It also creates the cause for our long life.

vi. Requesting the buddhas to turn the wheel of Dharma: This means asking them to teach the Dharma, showing us how to follow the path and attain enlightenment. Doing this counteracts any disrespect or indifference we may feel toward spiritual teachings and increases our appreciation of them. It also creates the cause to receive Dharma teachings in the future.

vii. Dedication: Just as it is important to have a positive motivation at the beginning of an activity such as meditation, it is also important to conclude by dedicating the merit—the good energy and insight—we have created. We can recall our initial motivation—wishing to attain enlightenment for the benefit of others—and dedicate our merit to that goal. It's also ideal to dedicate merit with the understanding that the three aspects involved—the one who created the merit, the merit itself, and the goal to which we dedicate it—are all empty of inherent, objective existence.[10] Such a dedication ensures that our positive energy is not lost and that it becomes a cause of enlightenment.

The fifth preparatory practice also includes making a mandala offering, of which there are two types: outer and inner. The outer mandala involves mentally transforming the entire universe—everything that exists—into a pure realm and offering it to the objects of refuge. With the inner mandala, we think of the people and things for which we have attachment, aversion, and indifference, mentally transform them into pure objects in the mandala, and offer them all to the buddhas with a pure attitude free of attachment and aversion.

Offering the mandala is an excellent way to accumulate merit, or positive energy, which is needed to transform our mind, attain realizations, and progress along the path.

6. Requesting blessings

Here we request the merit field (the Buddha and so on) for inspiration so that our practice of meditation will proceed well, and we will be able to overcome deluded states of mind and to develop correct, beneficial states of mind.

The practice for lamrim meditation in part 2 includes these preparatory practices. Further explanation of these practices can be found in Pabongka Rinpoche's lamrim text, *Liberation in the Palm of Your Hand.*[11]

MIND AND REBIRTH

Two themes that appear frequently in the lamrim, and in Buddhist literature in general, are mind and rebirth. Let's take a brief look at these before going further. *Mind,* or consciousness, is the part of us that thinks, perceives, remembers, meditates, feels happy or unhappy, experiences emotions, and dreams. It is present every moment, whether we are awake or asleep. In Buddhism, mind is not the brain nor a product of the brain, but a nonphysical phenomenon that exists in an interdependent relationship with our body while we are alive. It is not a single, static thing, like an organ located somewhere inside us, but an ever-changing stream of mental events, each arising and passing in the shortest span of time.

Buddhist scriptures contain detailed explanations of the mind and various mental states, such as those that are constructive and destructive, valid and nonvalid, virtuous and nonvirtuous. While it is not necessary to study these explanations before starting to meditate, if we wish to fully understand and practice the path to enlightenment, it is advisable to gradually learn more about the nature of mind and its different states. Although not a part of traditional lamrim texts, a meditation on the nature of mind has been included here, at the beginning of part 3, since many newcomers are unfamiliar with Buddhist notions of mind.

Mind and *rebirth* are connected because it is our mind—specifically, a subtle type of mental awareness—that continues to exist after death, takes rebirth in another body, and lives a new life. Many newcomers to Buddhism find the idea of rebirth challenging, perhaps due to the prevalent view that mind arises from the brain and ceases at death.

They nonetheless feel attracted to Buddhist philosophy and meditation and wonder if it's necessary to accept rebirth in order to practice these. When asked about this, the Dalai Lama has said that it is not necessary, as there are many meditations we can practice and benefit from without accepting rebirth, such as those for cultivating love, compassion, mindfulness, and concentration. However, he says it can be beneficial to accept rebirth provisionally:

> Even if you cannot ascertain the existence of future lives, you can tentatively accept it without any harm. Wishing to create the causes for fortunate future lives, you will endeavor to subdue your afflictions and cultivate your good qualities. This, in turn, will help you to be happier in the present because you will experience things freshly, without the confusion of attachment and anger. If you find it difficult to accept past and future lives, set the topic aside and focus on being a good person in this life. Do not create trouble for others and use your life to bring calm and peace in your own mind and in the world.[12]

He has also said that those who truly wish to pursue the Buddhist path and be Buddhist practitioners will at some point need to figure out what makes sense to them and what they actually believe.

Some skeptics go so far as to deny that rebirth is an integral part of the Buddha's teachings. Bhikkhu Anālayo addresses this idea in *Rebirth in Early Buddhism and Current Research*.[13] He quotes passages from sutras in which the Buddha spoke of rebirth and explains how it is an essential aspect of Buddhist views and teachings, such as those on karma and the twelve links of dependent arising.

In short, try to keep an open mind and, when you have time, explore resources on the topic of rebirth, such as near-death experiences and cases of people who remember past lives. As the Dalai Lama advises, if you find it too difficult to accept, leave it aside for now and focus on topics that enhance your happiness, well-being, and altruism, so that your life will be meaningful and beneficial, for yourself and others.

PART 2

PRELIMINARY MEDITATIONS

Before we even begin [making a] cake, we need to make careful preparations, buying all the ingredients, ensuring they are the best quality, having a good recipe, and so forth. Similarly, how rich our meditation is depends on how well we have prepared for it. Therefore, we should never skip or rush the preliminary practices, thinking they are not important.

LAMA ZOPA RINPOCHE, *The Power of Meditation*

Meditation on the Breath 3

THIS PRACTICE can be used on its own—for example, as a daily practice to increase mindfulness and concentration—or as a preliminary to other meditations. Some Tibetan teachers recommend observing the breath for a count of twenty-one breaths to calm the mind before doing meditation on the lamrim, but it's fine to spend more time on this practice.

Begin by sitting in the seven-point posture (explained on page 23) or in whatever position is most comfortable for you—but do try to keep your back straight. Spend a few moments settling and relaxing your body. If there is tension in any part of your body, let it dissolve and disappear. Let your breathing be natural. Do not try to control it; just allow your body to breathe as it naturally does.

If you are doing this practice on its own, rather than as a preliminary to lamrim meditation, generate a positive motivation; for example, "May this meditation bring benefit to me and all other beings, all over the world." That's just a suggestion; feel free to use whatever words and phrases are right for you.

If you are new to meditation, you can start with five to ten minutes of practice. Later, as your ability to sit still and concentrate improves, you can gradually increase the length of your session. At any rate, make the determination that you will keep your attention on your breath for the duration of the session, and bring it back to the breath when it wanders to something else.

Now focus your mind on your breathing. There are several ways you might place your focus:
- at your nostrils or upper lip, where you can feel the sensation of the breath entering and leaving your body;
- at your abdomen, where you can feel sensations of rising and falling, or moving in and out, with each breath; or

- on just the general sensations in your body as the breath is coming in and going out.

It's best to focus on just one of these throughout your session, rather than moving from one to another. But for the first few times you do the practice, you may want to experiment with different places to determine which works best for you. Once you have decided which place to focus on, keep your attention there for the whole session. Simply observe the sensations you feel for the entirety of each breath—both the inhalation and exhalation. Bring your mind back to this place each time it wanders away.

Counting

If you wish, you can count your breaths—this can help you stay focused on them. There are different ways of counting explained in Buddhist scriptures and by contemporary teachers. One way is to count each full inhalation and exhalation of the breath as one. You can say to yourself, "Breathing in, breathing out, one. Breathing in, breathing out, two . . ." and so on. Count up to five (if you are a beginner) or up to ten (if you are more experienced), then start again at one. If your mind wanders away partway through the counting, go back and start again at one. Continue counting in rounds of five or ten breaths and bring your attention back to the breath each time it wanders away. If your mind becomes more stable and is able to stay focused on the breath without needing to count, then you can dispense with that.

Distractions

Since our mind is usually very busy, we cannot expect it to stop thinking just because we decide to meditate. So don't be surprised when thoughts pop up and your attention is distracted by them. The ideal way of dealing with this is to notice the thought, let it go, and return your attention to the breath. Try to do this without being upset with yourself or your mind; rather, cultivate a neutral attitude toward your thoughts—neither liking nor disliking any of them. If liking or disliking—or any other emotional reaction such as worry, excitement, sadness, and so on—should arise, simply notice that and let it go, returning your attention to the breath. Don't worry or feel frustrated if you have to do this every few seconds. It takes time to change our habitual tendencies, so we need to be patient and persistent. Know that simply making the effort to keep your mind focused is itself meditation, and is highly beneficial.

One helpful technique from Buddhist masters is to think that your mind is like the sky and thoughts are like clouds. Just as clouds come and go in the sky—they appear, pass through, then disappear, without affecting the natural spaciousness of the sky—thoughts come and go in the clear space of your mind. They are transient, momentary, and are not *you*; they are just mental states arising and passing in your mind, so do not identify with them. If you can simply notice them and let them go, returning your attention again and again to the breath, the thoughts will disappear on their own.

Another helpful technique is to make simple mental notes of what arises in your mind, such as "thinking about dinner," "remembering a movie," "having an imaginary conversation," "feeling annoyed," "anxiety," "feeling bored," and so on. As soon as you have noted the thought or feeling, let it go, recalling its impermanent nature.

Your attention may also be distracted by sounds, smells, or sensations in your body, pleasant or unpleasant. Again, you can make mental notes—"hearing a sound," "smelling incense," "feeling warm," "pain," and so on—then let it go and return to the breath.

It's best to keep your body as still as possible, and not constantly shift your posture to avoid pain or discomfort. That doesn't mean you cannot move at all, like a stone statue. Here's a tip from experienced meditation teachers: adjust your posture only the third time you feel an impulse to move. In other words, the first time you feel an impulse to move, ignore it. If the impulse arises a second time, ignore it. If it arises a third time, then you can move, but do so slowly, mindfully, and quietly (especially if there are other meditators in the room). This will help to increase your mindfulness, maintain your mental stability, and strengthen your ability to put up with minor discomfort.[14]

Be content to stay in the present. Accept whatever frame of mind you are in and whatever arises in your mind; don't judge it as good or bad. Remember that all mental states are transitory, like clouds in the sky. Try your best to be free of expectations like "I want to feel blissful" or "I want to be the best meditator." If you notice such thoughts, let them go; they are just another kind of cloud.

Try to avoid clinging to pleasant experiences and having aversion to unpleasant ones. Since all experiences, pleasant and unpleasant, are transitory, it's pointless to have attachment or aversion to them; these attitudes just cause turmoil in your mind. Have no wish to be somewhere else, to be doing something else, or even to feel some other way. Be content with whatever is happening, right now.

When it's time to end the session, have a sense of joy and satisfaction about yourself and your practice. Don't be judgmental, thinking, "That was a lousy session," or "I'm hopeless. I can't keep my mind on my breath for more than a few seconds!" Remember that *just making the effort* to meditate is highly beneficial and meaningful, especially if it was done with a positive, altruistic motivation. Rejoice in the positive energy you have generated and dedicate it to all beings, wishing that their minds be free of disturbing thoughts and emotions, and full of beneficial states such as loving-kindness, compassion, joy, and peace.

A Practice for Lamrim Meditation   4

Note: As mentioned earlier, you can do an abbreviated version of the follow-ing practice by visualizing the Buddha—or another enlightened being such as Tara or Chenrezig—in the space in front of you, taking refuge and generating a positive motivation, and then doing the meditation on your chosen lamrim topic.

Motivation

FIRST take a few minutes to settle your body in a comfortable posi-tion for meditation and to relax, letting go of any tension you may feel. Once you have settled down, check your mind for any thoughts or emotions that might interfere with your practice and put these aside; you can return to them later, after your meditation, if they are important.

Generate a positive motivation for your meditation. You might like to use the one below or one you learned from your teacher or com-posed yourself. The most crucial thing is to keep your motivation free of harmful attitudes such as anger and greed, and in line with spiritual attitudes, especially the compassionate wish to benefit others.

Recite aloud or quietly in your mind the following motivation: "I am very fortunate to have a human life with an abundance of conducive conditions for spiritual practice. Recognizing the many ways I depend on others—relatives, friends, those who provide my food and other necessities, and so on—I wish to use my life to benefit them and other beings in the world, and to avoid harming anyone. To fulfill this wish, I need to work on my mind—decreasing incorrect, negative mental states and increasing positive ones—and that is my purpose for medi-tating. May this meditation be beneficial for myself and everyone else. May it be a cause for me to attain enlightenment in order to help all beings in the best possible way."

Visualization of the Buddha

Every aspect of your visualization is in the nature of light: transparent, intangible, and radiant. At the level of your forehead and about two meters away is a large golden throne adorned with jewels and supported at each corner by a pair of snow lions. These animals, which are manifestations of bodhisattvas, have white fur and a green mane and tail.

On the flat surface of the throne is a seat consisting of a large open lotus and two radiant disks representing the sun and the moon, one

on top of the other. These three objects symbolize the three principal realizations of the path to enlightenment: the lotus, renunciation; the sun, the correct view of emptiness; and the moon, bodhichitta.

Seated upon this is the Buddha, who has attained these realizations and is the embodiment of all enlightened beings. His body is of golden light and he wears the saffron robes of a monk. He is seated in the vajra, or full-lotus, posture. The palm of his right hand rests on his right knee, the fingers touching the moon cushion, signifying his great control. His left hand rests in his lap in the meditation pose, holding a bowl filled with nectar, which is medicine that cures our disturbing thoughts and emotions and other hindrances.

The Buddha's face is very beautiful. His smiling, compassionate gaze is directed at you and, simultaneously, at every other living being. Feel that he is free of all judging, critical thoughts and that he accepts you just as you are. His eyes are long and narrow. His lips are cherry red and his earlobes are long. His hair is blue-black and each hair is individually curled to the right and not mixed with the others. Every feature of his appearance represents an attribute of his omniscient mind.

Rays of light emanate from each pore of the Buddha's pure body and reach every corner of the universe. These rays are composed of countless miniature buddhas, some going out to help living beings, others dissolving back into his body, having completed their work.

Refuge and Bodhichitta

I go for refuge until I am enlightened
to the Buddha, the Dharma, and the Supreme Assembly.
By my practice of giving and other perfections,
may I become a Buddha to benefit all sentient beings.
(*Recite three times*)

The Four Immeasurable Thoughts

May all sentient beings have happiness and the causes
of happiness.
May all sentient beings be free from suffering and the causes
of suffering.

May all sentient beings be inseparable from the happiness that
is free from suffering.
May all sentient beings abide in equanimity, free from the
attachment and anger that hold some close and others
distant.

Seven-Limb Prayer

Reverently, I prostrate with my body, speech and mind;
I present clouds of every type of offering, actual and imagined;
I declare all my negative actions accumulated since beginningless time
and rejoice in the merit of all holy and ordinary beings.
Please, remain until the end of cyclic existence
and turn the wheel of Dharma for living beings.
I dedicate my own merits and those of all others to the great
enlightenment.

Mandala Offering: Outer and Inner

This ground, anointed with perfume, strewn with flowers,
adorned with Mount Meru, four continents, sun, and moon:
I imagine this as a buddhafield and offer it.
May all living beings enjoy this pure land.

The objects of my attachment, aversion, and ignorance—
friends, enemies, and strangers—
and my body, wealth, and enjoyments:
without any sense of loss, I offer this collection.
Please accept it with pleasure and bless me with freedom from
the three poisons.

idam guru ratna mandalakam niryatayami
(*I send forth this jeweled mandala to you precious gurus.*)

Request Prayer

> Please bless me to cease all deluded minds immediately,
> from disrespect for spiritual teachers to subtle dualistic
>   conceptions.
> Bless me to generate all unmistaken minds instantly,
> from respect for spiritual teachers to the realization of
>   emptiness.
> Bless me to completely pacify all outer and inner obstacles.

Mantra of the Buddha

> *tadyatha om muni muni maha muniye svaha*[15]

While reciting the Buddha's mantra twenty-one times or more, visualize white light and nectar flowing from the Buddha into you, purifying all sickness, negative karma, delusions, and obstacles, especially to the attainment of lamrim realizations. Imagine your body and mind becoming completely calm, clear, and pure. Then again recite the mantra twenty-one times or more while visualizing yellow light and nectar flowing into you, blessing your mind to attain all knowledge, qualities, and realizations of the path to enlightenment.

Lamrim Meditation
Now do an analytical meditation on one of the lamrim topics. When you have finished, you can recite the following text, or skip to the dissolution.

"The Three Principal Aspects of the Path" by Lama Tsong Khapa

Homage to the venerable and holy teachers!

> 1. I shall explain as well as I can
>   The essence of the Victorious Ones' teachings,
>   The path praised by their excellent children,
>   The gateway for the fortunate seeking liberation.

2. Unattached to the joys of worldly existence,
   Striving to use well their freedoms and riches,
   Trusting the path that pleases the Victors—
   Fortunate ones, listen with a pure mind.

3. Without the wish for freedom there is no way to calm
   The pursuit of pleasant effects in the sea of worldly existence.
   Since those with bodies are fettered by their thirst for being,
   First seek the wish to leave cyclic existence.

4. Freedom and riches are hard to find; life is fleeting—
   Familiarity with this stops clinging to this life's pleasures.
   Repeatedly considering actions, their unfailing effects
   As well as the suffering of cyclic existence
   Stops clinging to future pleasures.

5. When through such familiarity not even a moment's longing
   Arises for the marvels of cyclic existence,
   And if day and night you constantly aspire to freedom,
   You have developed the wish to leave cyclic existence.

6. Since this wish for freedom, if unaccompanied
   By the altruistic intention, will not act as a cause
   For the perfect happiness of unsurpassable enlightenment,
   The wise arouse the supreme intention to become
       enlightened.

7. Swept away by the strong currents of four great rivers,
   Bound by the tight bonds of actions which are hard to escape,
   Ensnared in the iron meshes of conceptions of a self,
   Beings are shrouded in thick darkness of ignorance.

8. Endlessly born in worldly existence, and in those births
   Incessantly tormented by three kinds of suffering—
   Reflecting on the condition of your mothers
   In such a predicament, arouse the supreme intention.

9. Though familiar with the wish to leave cyclic existence
   And with the altruistic intention, you cannot cut the root
   Of worldly existence without wisdom understanding reality,
   So make effort in the means to comprehend dependent
      arising.

10. Whoever sees that the causes and effects of all phenomena
    In cyclic existence and beyond are unfailing
    And thoroughly destroys the mainstay of misconceptions,
    Walks on the path that pleases the Buddhas.

11. So long as the understanding of appearances
    As unfailing dependent arising and of emptiness
    Free from all assertions seem disparate,
    You still do not comprehend the Subduer's thought.

12. When the two do not alternate but are simultaneous,
    And merely seeing dependent arising as unfailing
    Destroys through certainty how the object is perceived,
    Analysis with regard to the view is complete.

13. Further, when you know how appearances preclude the extreme
    Of existence and emptiness precludes the extreme of
       annihilation
    And how emptiness appears as cause and effect,
    You will never be enthralled by wrong views.

14. When you have correctly understood
    The essentials of these three principal paths,
    Child, seek seclusion and strengthen your effort
    To swiftly accomplish your future well-being.[16]

Dissolution of the Visualization

The Buddha then dissolves into you, and your body, speech, and mind become inseparable from those of the Buddha. This is a skillful way of getting in touch with your buddha nature—your potential to attain the same qualities and realizations as the Buddha. Imagine your body becoming pure and clear like crystal, and your mind becoming calm and blissful, free of disturbing thoughts and emotions. Remain in this state for a while, feeling confident that one day this will be your actual way of being at all times.

Dedication of Merit

> Due to the merits of these virtuous actions
> may I quickly attain the state of a guru-buddha
> and lead all living beings, without exception,
> into that enlightened state.
>
> May the supreme jewel bodhichitta
> that has not arisen, arise and grow,
> and may that which has arisen not diminish
> but increase more and more.

PART 3

MEDITATIONS OF THE INITIAL LEVEL

Knowing that this highly meaningful perfect human rebirth
is difficult to obtain and easily lost,
and realizing the profundity of cause and effect
and the unbearable sufferings of the lower realms,
I take refuge from my heart in the three precious sublime ones.
I will abandon negativity and practice virtue in accordance
    with the Dharma.
Please bless me with the potential to accomplish this.

VAJRADHARA LOSANG JINPA, "A GLANCE MEDITATION
ON ALL THE IMPORTANT POINTS OF LAMRIM"

The Nature of Mind 5

A BRIEF EXPLANATION of mind, or consciousness, as it is understood in Buddhism was given in part 1. Since the mind plays an important role in the lamrim—it is the very thing that meditates and becomes enlightened—it's helpful to become more familiar with what it is and some of its characteristics, so a meditation on the nature of mind is included here.

Mind is also instrumental in our everyday life. For example, two people stuck in a traffic jam can have very different experiences depending on what's happening in their mind. One becomes impatient, anxious, even enraged; the other remains calm and appreciates the opportunity to practice mindfulness or listen to an informative podcast. Anyone can learn how to transform difficult situations into conducive conditions for well-being and spiritual growth; it's a question of working with our mind, and the lamrim meditations contain many practical methods for doing so.

The following meditation begins with an explanation of the clear and knowing nature of the mind and asks you to try to recognize it. Be aware that this is not easy to do—ideally you would have received instructions on the mind's nature from an experienced teacher, and you are able to keep your mind calm and concentrated during meditation. The Dalai Lama says that he was once able to recognize the nature of his mind while doing retreat in Ladakh, but once he resumed his usual busy duties his mind returned to its original state. So do not be discouraged if you are unable to gain this experience or if your mind is uncontrollably scattered or sleepy. Just try your best and accept that more practice may be needed to progress further.

In addition to the clear and knowing nature of mind, the meditation invites you to contemplate three other characteristics of the mind: its impermanence, the possibility of transforming it, and its continuation beyond this life. Regarding the last point, it is natural to wonder where our mind comes from and what happens to it when we die. Many people believe that the mind is produced by the brain and ceases at death. However, neuroscientists admit that we lack even the tools to properly ask the question of what consciousness is, much less when it starts and ends. There are well-documented cases of near-death experiences and past-life memories, especially of children,[17] that can't be explained by current theories of consciousness—this should make us skeptical of our current reductive theories. Rick Hanson, the author of *Buddha's Brain,* recommends that we have a deep humility about our current understanding of the relationship between mind and brain; our full understanding may come only after two or three centuries.[18]

The Buddhist explanation is that our mind existed before we were born—as part of another being, in another life—and it will continue to exist after death, taking birth in a new life. The cycle of death and rebirth—samsara—will continue until one has completed the mental transformation needed to attain liberation (nirvana) or full enlightenment.

If you find such ideas overly challenging, you can put them on the shelf for now and focus on other aspects of Buddhism that you find helpful. On the other hand, it's worthwhile to explore them since they form the basis for many of the teachings and meditations included in the lamrim.[19]

If you have the time, you can contemplate all the points below in one session, but feel free to divide them over several sessions, to explore them more deeply.

THE MEDITATION

Start the session by sitting comfortably in a posture conducive for meditation. Spend a few minutes observing your breath to settle your thoughts. When your mind is calm, do the practice for lamrim meditation on page 35, in full or abbreviated form. After the mantra recitation, do the following meditation.

Turn your attention to your mind—the ever-flowing stream of mental events that includes thoughts, memories, perceptions, and emotions. Notice as many of these as you can.

What exactly is the mind? Tibetan Buddhist texts define it as clear and knowing. *Clear* means nonphysical—it is not composed of material particles like molecules or atoms and does not have any physical properties like shape, color, size, or weight. It cannot be seen with the eyes or measured with scientific instruments. The only way to observe the mind is by using mind itself—one part of the mind being aware of the other parts.

And that brings us to the other term in the definition: *knowing*. The function of mind is to know, experience, or be aware of things. Mind can know things in different ways: conceptually, such as when we have thoughts and memories, or nonconceptually, such as when we directly perceive visual forms, sounds, smells, and so on.

Simply remain in the present for a while, observing whatever comes up in your mind without getting caught up in it. Try to avoid judging, liking or disliking, or getting lost in stories. Just let things come and let them go. Be like a person sitting beside a river calmly watching the water flow past without interfering with it. In this way, you become more familiar with the clear and knowing nature of your mind.

If you find it difficult to be aware of the flow of mental events, you could use the note-taking method explained in the meditation on the breath. The mental notes can be as simple as "thinking," "hearing," or "pain," or could be more detailed, such as "thinking about coffee," "hearing a bird singing," "feeling pain in my knee," "feeling bored," and so on. Once you have noted an experience, let it go and be aware of the next one.

This practice provides the opportunity to understand another aspect of the mind: its impermanence. Mind is not static or frozen, always the same, but is changing every moment. Mental events are like bubbles—each one arises and instantly ceases, followed immediately by the next one, which also instantly ceases, and so on, without break. As you watch the stream of thoughts, perceptions, and other mental events, see if you can notice their impermanent nature.

The impermanent nature of the mind underlies its most marvelous quality: that it can be purified, transformed, and brought to the state of enlightenment. This is possible because the defilements clouding the true nature of the mind—mainly the delusions such as ignorance, greed, and hatred, along with their seeds and imprints—are not permanent but adventitious. They can be removed.

The Buddha spoke of this possibility in discourses that are found in both the Pali and Sanskrit traditions, such as the *Pabhassara Sutta* in the Pali canon: "Luminous, bhikkhus, is this mind, but it is defiled by adventitious defilements. Luminous, monks, is this mind, and it is freed from adventitious defilements."[20] The term for luminous (Sanskrit: *prabhasvara*) was translated into Tibetan as clear light, *osel,* and there is much discussion in Tibetan Buddhism on the clear light nature of the mind.[21]

The adventitious nature of defilements is good news for us: it means that no matter how many disturbing thoughts and emotions race through our mind every day, none are permanent. We can become free of them and fill our mind with only peaceful, beneficial mental states. Remain for a while in the awareness of that fact.

You might also like to contemplate the Buddhist explanation of the continuity of mind—that it existed before our present life, as part of another person, and that it will continue beyond this life, take rebirth, and become part of yet another, future person. If you notice resistance to this idea, investigate why; what are your reasons? Is it because you are not familiar with it? It was not part of your upbringing and education? You want proof of it? If so, what type of proof would convince you? Remember, the mind is nonphysical, therefore it cannot be detected or measured with current scientific instruments and technology. You can also investigate if there is solid proof for the opposite view, that mind is produced by the brain and ceases at death. These are difficult questions that you probably won't be able to answer during your meditation session, but it's important to explore them. As part of your conclusion to the meditation, you can resolve to continue investigating these points.

Conclusion

Review the key points of the meditation:
- The mind is clear (nonphysical) and knowing (aware).
- The mind is impermanent, changing every split second.
- The mind can be transformed such that it becomes free of all disturbing thoughts and emotions and fully perfected in every positive quality.

- The mind is a flow of mental events, coming from past lives and continuing beyond the present life.

Appreciate the opportunity to begin exploring your mind. Resolve to continue learning and meditating to gain a deeper and broader understanding of it, for the benefit of yourself and all other beings.

Dedication

If you started the session with the practice for lamrim meditation, complete the remaining steps of that, dedicating the merit of the session to your attainment of enlightenment for the benefit of all sentient beings.

The Precious Human Life   6

Having gained this rare ship of freedom and fortune,
hear, think and meditate unwaveringly night and day
in order to free yourself and others
from the ocean of cyclic existence—
this is the practice of bodhisattvas.

TOGME SANGPO, *The Thirty-Seven Practices of Bodhisattvas*

O
NE OF the most beautiful and inspiring teachings in Mahayana
Buddhism is that of buddha nature—every living being's potential to transform themselves, emerge from suffering and confusion,
and become fully enlightened. Although this potential abides in all
of us, special circumstances are needed to actualize it and a precious
human life provides the ideal situation for this spiritual work.

A precious human life is not just any human life, but one having
eighteen aspects—eight freedoms and ten fortunes, which will be
explained in one of the meditations below. Being endowed with these
means we possess the most conducive outer and inner conditions for
practicing the Dharma and following the path to enlightenment. Such
a life is rare—among the countless beings in existence, only a small
number have such conditions. The purpose of meditating on the precious human life is to check whether we have one and, if so, to realize
how fortunate we are. We then generate joyful energy to use our life to
benefit ourselves and others. Meditating on this topic is also an effective antidote to depression, feelings of hopelessness or unworthiness,
or confusion about the purpose of life.

Here, this topic is divided into four separate meditations. The
first—recognizing a precious human life—explores the criteria and
significance of such a life. The second meditation—how a precious
human life is meaningful—looks at the beneficial ways we can use our
life. With the third— how a precious human life is rare and difficult to

attain—we learn why it is difficult to be born in such a situation and how there is no guarantee we will attain another one in our next life. The fourth and final meditation in this section is on the eight worldly concerns, factors in our mind that can interfere with the spiritual path and lead us to waste our precious human life.

Remember to begin each session of meditation by generating a positive, altruistic motivation and doing one or both of the preliminary practices in part 2. At the end of each session dedicate the merit to the enlightenment of all beings.

1. Recognizing a Precious Human Life

Two ways of meditating on this topic are presented here. The first is a nontraditional reflection on the excellent conditions and opportunities of our present life, aimed at dispelling any feelings of despair or depression that we might have and replacing them with appreciation and gratitude. It does not involve reflecting on rebirth and other realms of existence and thus offers an opportunity to engage with this topic for people who have difficulty accepting those aspects of the Buddha's teachings. The second is a traditional presentation of the eighteen characteristics that define a precious human life: the eight freedoms and ten fortunes.

1. Nontraditional Presentation

The Meditation

Start the session by sitting comfortably and observing your breath for a while to settle your thoughts. When your mind is calm, do the practice for lamrim meditation (page 35) in full or abbreviated form. After the mantra recitation, do the following meditation.

Start by checking how you feel about yourself and your life. Do you often feel unhappy or dissatisfied? Do you ever think that life is meaningless or hopeless?

Such feelings may indicate that we do not recognize how fortunate

THE PRECIOUS HUMAN LIFE   53

and precious our life is; we do not realize the wonderful potential that we have.

Abiding within each person, at all times, is our buddha nature. The mind is by nature clear and pure and has the potential to become enlightened—the state of being free of all disturbing thoughts and emotions, and fully perfected in all positive qualities, such as love, compassion, and wisdom. No matter how confused, deluded, and negative we may sometimes feel, our buddha nature is always there; it can never be lost or damaged. Let this awareness sink deep within you; allow it to bring lightness and joy to your mind.

Although all beings have the potential for enlightenment, due to their circumstances most are unable to recognize and develop it. For example, animals face many difficulties simply staying alive. Even those in comfortable conditions, such as pet dogs and cats, lack the intelligence needed to understand basic teachings like karma—how to refrain from nonvirtue and engage in virtue. This makes it almost impossible for them to create the causes for better rebirths in future lives, much less for enlightenment. As human beings we are in a much better situation than animals; with our human intelligence we can understand karma, ethics, and other aspects of the spiritual path and start practicing them. See if you can appreciate how fortunate you are to have a human body and mind, rather than those of an animal.

But even among human beings, not everyone has the ideal conditions to develop their potential for enlightenment. Imagine, for example, being born in an impoverished family in a country suffering from famine, drought, or war. Even if you knew about the path to enlightenment and wished to practice it, most of your time and energy would be spent simply trying to keep yourself and your family alive; you would have little time to think of anything else, such as spiritual practice.

Other people do not have access to spiritual teachings that explain enlightenment and how to attain it. Imagine spending your life in a remote village in the forest or mountains, cut off from the rest of the world, with no opportunity to learn about your potential for enlightenment.

Some people live in prosperous, developed countries where they *could* learn and practice spiritual teachings, but they are not interested. They are preoccupied by other affairs—accumulating wealth, property, and possessions; acquiring worldly knowledge or skills; or just experiencing as much pleasure as possible. It may never occur to them that these things will be left behind when they die, like a dream that vanishes when we wake up, and that only their mind will continue to the next life. Think of people you know who have such attitudes and appreciate the fact that you recognize the value of spiritual teachings and practice.

Some people even use their lives in destructive ways—committing violent crimes or scams, producing and selling illegal drugs, being abusive—not realizing that these actions are harmful to themselves as well as to others and will bring even more suffering in the future. Recognize your good fortune in being interested in spiritual practice and using your life to benefit yourself and others.

Now think about the advantages you have. You are a healthy human being with a mind that can appreciate and understand the Dharma. You have opportunities to learn about the path to enlightenment from compassionate and wise spiritual teachers and wish to learn and practice this path. You have sufficient resources allowing you time to study and practice the Dharma, and there are people who care about and support you—family, friends, and spiritual teachers.

Your mind might object: "Yes, I know I am fortunate, but my life isn't perfect; I have lots of problems." This may be true, but everyone in samsara has problems, even the rich and famous. If you think about the difficulties many others face, you might realize that your troubles are relatively minor and manageable. Most problems are temporary and are not necessarily bad—it depends on how we view them. There are methods for using difficulties in our spiritual practice, helping us progress on the path; some of these will be explained in the meditation on the perfection of patience (part 5). And it's always helpful to remember that you have the potential to become free forever from all difficulties and their causes, and to help others do the same.

Conclusion

If contemplating these points gives rise to joy, or at least an appreciation for the good fortune you have in this life, keep your mind focused on that positive experience for several minutes to familiarize your mind with it.

Finally, conclude the meditation by making a resolution to use your precious human life in ways that are meaningful and beneficial, both for yourself and all other beings.

Dedication

Complete the practice for lamrim meditation and dedicate the merit of doing the meditation that all sentient beings may become enlightened.

2. TRADITIONAL PRESENTATION

This meditation contains numerous points to reflect on, so feel free to divide them among several sessions—you could reflect on the eight freedoms in one session and the ten fortunes in another; the ten could also be divided between two sessions. Once you are familiar with all eighteen you can do a quick review of all of them in a single session.

THE MEDITATION

Start the session by sitting comfortably in a conducive posture for meditation. Spend a few minutes observing your breathing to settle your thoughts. When your mind is calm, do the practice for lamrim meditation (page 35) in full or abbreviated form. After the mantra recitation, reflect on the points of the following meditation.

The eight freedoms

A precious human life is free from eight states or situations in which it would be difficult to practice Dharma and follow the path to enlightenment. Lama Zopa Rinpoche recommends imagining yourself in each of these states to recognize their disadvantages and appreciate your present situation. The teachings say that we have been born in these situations numerous times in previous lives, so we are fortunate to be free of them now.

The first four of these unfree states involve birth in nonhuman realms. These rebirths are temporary, not eternal, but during such a life it is nearly impossible to engage in Dharma practice.

1. *Being born in hell.* This is the realm of greatest suffering that results from the most destructive negative actions. Hell-beings experience constant physical and mental torment, so it is extremely difficult for them to focus their minds on spiritual practice. To get a sense of this, recall an experience of intense

physical pain and check whether you would be able to meditate at that time.

2. *Being born as a hungry ghost.* These beings have karmic obstacles to finding food and drink. Human beings cannot survive more than a few days without food and water, but hungry ghosts spend their entire lives in such conditions and their suffering of extreme hunger and thirst prevents them from thinking of anything else, such as Dharma. Imagine trying to meditate when you've had nothing to eat or drink for just a day.

3. *Being born as an animal.* It may be hard to accept the existence of hungry ghosts and hell-beings since most of us cannot see them, but animals are all around us. Documentaries reveal the suffering of animals in the wild and in the oceans—hunger and thirst, heat and cold, being hunted and killed by other animals and humans. Domesticated animals have their share of miseries such as being kept in inhumane conditions then slaughtered for their meat, feathers, or skin. But the greatest obstacle for animals is having limited intelligence and being unable to understand and practice Dharma; even our beloved pets are afflicted with this problem. Imagine being in such a situation.

4. *Being born as a long-life god.* These are worldly gods born in celestial realms as a result of virtuous karma.[22] They have long lives and splendid enjoyments but are so distracted by pleasure that they have little or no interest in learning and practicing the Dharma. To get a sense of this, imagine winning an all-expenses-paid holiday for two on a tropical island, where you stay in a stunning five-star resort that offers gourmet food 24/7; on-demand movies, music, and massages; and endless exciting activities. Would you feel like meditating in such a situation? And if you tried, would it be easy to keep your mind concentrated?

The remaining four unfree states are situations in the human realm that have obstacles to spiritual practice. As before, imagine yourself in these situations to appreciate your good fortune in being free of them.

5. *Living in an uncivilized society.* This is a place where you have no access to spiritual teachings, such as a remote or politically troubled country where religion and spirituality are unknown or outlawed. You could spend your entire life unaware of your potential for enlightenment and the path to attain it.

6. *Being born during a dark age.* This is a place and time where no buddha appeared in the world and taught the Dharma. According to Buddhism, there are multiple universes and planets; in some of these, at certain times, the inhabitants' karma is such that they would not benefit from a buddha's teachings, so the buddhas do not go there to teach.

7. *Having severe physical or mental impairments.* Such impairments would restrict your ability to learn and practice the Dharma. For example, due to a congenital health issue or an illness or injury, a person's brain might be unable to function at full capacity, and they may remain in a vegetative state for years or even their entire life. In places that lack sign language and high literacy rates, being deaf could pose an obstacle to learning Dharma.

8. *Holding wrong views.* These include such views as denying karma, the law of cause and effect, or the possibility of attaining liberation and enlightenment. With such views, one would see little or no purpose in practicing Dharma.

The ten fortunes

The ten fortunes consist of two groups: five personal fortunes and five external fortunes that depend on others. The five personal fortunes are

1. *Being born as a human being.* Generally, a human body and mind possess the ideal qualities needed to learn, comprehend, and practice the Dharma and thus create the causes for enlightenment.

2. *Living in a central land.* This is a place where the four types of Buddhist followers abide: fully ordained monks and nuns, and laymen and laywomen who keep the five precepts, or vows. In such a place one can take precepts and practice pure ethical conduct, an essential aspect of the path to enlightenment.

3. *Having a healthy body and mind.* One is free of impairments that would interfere with spiritual study and practice.

4. *Not having committed any of the five extreme negative actions.* These are killing one's father, killing one's mother, killing an arhat (a person who has attained nirvana), severely injuring a buddha, or causing a schism in a sangha (a group of four or more fully ordained monastics). Committing any of these results in severe internal obstacles to successful Dharma practice.

5. *Having faith in the Three Baskets* (Sanskrit: *Tripitaka*). These are the collections of the Buddha's teachings on three topics: ethical conduct, concentration, and wisdom.

The five external fortunes involve living in a situation where

6. a buddha appeared in the world;

7. that buddha taught the Dharma;

8. those teachings still exist and are being taught and practiced;

9. there are people who follow the buddha's teachings, demonstrating that it is a living tradition that we can follow as well; and

10. there are kind-hearted people willing to support Dharma practitioners with their needs, such as food, shelter, and so on.

Conclusion

If you recognize that you possess all eighteen of these factors, feel joyful and enthusiastic about using your life in meaningful, beneficial ways, both for yourself and all other beings. But if you notice one or more of these factors are missing in your life—you may lack faith in the Three Baskets, for instance, or people who support your practice—think of ways you could create the causes for these so you will eventually have the full set of eighteen.

Dedication

Return to the practice for lamrim meditation and complete the remaining steps, then dedicate the merit you have created to enlightenment for the benefit of all sentient beings.

2. How a Precious Human Life Is Meaningful

Here we look at how a precious human life is meaningful or valuable. People often wonder what the purpose of life is. Is it simply to follow the usual pattern of going to school, getting a job, buying a house, raising a family, retiring, traveling, and so on? Or should we follow our heart and create beautiful works of art, music, or literature? Ask yourself: What do *you* think the purpose of your life is?

This is a question each person needs to explore in order to discover an answer that feels right for them. But it can be useful to consider the Buddhist response: the purpose of human life is to engage in spiritual practice, develop our positive potential, and benefit others as much as we can. The following meditation on the various ways we can use our precious human life can help you gain clarity about this important question.

The Meditation

Begin by sitting comfortably in a posture conducive for meditation. Spend a few minutes observing your breathing to settle your thoughts. When your mind is calm, perform the practice for lamrim meditation (page 35) in full or abbreviated form, and contemplate the points of the following meditation after the recitation of the Buddha's mantra.

The lamrim explains three ways of living that will make our precious human life meaningful: for temporal goals, for ultimate goals, and as if every moment of our life can be beneficial.

1. For temporal goals
This means we make our life meaningful by creating the causes for good rebirths in our future lives. Our long-term goal may be enlightenment, but that usually takes lifetimes to attain. We need to ensure that in all those lives we will have ideal conditions to continue following the path—this is the meaning of *temporal goals.*

Being born with such conditions depends on the karma we create—we need to avoid nonvirtuous karma, the cause of birth in unfavorable situations, and accumulate virtuous karma, which brings birth in favorable situations. By living this way to the best of our ability, when this life comes to an end and our consciousness travels to the next life, we will land in a good situation—such as another precious human life—with the most suitable conditions to continue following the path to enlightenment.

Even if you have difficulty accepting rebirth, living in the above way makes sense because it will benefit your present life. Refraining from harmful actions and acting ethically and compassionately results in greater happiness and mental peace, and fewer worries and regrets. Your relationships and interactions with others will be more satisfying, and you will die with a tranquil mind, feeling positive about the way you lived.

2. For ultimate goals

This means using our life to attain liberation and enlightenment, which are ultimate in the sense of being irreversible. Once attained, they are never lost. With our precious human life, we can start creating the causes for liberation from samsara—the cycle of death, rebirth, and suffering—and for buddhahood, with the ability to benefit all other beings. Contemplate how fortunate you are that you can begin working toward these states in this life.

3. Each moment of our life can be beneficial

We can make our life meaningful and beneficial for others even now, by comforting those who are depressed or anxious, lending a hand to someone who needs help, or simply being kind and friendly.

In the lamrim, this point mainly refers to acting with a bodhichitta motivation. Anything we do with the motivation of attaining enlightenment to help all sentient beings creates a vast amount of merit, even in one moment. For example, reciting a few mantras, giving food or money to a homeless person, or offering a candle to the Buddha— these actions require little time and energy, but if they are done with bodhichitta, they become highly meritorious and bring us closer to enlightenment. If this is true for minor actions, there's no need to mention greater ones such as studying the Dharma, meditating, or offering service to our spiritual teachers. Feel fortunate that you can create vast and powerful causes for enlightenment, even in one moment, for the benefit of all beings.

Conclusion

Recall the key points of the meditation:

- A precious human life can be used to create the causes of fortunate rebirths in future lives and for other temporal goals.
- It can be used to create the causes of the ultimate goals of liberation and enlightenment.
- Each moment of this life is precious because it can be used for positive, beneficial actions that have long-lasting consequences for oneself and others.

Recognizing the many meaningful aims you can accomplish with your life, feel joyful and enthusiastic about using your life to benefit yourself and others. Hold that experience in your mind as long as possible.

Dedication

Complete the practice for lamrim meditation and dedicate the merit of the session to the happiness and enlightenment of all living beings.

3. RARE AND DIFFICULT TO ATTAIN

The third meditation on the precious human life looks at how such a life is rare and not easy to attain. It is important to reflect on this, otherwise we might think, "It's okay if I don't practice Dharma in this life. I can do it in my next life." This is unwise because a precious human life is difficult to come by; there's no certainty we will get another one next time.

THE MEDITATION

Start by sitting in a comfortable and conducive posture and observe your breathing for a while until your mind is calm. Perform the practice for lamrim meditation, in full or abbreviated form. After the mantra recitation, do the following meditation.

There are three reasons for understanding that a precious human life is rare and difficult to attain.

The first reason is in terms of its *causes*. A precious human life is the result of numerous causes; the fact that we now have one indicates that we created those causes in past lives. The main cause is ethical conduct—refraining from negative actions such as the ten nonvirtues, keeping whatever precepts we have taken, and creating virtuous karma. Reflect on how you are creating these causes in your present life.

Other causes for a precious human life include practicing generosity, patience, joyful effort, concentration, and wisdom, as well as praying to attain a precious human life in the future. Who do you know is creating these causes? Are you?

The second reason is in terms of *numbers*. We can understand the rarity of a precious human life by comparing human and animal populations. There are now over eight billion people on this planet but there are many more mammals, birds, fish, reptiles, insects, and so on. It would be difficult to count all of them, but one researcher's estimate is twenty quintillion.[23] Even that staggering number is small compared to beings in the two other unfortunate realms. Buddhist tradition says there are more hungry ghosts than animals and more hell-beings than hungry ghosts. That should give you a sense of the rarity of human life.

But remember that not all human beings have a precious human life with all eighteen characteristics—such people are very rare. Contemplate this and check: When you die and your mind travels on, is it certain that it will find a precious human life?

The third reason is by way of an *example*. In the *Balapandita Sutta*, the Buddha used an analogy to illustrate the difficulty of obtaining a precious human life:

> "Suppose a man threw into the sea a yoke with one hole in it, and the east wind carried it to the west, and the west wind carried it to the east, and the north wind carried it to the south, and the south wind carried it to the north. Suppose there were a blind turtle that came up once at the end of each century. What do you think, bhikkhus? Would that blind turtle put his neck into that yoke with one hole in it?"
> Bhikkhus: "He might, venerable sir, sometime or other at

the end of a long period." "Bhikkhus, the blind turtle would take less time to put his neck into that yoke with a single hole in it than a fool, once gone to perdition, would take to regain the human state, I say."[24]

Pabongka Rinpoche explains that in this analogy, the sea represents our samsaric state; the turtle is ourselves; its blindness is ignorance; the yoke is a Buddha's teachings.[25] It is thus rare to obtain a human birth with the opportunity to learn a Buddha's teachings; now that we have this situation, we should use it wisely. Reflect on this example and its meaning in terms of your own life.

Conclusion

The purpose of contemplating these points is not to feel anxious or hopeless but rather to feel joyful that the life we have is extremely precious—more precious than money or gold. Even if we had all the wealth in the world, we could not buy enlightenment, but enlightenment can be attained with a precious human life.

It's up to us: we can spend our life in meaningless pursuits or use it to do what is positive and beneficial and refrain from what is negative and harmful. If you feel inclined toward the latter choice, resolve to spend your life in that way. Stay focused on this thought for a few minutes or longer to deeply familiarize yourself with it.

Dedication

Complete the practice for lamrim meditation, dedicating the merit of the session to your attainment of enlightenment for the benefit of all sentient beings.

4. THE EIGHT WORLDLY CONCERNS

Knower of the world! Gain and
loss, well-being and misery, fame and disrepute,
praise and censure; be indifferent to these eight worldly
dharmas and let them not enter your mind.
NAGARJUNA, *Nagarjuna's Letter*

A life with freedoms and fortunes is a precious opportunity: it can be used to create the causes for favorable rebirths, complete liberation from samsara, and full awakening—states that are beneficial for our-selves and others. It would be a great shame to have this opportunity and use it to create suffering rather than happiness. That would be similar to a person from a low-income family who is awarded a schol-arship to a prestigious university, but they spend their time partying rather than studying and eventually get kicked out. Sadly, this is what can happen if we fail to differentiate Dharma and non-Dharma.

The Sanskrit term *dharma* has different meanings, but in the con-text of spiritual practice, it means "that which protects from suf-fering." In that sense, Dharma is virtue, the cause of happiness; it includes virtuous mental states like faith and compassion and actions motivated by these. Nonvirtuous mental states such as anger and crav-ing for sense pleasures, as well as actions done under their influence, are not Dharma because they lead to suffering. Further details about virtue and nonvirtue will come later, in the chapter on karma. But one type of non-Dharma that we need to look out for in the early stages of our practice are the eight worldly concerns.

Buddhist texts refer to these as the eight worldly dharmas—*dharma* with a small "d" usually means phenomenon, something that exists. The eight worldly dharmas are attitudes that involve being happy and delighted about four pleasant experiences—gain, praise, fame, and pleasure—and being averse to four unpleasant ones—loss, blame, dis-repute, and pain. They are rooted in a narrow, self-centered attitude that is exclusively concerned about this present life, such as thoughts of "I should have only perfect, enjoyable experiences, and not even the slightest problem." If we are not careful, our precious opportunity can be sabotaged by these eight concerns.

Looking honestly at our mind, we might notice that it's focused on experiencing pleasure and avoiding what is unpleasant, concerned only for this life. All day long we make choices and decisions based on this tendency—eating tasty food, listening to enjoyable music, looking at beautiful scenery, experiencing pleasant bodily sensations, getting positive feedback from others about how we look or how well we accomplished a task. How many of our thoughts and decisions are based on longer-term goals—our future lives or enlightenment?

Being principally preoccupied with the affairs of this life is a hindrance to spiritual practice. We may become so busy with work, relationships, acquiring possessions, and enjoyments that we find little time to study or meditate. Even when we do, our motivation may not be pure Dharma but tainted by worldly concern. Meditating just to feel good or impress others is not pure Dharma, nor is teaching Buddhism and meditation out of desire for wealth or fame. The minimum motivation for pure Dharma practice is aspiring for fortunate rebirths with conducive conditions in future lives.

Overcoming the eight worldly concerns is not easy because our mind has been under their control for a very long time. We will not be completely free from them until we directly realize emptiness. For now, we can become aware of them with mindfulness and introspective awareness and use antidotes such as the meditations on impermanence and death to weaken their hold on our mind.

Working on them does not mean we cannot enjoy life, nor that we should give away all our things and be homeless. It also does not mean we shouldn't seek solutions to problems such as sickness, pain, and financial loss. We *should* take care of our health, our family and friends, and our possessions. The problem is being concerned *exclusively* with the present life's happiness and comfort, while having no interest in developing our spiritual potential, working for the benefit of others, and creating the causes for positive experiences in future lives. The Dalai Lama has said:

> Dharma practitioners are warned about seeking the temporary happiness of *only* this life, not because it is bad or "sinful" but because it impedes us from actualizing the spiritual realizations that will bring long-term happiness.[26]

The solution is training our mind to be balanced, equanimous, and resilient: refraining from strong excitement and attachment to pleasant experiences as well as strong despondency and aversion to unpleasant ones. Among the most effective methods for accomplishing this are the meditations on death and impermanence—the next topic in the lamrim.

We can take advice from the Buddha on how a "wise and mindful person" regards the eight worldly concerns:

The wise and mindful person knows them
and sees that they are subject to change.
Desirable conditions don't excite his mind,
nor is he repelled by undesirable conditions.[27]

The eight worldly concerns also interfere with our happiness here and now. We are unable to control everything that happens in life; we can't always get what we want and can't always avoid problems. If our mind is enslaved by the eight concerns, it will be tossed up and down on waves of attachment and aversion, our likes and dislikes, one moment feeling elated and the next miserable. Is that happiness? Also, with such an unstable mind, we will be unable to stay focused and clear during meditation, so our attempts to attain long-term happiness will not succeed.

The only way to free ourselves completely from the eight worldly concerns is to directly realize emptiness, and that takes time. In the meantime, we can learn to notice them in our mind and recognize their disadvantages so we will be less likely to follow them. At my first one-month meditation course at Kopan Monastery in Nepal in 1974, Lama Zopa Rinpoche spoke about the eight worldly concerns every day, several times a day, for the first two weeks. We all became proficient at noticing them in our minds and understanding their faults![28]

Below is a suggested reflection on the eight worldly concerns, arranged in four pairs of opposites. Think of examples of these in your own experience and from your observations of others so that you may become more familiar with them and the difficulties they cause.

The Meditation

Begin as usual by sitting comfortably and settling your mind by observing your breathing for a while. When your mind is calm, do the practice for lamrim meditation, and insert the following meditation after the mantra recitation.

1. and 2. Gain and loss
- Do you feel excited and joyful when receiving a gift or promotion, or when you buy something for yourself?
- How long do these feelings last?

- Do you notice any unpleasant side effects of these experiences?
- How do such experiences affect your Dharma practice?

Now consider how you react when you lose a cherished possession or fail to get something you want.
- Do you feel miserable, depressed, or angry?
- How do these feelings affect your practice?

There's nothing wrong with receiving nice things and feeling happy about it. The problem is being attached to material things, never satisfied with what we have, and always craving more. Likewise, there is nothing wrong with feeling sad over experiences of loss and seeking solutions—trying to recover a stolen possession, for example, or relying on emotional support after the death of a loved one. But sinking into despair, as if such misfortunes were permanent and irreparable, is not helpful. Spiritual practice enables us to remain balanced, during good times and bad.

3. and 4. Praise and blame
- When you are praised or complimented, do you feel elated?
- Is this genuine happiness, or transitory, self-centered pleasure?
- Does praise help you become a better person, or does it increase delusions such as arrogance and attachment?
- Does concern about praise help or hinder your spiritual practice?

When we encounter blame or criticism, it's natural to be upset, but are these truly harmful? Consider the saying, "Sticks and stones may break my bones but words will never hurt me." There are constructive ways to think about blame and criticism that can soften the blow and help us grow spiritually. One solution is to examine whether the person's criticism is true or not—when angry, people often speak without thinking and their words may have no basis in reality. After an honest assessment of yourself, if you conclude that the criticism is not true, you can regard it as meaningless words—like someone saying you have horns on your head—and simply ignore it. But if it's true, take it as constructive criticism to help you become a better person. Either way, being upset does not help.

With regard to praise, we might think it's best to stop people from expressing it in order to avoid getting attached or arrogant, but that isn't necessary. In fact, recognizing and admiring our good qualities and deeds is beneficial for them, a way to create virtue. But we need to observe our mind, and if we notice our ego swelling up with pride and craving for more, understand the dangers of such attitudes and avoid following them. Recalling the impermanent nature of such experiences is a helpful solution—the person who praises you today might criticize you tomorrow, and vice versa. With practice, we can gradually learn to be more even-minded and not so easily affected by either praise or criticism.

5. and 6. Fame and disrepute
- Do you long to be famous, and feel delighted when your accomplishments are recognized?
- Do you feel unhappy or even angry when you are not known or recognized, and jealous of those who are?
- Think about it: if fame brought genuine, long-lasting happiness, celebrities would be the most contented people on the planet—is that true?
- How do attachment to fame and aversion to being unknown affect your spiritual practice?

In *The Jewel Rosary of a Bodhisattva*, Atisha expresses the ideal attitude of a Dharma practitioner regarding fame and other worldly things:

> Reject acquisitions and honors
> and always reject desire for fame.[29]

By recognizing the futility of fame and the disadvantages of craving for it, we can gradually free ourselves from this pair of concerns—fame and disrepute—and cultivate even-mindedness toward them.

7. and 8. Pleasure and pain
- Are you attached to delicious food, beautiful music, and other sensual enjoyments?
- Is such pleasure truly satisfying and long-lasting, or fleeting?

- What is your usual way of responding to unpleasant or painful sensory experiences? Is it reasonable or exaggerated?
- How do these ways of reacting affect your life and your spiritual practice?

There is nothing wrong with pleasure; it's simply an experience that comes and goes. It becomes problematic when we crave it and spend a great deal of our time and energy pursuing it.

There's also nothing wrong with trying to avoid pain and seeking remedies to it. But if we become overly upset about the slightest discomfort or unpleasantness and obsessively try to avoid them, we just create additional problems for ourselves and others. Making ourselves familiar with the ephemeral nature of both pleasant and unpleasant experiences will enable us to avoid the difficulties arising from this pair of concerns.

Conclusion

Understanding the problems that arise from being addicted to the eight worldly concerns, resolve to watch out for them in your mind, try your best to not follow them, and instead apply antidotes, such as contemplating the impermanent nature of all experiences, good and bad.

Dedication

Return to the practice for lamrim meditation and dissolve the visualization of the Buddha. Then dedicate the merit you created to all beings' attainment of happiness, up to the highest happiness of enlightenment.

Death and Impermanence 7

Loved ones who have long kept company will part.
Wealth created with difficulty will be left behind.
Consciousness, the guest, will leave the guesthouse of the body.
Let go of this life—
this is the practice of bodhisattvas.

TOGME SANGPO, *The Thirty-Seven Practices of Bodhisattvas*

MEDITATING on the precious human life opens our mind to a unique, constructive way of looking at our life and arouses interest in using it for spiritual practice. For those who wish to practice the path to enlightenment, lamrim texts divide this path into three sections, known as the three levels, or scopes: initial, intermediate, and advanced.

The initial-level section of the lamrim begins with meditation on death—a topic many people don't like to hear or think about, even though it is something we will all have to face one day. The Buddhist approach to death is realistic and practical: we are advised to think about death during our life—every day, in fact—to prepare ourselves for it and be able to die with a positive, peaceful state of mind, rather than a mind overwhelmed by fear or other disturbing emotions. Accepting the reality of death does not make us morbid; on the contrary, it instills a sublime sense of the preciousness of each day and moment of our life and the wish to live it fully, with compassion and wisdom.

Meditating on death in the context of the lamrim involves contemplating that we will definitely die at some point, that we have no way of knowing when, and that the most helpful thing at that time is Dharma—our spiritual practice. This is mainly because death is followed by rebirth, and the circumstances and experiences of our next life depend on how we live and die in this one. Since we naturally want happiness and not suffering, we need to learn how to create the causes of good experiences and avoid the causes of problems and misery. In Buddhism, this starts with taking refuge and living in accordance with karma—the subjects of chapters 9 and 10.

This chapter includes three meditations. The first is on the disadvantages of not being aware of death and the benefits of being aware of it. Contemplating these can help us overcome any resistance we might have to death as a "taboo" topic. That is followed by the nine-point meditation on death, divided into three parts. Finally, there is a meditation on subtle impermanence, the ever-changing nature of things.

1. Disadvantages and Benefits

Being aware of death means not denying it or pretending that we will live forever. Instead, we accept that our life will definitely end and remain aware of that fact as much as possible. The lamrim mentions six disadvantages of not making a conscious effort to accept and remain aware of death, and six benefits, or advantages, of doing so.

The Meditation

Begin by sitting comfortably in a conducive posture for meditation. Spend a few minutes observing your breathing to settle your thoughts. When your mind is calm, do the practice for lamrim meditation on page 35 in full or abbreviated form. Pause after the mantra recitation and do the following meditation.

First, consider the disadvantages of not being aware of death. To understand these better, think of examples of them from your own and others' lives.

1. *We will not remember the Dharma.* All our time and energy will instead be spent trying to achieve only the goals of this life such as wealth, fame, power, and so on.

2. *Even if we remember the Dharma, we will not practice it.* Due to procrastination, we will think about practicing Dharma later

in our life when we are less busy. Our life may end before that time comes.

3. *Even if we practice the Dharma, we will not practice it purely.* Without awareness of death, our practice may be polluted by the eight worldly concerns such as hoping to receive material gain, recognition, or praise.

4. *Our practice will lack persistence.* We may give up if things get tough or we don't get the results we expected.

5. *We may commit many nonvirtuous actions.* Such actions will bring suffering both now and in the future.

6. *We may die with regrets.* At the time of our death, we may have many things to regret—things that we wish we hadn't done and things we should have done but did not.

There are six benefits of being aware of death. Contemplate these to generate enthusiasm for this practice.

1. *Our actions and our life will become beneficial.* We will practice Dharma sincerely and energetically.

2. *Our Dharma practice will become very powerful and pure.* By being aware of death, our practice will be free of the eight worldly concerns.

3. *It is important at the beginning.* It will help us to recognize the value of practice and start doing it.

4. *It is important throughout our practice.* It will help us continue practicing even when the going gets tough.

5. *It is important at the end of our practice.* Being aware of death will help us reach the final goals: liberation and enlightenment.

6. *We will die with a peaceful, positive state of mind, free of regrets.* Awareness of death's inevitability will make us careful of our actions—refraining from harmful ones and doing those that are positive and beneficial. Living in this way ensures that our mind will be positive and peaceful at the time of death, rather than tormented by regrets and fear.

Conclusion

Understanding the benefits of maintaining awareness of death and the disadvantages of not doing so, resolve to keep in mind the fragility of your life and the certainty of your death and to use this awareness to live your life wisely and compassionately. Focus on this experience for a few minutes.

Dedication

If you started the session with the practice for lamrim meditation, complete the remaining steps of that, then dedicate the merit you created to enlightenment for the benefit of all sentient beings.

2. THE NINE-POINT MEDITATION ON DEATH

This meditation on death consists of three main *roots*; nine reasons or points, three for each root; and three conclusions, one at the end of each root. The three roots are (1) the inevitability of death, (2) the uncertainty of the time of death, and (3) only Dharma helps at the time of death. The three reasons for each root will be explained below.

Depending on your time and inclination, you can meditate on all nine points in one session, in three sessions (one on each of the three roots), or in nine sessions (one on each point).

THE MEDITATION

Whichever of the suggested ways you choose to meditate on the nine points, begin each session by sitting in a conducive posture and calming your mind with a few minutes of meditation on the breath. Do the practice for lamrim meditation on page 35 in full or abbreviated form, then do the meditation on death below following the mantra recitation. When you have finished contemplating your chosen number of points of the death meditation for that session, complete the practice for lamrim meditation and, finally, dedicate the merit to the benefit of all beings.

THE FIRST ROOT: THE INEVITABILITY OF DEATH

1. Everyone has to die.

Bring to mind people from the past: powerful leaders like kings, queens, presidents, or generals; talented artists and musicians; brilliant scientists and philosophers; spiritual leaders like Buddha and Jesus. No matter how powerful, intelligent, or holy these people were, they all had to die. Can you think of anyone who lived on this earth but did not have to die?

Recall people you have known in your life who have already died and reflect that one day you will also die.

Think of people you know who are still alive—family members, friends, neighbors. Contemplate that each of these people will die one day, and so will you.

At present there are more than eight billion people in the world, but in a hundred years most of them will have died, except for a few who are now infants. You yourself will have died. Imagine the world going on without you and most of its current inhabitants.

2. Your lifespan is decreasing continuously.
As time passes—seconds, minutes, hours, days, months, and years—your lifespan is running out and you are moving ever closer to death. Imagine an hourglass with the sand trickling down; the time you have left to live is like the grains of sand, continuously running out.

You can also get a sense of moving continuously toward death by imagining yourself on a train traveling at a steady speed. It never slows down or stops and you are unable to get off. This train is like time bringing you closer and closer to its destination: the end of your life. Try to really get a sense of this.

3. The amount of time you have for spiritual practice is very small.
Since you are continuously traveling toward death, what are you doing to prepare for it? The best preparation for death is spiritual practice. Practicing Dharma during our life—cultivating mindfulness, living ethically, meditating on compassion, and so on—will enable us to keep our mind positive and peaceful at the time of death rather than confused and fearful, and it will ensure a fortunate rebirth. Only our mind and the imprints of our actions will continue after death. It's hard to find anything other than spiritual practice that can truly benefit the mind at that point. But how much of your time do you devote to spiritual practice—working to decrease disturbing emotions such as anger and attachment, and developing positive aspects of the mind such as kindness and wisdom?

Conclusion

Understand the importance of Dharma practice: that it should be one of your main priorities in life. Generate the thought, "I must practice Dharma in order to prepare for death and the next life," then focus on this single-pointedly for several minutes.

THE SECOND ROOT: THE UNCERTAINTY OF THE TIME OF DEATH

We might accept the inevitability of death but think we don't need to be concerned about it now because it won't happen soon. This is unrealistic; we have no way of knowing when we will die. It could happen any time—this year, this month, even today. Let's look at the reasons for this.

4. The human lifespan is uncertain.

We are not guaranteed a certain number of years to live. Some people live into their eighties or nineties, but some die long before that—even in their twenties or thirties, or as children. Bring to mind examples of people you know or have heard of who died at different ages, even before they reached your current age.

Recognize that it would be foolish to think thoughts such as "I won't die soon. Only old people die, and I'm not old." Understand that your present age has nothing to do with your remaining lifespan because death can happen at any age.

5. There are many causes of death.

People die in various ways. Some die in natural disasters such as earthquakes or floods; others die due to human activity such as war, murder, terrorist attacks, or car accidents. But most people die from illness, especially heart disease, cancer, and strokes. There are also cases of healthy people who die mysteriously in their sleep. Think of examples that illustrate the various ways people can die.

Ironically, even things that normally support life can become the cause of death. We need food to stay alive, but people sometimes die as a result of eating—choking on their food or getting food poisoning. Medicine normally prolongs life, but people can die after taking the wrong medicine or the wrong dose. Houses and apartments enable us to live comfortably, but they sometimes catch fire or collapse, killing their occupants.

We have no way of knowing how we will die. Even if we care for our health and eat wisely, we could unexpectedly encounter conditions that cause our death—anywhere, anytime, even today.

6. Our body and life are very fragile.
We may feel strong, full of energy, and as if nothing could harm us, but this is an illusion. It does not take something enormous and dramatic like a tsunami, a plane crash, or a tiger to end our life. Death can be caused by a small bullet or a microscopic virus. It can also happen very quickly; due to a heart attack or stroke, a person who was bursting with energy one moment can suddenly become a lifeless corpse. Death is simply a matter of exhaling one last time and not inhaling again.

Conclusion
Since we do not know when death will occur, it is unwise to procrastinate or be lazy. If we see the value of practicing Dharma, we should start doing so now. Generate this thought in your mind and concentrate on it for a few minutes to deepen your familiarity with it.

The Third Root: Only Dharma Helps at the Time of Death

According to Buddhism, dying with a positive, peaceful state of mind is crucial for a favorable rebirth in the next life. What can help us die with such a mental state? Imagine yourself at the time of death while contemplating the following three points.

7. Family and friends cannot help.
We probably wish to have our loved ones with us when we die, to support and comfort us. But is it certain they will be there? Death could happen when we are away from home, away from our family and friends.

Even if they are with us as we are dying and able to take care of our physical needs, could they help with our emotional needs—if we are frightened, angry, or sad about all we are leaving behind? They might be overwhelmed by their own emotions and unable to help us with ours.

As we die, our mind gradually withdraws from the outer world and sinks into subtler levels. We lose the ability to see, hear, speak, move, and be aware of others. Finally, we separate from them and travel alone through the process of dying and the intermediate state[30] to the next life. No one can accompany us on that journey.

Also, clinging to loved ones with the wish to never separate from them can make it difficult to die peacefully. Instead, our mind may be troubled by sadness, longing, and anxiety. Such clinging is a type of attachment, which the Buddha recognized as one of the main causes of suffering because it denies the impermanent nature of things, such as people and relationships, and often incites us to commit unwholesome actions. Attachment to people is not the same as love, as will be explained later in chapter 13. Love is concerned for the happiness of others, while attachment is self-centered; under its influence, we use people to fulfill our own needs and wants. Understanding the problems that arise from attachment motivates us to work on decreasing it while continuing to love and care for family and friends, setting the stage for a more peaceful death.

8. Our possessions and enjoyments cannot help.

Much of our time and energy is devoted to our material possessions, wealth, and property—managing them, protecting them, acquiring more. These are useful while we are alive, but can they help us at the time of death? Our money can provide physical comfort, like having a private room in the hospital and good medical care. But it cannot stop death from happening, and we can't take even one cent with us when we die.

We do need a certain amount of material resources for ourselves and our family, but we often crave more than we really need. Moreover, attachment to our money and property can make it difficult to die peacefully—our mind may be overwhelmed by sadness about leaving them behind or worry about who gets what and whether they will take proper care of our things.

9. Our body cannot help.

Our body has been a constant companion since birth, and our sense of self is deeply entangled with it—we easily get upset when someone insults it or bumps against it. We have spent countless hours caring for it, keeping it comfortable and healthy, beautifying it, and using it to enjoy sensory pleasures.

At death, our mind separates from this body and departs for the next life, and our body will become a lifeless corpse to be buried or cremated. Not only is it unable to help us as we are dying, but it can be a source of intense pain and suffering. Being attached to and identified with our body at that time could also make our mind disturbed, frightened, and unpeaceful.

So what *can* help us at the time of death? Spiritual teachers and Dharma friends can help us with advice, prayers, and their peaceful presence. However, since it's not certain that such people will be present when we die, it is important to learn how to manage that experience on our own. Training our mind in spiritual practice while we are alive will enable us to remember it and use it to keep our mind positive at the time of death.

Conclusion

Recognizing that unhealthy attachment to people, possessions, and our body can interfere with a peaceful death, resolve to overcome such attachment and to engage in Dharma—spiritual practice—as much as you can during your life. This will benefit you throughout your life and especially at the time of death.

Dedication

If you started the session with the practice for lamrim meditation, complete the remaining steps of that. Recall the altruistic motivation you generated at the beginning of the session and dedicate the merit you created to enlightenment for the benefit of all sentient beings.

3. Meditation on Subtle Impermanence

If you look closely at and contemplate deeply
the people and things that appear around you,
you can see that all are in constant flux.
Everything becomes the teacher of impermanence.
THE SEVENTH DALAI LAMA, *Meditations to Transform the Mind*

Buddhism explains two levels of impermanence: coarse and subtle. Coarse impermanence is visible to our senses: a person dies, a house burns down, a glass smashes into tiny fragments. Subtle impermanence refers to the changes taking place constantly in conditioned phenomena—things that arise from causes and conditions. For example, the tiny particles that make up our bodies and all other material things are always changing, not remaining the same from one moment to the next. It is precisely because of these momentary changes that our body and other physical phenomena age and eventually die or go out of existence. Coarse impermanence is thus contingent on subtle impermanence.

Our minds are also constantly changing. Each moment, different mental states—perceptions, thoughts, emotions, memories—arise and disappear. Nothing in our mind is permanent, fixed, or always the same.

It is important to understand and become familiar with the subtle, transient nature of our bodies, minds, and all the things we perceive around us. Doing so will help us adopt more realistic attitudes about life and death and be less caught up in disturbing emotions such as attachment and hatred.

THE MEDITATION

Begin by sitting in a comfortable, conducive posture for meditation. Spend a few minutes observing your breathing to settle your thoughts. When your mind is calm, do the practice for lamrim meditation on page 35 and then insert the following meditation after reciting the Buddha's mantra.

Focus your attention on your body. Be aware that it is not a single, indivisible thing, but a collection of many distinct components: skin, bones, blood, organs, muscles, and so on. Each of these larger parts is in turn composed of tiny cells that are constantly changing—coming into existence, moving about, reproducing, dying, and disintegrating.

On an even subtler level are molecules, atoms, and subatomic particles, each of which is likewise changing constantly. Although you are sitting still on your meditation seat, your body is anything but still; it is changing every moment. Stay with this awareness for a while.

Next, turn your attention to your mind. The mind is also composed of parts—thoughts, perceptions, feelings, memories, emotions—that arise and vanish like bubbles. Remain for some time observing this stream of experiences as though you are standing on a bridge watching a river flowing beneath. Avoid getting involved with any of the mental activity; don't judge or make comments. Simply observe and be aware of the impermanent, ever-changing nature of your mind.

After spending some time observing the subtle impermanence of your body and mind, turn your attention to the outer world. All the things around you are likewise changing every moment. Start with the house or building you are sitting in: the wood, bricks, concrete, glass, and metal it is made of, as well as the furniture, carpets, and electrical appliances within it, are composed of particles that do not remain the same from one moment to the next. You cannot see subtle impermanence with your eyes—things appear still and unmoving—but you can understand it conceptually. Stay focused on that awareness for some time; allow it to sink deep within you.

Expand your awareness to the surrounding environment—other buildings and houses, roads, cars, trees, hills and mountains, lakes and rivers, people and animals. Understand that all these are changing every moment. Get a sense that everything in the world around us, and the world itself, is constantly changing, not remaining the same from one moment to the next. Concentrate on this experience as long as you can.

Conclusion

Since all conditioned things are impermanent and subject to change, it is unrealistic to be attached to attractive things, hoping they will remain forever. It also makes no sense to be despondent about problems, as if they will never go away. Resolve to stay mindful of the impermanent nature of things and use this understanding as a remedy to disturbing emotions.

Dedication

Complete the remaining steps of the practice for lamrim meditation, then dedicate the merit you created to all beings' attainment of happiness, up to the highest happiness of enlightenment.

Rebirth and the Three Unfortunate Realms   8

W HAT HAPPENS to our mind when we die? Does it simply vanish, like a candle flame that has gone out, or does it continue? Numerous people have had near-death experiences that point to the feasibility of consciousness continuing after brain functions have ceased. Evidence of the survival of consciousness beyond death can also be found in cases of past-life memories, some of which have been publicly verified. Several religions, including Buddhism, teach rebirth, and surveys show that between 25 to 45 percent of Western people believe in it. It is difficult to prove scientifically but also difficult to disprove, so it's best to keep an open mind.

According to Buddhism, death is the separation of our body and mind, after which the mind takes another rebirth. Where we are born is not a matter of choice unless we happen to be highly accomplished bodhisattvas, who can direct their consciousness at the time of death. Instead, the place of our birth, our parents, and the kind of body and experiences we will have in our next life are determined by karma and our mental state as we die. If we have an abundance of virtuous karma and a positive mind at death, we will be born in a fortunate situation— as a human, deva, or asura.[31] On the other hand, an excess of nonvirtuous karma and a negative mind at death will probably cause rebirth in one of three unfortunate realms—animal, hungry ghost, or hell.

Especially for those of us who might not have been raised in a Buddhist household, the existence of some of these realms may be challenging, as may be the idea of humans being reborn in them. If you fall into that camp, don't simply dismiss these notions without investigation. They were taught by the Buddha based on his meditative experiences—on the eve of his enlightenment, he remembered his own previous lives and perceived other beings dying and taking rebirth according to their karma. Over the centuries since then, numerous meditators who attained high levels of concentration have confirmed the Buddha's findings; we too can experience them first-hand by training in meditative stabilization. Rejecting rebirth and other realms on the grounds that ordinary people do not perceive them and scientists have not discovered them is not reasonable. Conscientious scientists admit there are many things they cannot explain.

The meditation below involves contemplating the sufferings of the three unfortunate places of rebirth. It is crucial to be aware of the disadvantages of these situations—not to become depressed or paralyzed with fear, but to be careful about our behavior and avoid creating their causes. Contemplating them also helps us to realize our good fortune in having a human life and to generate compassion for the beings who are currently in these unfortunate states.

When doing this meditation, it is recommended that you imagine yourself experiencing the sufferings of these realms, realize how disadvantageous they are, and generate the determination to avoid them at all costs. Keep in mind that they are temporary and not eternal—such rebirths are the result of karma, and karma also determines how long you remain in them.

If you have difficulty believing in the existence of these realms, think of human experiences that are similar to them. Being burned in a fire or tortured are comparable to a hell rebirth; experiencing famine and drought or having a drug addiction are comparable to hungry ghost sufferings. Since we share our world with animals, we can understand their sufferings by observing pets and domesticated animals and watching documentaries about animals in the wild.

It is also useful to think of these realms as the product of mental states driven by intense hatred, greed, or confusion. In his classic text *A Guide to the Bodhisattva's Way of Life*, Shantideva said:

> Who intentionally created
> all the weapons for those in hell?
> Who created the burning iron ground? [. . .]
> The Mighty One has said that all such things
> are (the workings of) a negative mind.[32]

We should not take this too far and presume that all suffering is "only in your mind." Saying that to someone experiencing intense pain or grief would be cruel—physical and mental sufferings are very real to those facing them. Shantideva's point is that they are caused by deluded mental states and negative karma and if we want to be free of them, we need to stop creating their causes.

THE MEDITATION

Begin by sitting comfortably in a conducive posture for meditation. Observe your breathing for a few minutes to settle your thoughts. When your mind is calm, do the practice for lamrim meditation on page 35, in full or abbreviated form. Pause after the mantra recitation and do the following meditation.

Animals

Beings are born as animals due to minor nonvirtuous actions, such as stealing, unwise and unkind sexual behavior, or lying. Most animals live in the wild—mountains, forests, deserts, and oceans—where they encounter such sufferings as hunger, thirst, heat, cold, being hunted, and so forth. Those living in deserts or snowy wastelands sometimes go without food or water for long periods of time, and while searching for these are at risk of being killed by other animals or humans. They often face extreme weather conditions with little protection and have no access to medical care when they are injured or sick.

Domesticated animals have other problems, such as the lack of freedom. They may be tied up or confined to a cage or pen, not free to come and go as they wish, nor to eat what and when they like. Their owners may decide to kill them—for meat or hides, or simply because they are old, sick, or troublesome.

The main suffering experienced by all animals is limited intelligence, especially when it comes to Dharma. They are unable to understand and practice the methods for attaining liberation and enlightenment, or even a better rebirth. Instead, most of their actions are motivated by delusion—attachment, anger, and ignorance—and therefore will lead to further suffering in unfortunate rebirths.

Hungry ghosts

The causes of being born in this situation are middling nonvirtuous actions and habitual attitudes such as craving, miserliness, and covetousness.

To get a sense of what such a rebirth is like, imagine being lost in a desert without food or water. The sun is intensely hot, the environment is dry and barren, and your mind can think of nothing other than finding something to drink and eat.

If we human beings were in such a situation, we would not survive more than a few days, but hungry ghosts live without food and water for many years and do not die, but continuously experience unbearable hunger and thirst.

Hungry ghosts are said to be more intelligent than animals and thus have a greater capacity to understand the Dharma, but they are unable to practice it due to their severe suffering. Imagine trying to meditate when you've had nothing to eat or drink for several days.

Hell

Beings are born here as a result of the heaviest negative actions, such as killing or harming others out of strong anger or hatred. The worst of all realms, hell has various levels and types of suffering. Beings in the hot hells are surrounded by fire, intense heat, and torturers intent on causing pain. We humans find it unbearable when the temperature rises above 100 degrees Fahrenheit or if someone criticizes us. The torments of hell are far worse than any human hardship, so it should be easy to recoil from the thought of spending even a moment there.

There are also cold hells. You can get a sense of them by imagining yourself in Antarctica during the winter, when for months the sun doesn't appear to provide a bit of light and warmth. You have no clothing to keep you warm, no shelter from the freezing wind and snow, and no hot food or drinks. A human being would quickly die in such conditions, but a hell-being continues to live with these intense and relentless sufferings for a very long time.

Conclusion

Review the key points:

- After we die, it's possible we could take birth in one of the three unfortunate states—as an animal, as a hungry ghost, or in hell.
- In each of these situations, we would face numerous sufferings and problems and it would be nearly impossible to practice Dharma, even the most basic practice of refraining from nonvirtue.
- As these rebirths are the result of nonvirtuous actions, gener-

ate a strong determination to avoid such actions and to purify those created in the past.[33]

Resolve to learn about karma and do your best to live according to it in order to always be born in conducive conditions to practice Dharma and follow the path to liberation and enlightenment, for the benefit of all beings.

Dedication

If you did the practice for lamrim meditation at the beginning of your session, return to that and complete the remaining steps. Then dedicate the merit you created to your attainment of enlightenment in order to help all sentient beings become free of samsara—especially the unfortunate realms—and lead them to full enlightenment.

Refuge

 9

Thus, the unbearable sufferings of the hells,
of pretas[34] and of beasts are hard to endure.
Whoever else I go to for refuge, except
the Three Supreme Ones, cannot protect me from them.

How can I be protected by the Three Jewels?
The Dharma's the actual refuge, which saves from these fears.
The Buddhas are the Teachers of this Dharma,
the Sangha, my helpers in the Dharma's practice.
YESHE TSONDRU, IN *The Essential Nectar*

MEDITATING on the previous two topics—death and the possibility of an unfortunate rebirth—might make us feel uneasy, even anxious. We may wonder where to turn for help and whether there are methods we can use to deal with these challenges. The next two topics—refuge and karma—provide the Buddhist answer to these questions.

The topic of refuge explores the Three Jewels—Buddha, Dharma, and Sangha—that Buddhists have trust in and rely on to avoid suffering and attain ever-higher forms of genuine happiness. Taking refuge in the Three Jewels is not an act of blind faith, but a carefully considered decision arising from in-depth study, reflection, and meditation on the Buddha's teachings. This process enables us to correctly understand that the Three Jewels help not by magically removing our suffering and transferring realization to us, but by showing the path we need to follow to find true happiness and develop realization for ourselves. A scripture says:

Buddhas do not wash away negativities with water,
clear away beings' duhkha with their hands,

or transfer their realizations to other beings:
they liberate them by teaching the truth of reality.[35]

No one, not even a buddha, can liberate us from suffering and its causes; we must do that ourselves, but the buddhas teach us how. One of the first steps in this process is learning about karma and putting it into practice in our lives—the topic covered in the next chapter.

There are three meditations in this chapter on refuge: the qualities of the Three Jewels, to help us generate confidence in them; the mental states that are the causes of taking refuge; and the benefits of taking refuge.

1. THE QUALITIES OF THE THREE JEWELS

Taking refuge in the Three Jewels involves relying on their guidance in the way we live our life. Taking refuge is primarily an attitude or state of mind, not simply the act of reciting a verse, such as "I take refuge in the Buddha, Dharma, and Sangha." Generating this state of mind depends on understanding their qualities, so the following meditation involves contemplating some of these.

You may have doubt about the qualities ascribed to the Buddha or wonder how we can be sure he really has them. One way to gain confidence in the Buddha's attributes and realizations is to investigate his teachings to determine whether they make sense and accord with our experiences. That is why we are advised to study, reflect, and meditate on the Dharma. Another way is to experiment with meditation and other methods he taught, such as living ethically and compassionately. If these make us happier, more peaceful, and better able to get along with others, we will feel more certain that the Buddha is someone we can rely on.

THE MEDITATION

Start the session by sitting in a conducive posture and take a few minutes to settle your thoughts by observing your breathing. Then perform the practice for lamrim meditation on page 35, in full or abbreviated form, inserting the following meditation after the mantra recitation.

To make this meditation more effective, focus on the visualization of the Buddha in front of you—or imagine traveling back in time and sitting in the Buddha's presence as he is teaching—and contemplate the following qualities.

1. Qualities of the Buddha

A buddha is someone who has freed him- or herself from all negative aspects—ignorance, disturbing emotions, karma, and suffering—and has fully perfected all positive qualities. A buddha's excellent traits can be condensed into four categories: qualities of body, speech, mind, and enlightened activities.

One of the qualities of a buddha's *body* is the ability to manifest in countless different forms at the same time—as a human or animal, a work of art, an awe-inspiring natural phenomenon, an image appearing in a dream. These manifestations arise effortlessly due to a buddha's wisdom and compassion as skillful means to help sentient beings in whatever way is appropriate to them, especially teaching them the Dharma.

One quality of a buddha's *speech* is being able to communicate the Dharma to many beings simultaneously in their respective languages and in ways that are suitable to their minds. The sound of a buddha's voice causes listeners to feel relaxed, peaceful, and inspired. A buddha's many *mental* qualities can be summarized in three: (1) *knowledge*: a buddha's mind is omniscient, seeing all things (both conventional and ultimate truths) directly and simultaneously, every moment; (2) *compassion*: a buddha regards every sentient being with pure, unconditional love and compassion, which are far greater than the love and compassion of, for example, parents for their children; (3) *power* or *ability*: a buddha has no obstruction to acting in compassionate and skillful ways to help others. However, individual beings may sometimes be unable to receive a buddha's help due to their own karmic obstructions.

A buddha's *enlightened activities* are always motivated by pure compassion; they occur spontaneously and effortlessly and are accompanied by perfect wisdom. Although a buddha can assist sentient beings in various ways, the supreme way they help is by teaching the Dharma—the methods whereby sentient beings can become free from samsara and attain the perfect peace and happiness of enlightenment. Providing material aid like food, shelter, and medicine is of course beneficial, but only temporarily because they do not eliminate the root causes of suffering.

We can also feel confident in the buddhas and inspired to follow them by reflecting on their four "bodies" (Sanskrit: *kayas*). These are not physical bodies like ours, made of skin, bones, and so on, but different aspects of an enlightened being:

1. Wisdom truth body (*jnana dharmakaya*): the omniscient mind of a buddha, which is purified of all obscurations and perfect in all excellent qualities.
2. Nature truth body (*svabhavika dharmakaya*): this refers to the true nature of the buddha's mind, its emptiness of inherent existence. It is due to emptiness that an unenlightened mind can be transformed into an enlightened one.
3. Enjoyment body (*sambhogakaya*): a form body manifested by a buddha in a pure land to teach arya bodhisattvas, those who have directly realized emptiness.
4. Emanation body (*nirmanakaya*): form bodies manifested by a buddha to teach ordinary beings, those who are not arya bodhisattvas. Emanation bodies can appear in various ways—as people, animals, or inanimate objects like trees or bridges.

2. Qualities of the Dharma

The word *Dharma* is often used to refer to Buddhist texts, teachings, and practices, but the *actual* Dharma consists of true cessations and true paths—the last two of the four noble truths. A true cessation is a state of having abandoned forever some portion of mental obscurations that prevent the attainment of liberation and enlightenment, such as anger. To better understand this, imagine having abandoned anger such that it never again arises in your mind. No matter what anyone does, you never feel the slightest unhappiness, aversion, or impatience.

A true path is a realization that enables us to attain a true cessation. The main true path is the wisdom directly realizing emptiness, which

is the true nature of all things. When this realization is achieved—
as the culmination of learning, thinking about, and meditating on
emptiness—ignorance and disturbing emotions are abandoned and
no longer arise. This abandonment occurs gradually, in stages, as one
progresses along the path to liberation or enlightenment.

Dharma is said to be the actual refuge; it is like the medicine that
cures our suffering and its causes.

3. Qualities of the Sangha

Although the term *Sangha* is normally used for Buddhist monastics—
monks and nuns—and sometimes one's lay Buddhist community, the
actual Sangha we take refuge in is composed of arya beings, those who
have attained true paths and true cessations. Imagine what it would
be like to meet an arya: someone who has realized the true nature
of things, and whose mind and behavior are exceptionally subdued
rather than being under the control of anger, attachment, jealousy,
and so forth. Get a sense of how helpful it would be to associate with
such a person.

An analogy is used to illustrate the role of the Three Jewels in our spiritual practice:

- We are like a patient afflicted by a serious illness because our
  minds have been under the control of delusions (mental afflictions) from beginningless time and these cause numerous types
  of suffering.
- The Buddha is like the doctor who understands our illness and
  prescribes medicine to cure it.
- The Dharma is like the medicine that actually cures our illness.
- The Sangha are like nurses and caregivers who help and support us while we are recovering.

The Buddha, Dharma, and Sangha are known as objects of *causal
refuge*: external objects we rely on while following the spiritual path.
Buddhist scriptures also speak of objects of *resultant refuge* (sometimes
called *inner refuge*): the buddha, dharma, and sangha we will one day
actualize. Contemplating that we have within us the potential to be a
source of refuge for others can greatly inspire us in our practice.

Conclusion
Review the key points of the meditation: that, due to their qualities and abilities to help us, the Buddha, Dharma, and Sangha are like the doctor, medicine, and caregivers who cure us from suffering. If feelings of inspiration and confidence in the Three Jewels arise in your mind from contemplating these points, focus on them single-pointedly as long as possible to deepen the experience.

Dedication
Complete the remaining steps of the practice for lamrim meditation, then dedicate the merit of the session to all beings' attainment of happiness and enlightenment.

2. The Causes of Taking Refuge

As mentioned above, taking refuge is primarily a state of mind or attitude; this attitude arises from two causes. The first is traditionally called *fear*, but could also be called concern, alarm, or trepidation. The second, *faith*, could be called trust or confidence. Feel free to use whichever of these terms you are most comfortable with. Contemplate the following points to generate these factors in your mind.

The Meditation

Sit in a comfortable and conducive posture for meditation and settle your mind by observing your breathing for several minutes. When you feel ready, do the practice for lamrim meditation on page 35 and insert the following meditation after the recitation of mantra.

1. Concern or fear
The concern or fear that results in taking refuge in the Three Jewels is a reasonable, healthy fear, like being afraid of a car accident if we don't drive carefully. Just as that fear motivates us to be cautious and obey the traffic laws, the fear involved in taking refuge motivates us to rely on the Buddha's guidance and live in accordance with the "law" of karma to the best of our ability.

There are three levels of this fear. The first, related to the initial level of the lamrim, is fear of rebirth in an unfortunate realm. When we hear about these realms we might think, "Oh, that won't happen to me. I haven't committed any major negative actions in my life." That may be true, but the karmic imprints in our mind are not exclusively those accumulated in our present life; they also include imprints from previous lives. Can you be certain that you did not create any major negative actions in past lives? For instance, if you ever thought or dreamed about killing someone, this might be due to imprints in your mind from having killed in a past life.

Also, rebirth in unfortunate states is not caused only by *major* negative actions, but also by minor ones that have not been purified, such as telling little white lies or stealing office supplies from your workplace. Can you really be certain that you do not have the causes of an unfavorable rebirth in your mindstream?

Another factor that determines our next rebirth is our mental state at the time of death. We may have accumulated a lot of virtuous karma but if our mind is overwhelmed by negative thoughts and emotions as we are dying, a seed of nonvirtuous karma could be activated and lead to an unfortunate rebirth. During our life, even when we are healthy and things are going smoothly, our mind sometimes gets swept away by a tsunami of negative energy. The same could happen at the time of death, when everything in our life is falling apart and the situation around us may be chaotic.

Therefore, we cannot be absolutely certain that when our mind separates from our body at the time of death and begins its journey to the next life, we will arrive in a good situation. Contemplating this, we will probably feel alarmed and wonder who or what can help us avoid an unfavorable rebirth. Buddhism says that the Three Jewels can give us the help we need. One way this occurs is by simply remembering them—all three or just one, such as the Buddha—as we are dying and requesting their help. Taking refuge at the time of death will prevent rebirth in an unfortunate realm.

However, the supreme way of receiving help from the Three Jewels is by relying on the Buddha's teachings during our life, especially by living ethically, being kind and compassionate, cultivating wisdom, and so on. The greater our familiarity with such Dharma practices, the greater our chances of being in a positive state of mind at the time of death, thus activating a good karmic seed and obtaining a fortunate rebirth.

The second level of fear, related to the intermediate level of the lamrim, involves fear of cyclic existence: taking rebirth again and again in the cycle of samsara and experiencing its manifold sufferings. This fear leads to taking refuge in the Three Jewels and relying on their guidance to attain liberation, the state of being free forever from all suffering and its causes.

The third level of fear, related to the advanced level, involves extending the fear of samsara to all sentient beings and wishing them to be free of its sufferings. In this section of the lamrim, we cultivate universal love and compassion and eventually commit ourselves to do whatever we can to help sentient beings be free of suffering and its causes and attain the supreme peace and happiness of enlightenment. Fulfilling this commitment entails becoming enlightened ourselves. Realizing that we are unable to attain enlightenment without the help of the Buddha, Dharma, and Sangha, we rely on the Three Jewels to attain full enlightenment, or buddhahood, for the sake of all beings. This is Mahayana refuge.[36]

2. Confidence or faith

The second cause for taking refuge is a confident recognition that the three objects of refuge—Buddha, Dharma, and Sangha—can give us the help we need to avoid unwanted sufferings and problems, such as an unfortunate rebirth. It arises from contemplating the qualities of the Three Jewels, as explained above. In addition, the lamrim explains four reasons why the Buddha is a worthy object of refuge.

(1) *He himself is free of all fears,* due to having overcome all suffering and its causes: karma and delusions. The Buddha was once like us—trapped in samsara, uncontrollably experiencing its myriad sufferings—but by following the path, he purified his karma and delusions, especially ignorance, which are the main causes of suffering. As a result, he will never again experience even the slightest problem and has nothing to fear.

(2) *He knows how to help others become free of fear.* Because he found the way out of samsara, he is someone we can rely on to free ourselves of suffering and its causes. If you and some friends were lost in the wilderness without a map, you would be overjoyed to meet a forest ranger

who is familiar with the terrain and trails and can show you the way out. The Buddha is similar—he knows thoroughly the causes of suffering and the causes of happiness and can guide us to avoid the former and follow the latter.

(3) *He has great compassion* and wishes to help us become free of suffering. If the forest ranger was preoccupied with his own work and refused to help you, you would be devastated. Likewise with the Buddha—if he remained meditating in the peace of nirvana and did nothing to help others, how would anyone find their way out of samsara? Fortunately, due to his ever-flowing great compassion for every sentient being, he is totally dedicated to helping us until we have all become free from samsara.

(4) *His great compassion extends to all sentient beings without exception* because he has no prejudice, only perfect equanimity. How would you feel if the forest ranger was biased and willing to help only some members of your party but not everyone? It is said that if there are two people, one who is devoted and makes offerings to the Buddha and another who is hateful and tries to harm him, the Buddha's feelings toward both are exactly the same—equally loving and compassionate, equally dedicated to helping them become free of suffering and attain enlightenment.

Conclusion
Review the key points of the meditation:
- The first cause of taking refuge is the wish to be free of suffering, starting with unfortunate rebirths in future lives.
- The second cause is confidence that the Three Jewels can help us become free of suffering, mainly by revealing the path to liberation and enlightenment.
- We can develop this confidence by contemplating how the Buddha himself has gone beyond all problems and their causes and is compassionately dedicated to helping all other beings do the same.
- Confidence in the Buddha enables us to trust his teachings, the Dharma, and those who follow these teachings, the Sangha.

To whatever extent you feel confidence in the Three Jewels, keep your mind focused single-pointedly on that feeling for several minutes.

Dedication
Complete the practice for lamrim meditation and dedicate the merit you created to enlightenment for the benefit of all living beings.

3. The Benefits of Taking Refuge

Knowing the benefits of taking refuge in the Three Jewels will inspire us to cultivate this state of mind and make it a part of our daily life.

The Meditation

Start the session as usual: sitting comfortably, then settling your thoughts with a few minutes of meditation on the breath. When your mind is calm, do the practice for lamrim meditation on page 35, in full or abbreviated form. Pause after the mantra recitation and do the following meditation.

Contemplate the following results of taking refuge:
1. *You become a Buddhist.* This is not like joining a club, but becoming a person dedicated to bringing about a positive transformation of their mind. The Tibetan term for Buddhist literally means an "inner being"—someone who looks inside for genuine happiness and peace.
2. *You are qualified to take precepts,* or vows, such as the five lay precepts. Taking and keeping precepts is a powerful way to purify karma, create virtue, and make progress on the path.
3. *Your negative karma and delusions will gradually decrease* and will eventually be completely purified.
4. *You quickly accumulate a vast amount of merit,* or positive energy, an essential factor for spiritual progress.
5. *You will avoid unfortunate rebirths.* Taking refuge as you die will prevent an unfortunate rebirth in the next life, and practicing the Dharma—especially ethical conduct—protects you from unfortunate rebirths in later lifetimes.

6. *You are not harmed by obstacles,* whether they are human or nonhuman. There are numerous accounts of people freeing themselves from difficult situations by taking refuge.

7. *Your wishes, both temporal and ultimate, are more easily fulfilled.* This is due to the virtue created by taking refuge and practicing the Dharma.

8. *You will attain buddhahood swiftly* due to following the Buddha's guidance in your thoughts and actions.

Conclusion

Consider what you wish to achieve in terms of the spiritual path, and whether relying upon Buddha, Dharma, and Sangha will help you to achieve those goals. If the wish to take refuge in and follow the guidance of the Three Jewels arises in your mind, stay focused on that for a few minutes. Finally, resolve to live your life in that way to the best of your ability.[37]

Dedication

If you did the practice for lamrim meditation at the beginning of your session, return to that and dissolve the visualization of the Buddha. Then dedicate the merit you created to all beings' attainment of happiness, up to the highest happiness of enlightenment.

Karma

10

This body and life are changing, like a water bubble;
remember how quickly they perish and death comes.
After death, just like a shadow follows the body,
the results of negative and positive karma follow.

When I have found definite conviction in this,
please bless me always to be conscientious
in abandoning even the slightest collection of shortcomings
and in accomplishing all virtuous deeds.
TSONGKHAPA, "THE FOUNDATION OF ALL GOOD QUALITIES"

WE NOW have a precious human life, but it will someday end and our mind will travel to its next rebirth. Naturally we wish to be born in a favorable situation rather than an unfavorable one, and taking refuge will facilitate that. However, since it is mainly our karma, or actions, that determines the realm and circumstances of our next life, it is important to understand karma and do our best to live according to it. Otherwise, even if we attain another human rebirth, our life might be short or plagued with problems.

Like rebirth, karma is another Buddhist topic people sometimes have trouble accepting. Remember, the Buddha said we should investigate things for ourselves and not blindly believe them. When talking about karma, Lama Yeshe would say that we can see evidence of it in our daily life. We sometimes wake up in a bad mood—unhappy with ourself, our life, job, partner, and so on. What kind of experiences will we have that day with such a mental state? Mostly bad ones. On the other hand, if we start the day feeling cheerful and loving, wanting to be kind and helpful to others as much as we can, we are more likely to have positive experiences. This illustrates the basic principle of karma:

whether we are happy or suffer is mainly up to us. We are the creators of our experiences.

In this chapter you will find four meditations on the topic of karma: its general characteristics, specific details, and results, as well as the way to purify negative karma.

1. Four General Characteristics of Karma

The Buddhist teachings on karma are complex, containing many details regarding the types of karma that are virtuous and nonvirtuous, the various results of these, and so on. Before diving into those, it's helpful to start by looking at general characteristics of karma to understand better what it is and how it works.

You will likely note that there are a variety of terms found in different books for the two main types of karma: virtuous and nonvirtuous, positive and negative, skillful and unskillful, wholesome and unwholesome, constructive and destructive. Some of these are used in this book. Traditional Sanskrit and Tibetan texts sometimes use white and black, but given the racialized connotations of these terms, they are best avoided. You may be uncomfortable with some of the other terms, so feel free to adopt the ones you find most appropriate for your personal study and practice.

The Meditation

Sit in a comfortable posture that is conducive for meditation. Observe your breathing for a few minutes to settle your thoughts, then do the practice for lamrim meditation on page 35. Pause after the mantra recitation and do the following meditation.

1. Karma is definite.
Karma is the Sanskrit term for action; it refers to actions we do with our body, speech, and mind. It is sometimes called the "law of cause and effect" because our actions are the *causes* of *effects* that we will experience in the future. However, it is a natural law, like gravity, and not one fabricated by anyone, including the Buddha—he merely discovered the workings of karma while in deep meditation.

The first general characteristic of karma—that karma is definite—means there is a definite correlation between the actions we do and the experiences we will have later: nonvirtuous actions bring suffering, not happiness, and virtuous actions bring happiness, not suffering. This is like what we observe in nature: cauliflower seeds bring cauliflower, not tomatoes, and tomato seeds bring tomatoes, not cauliflower.

How do we know if an action is nonvirtuous or virtuous, negative or positive? One way is according to the motivation: negative actions are those motivated by delusions such as anger, attachment, jealousy, and ignorance,[38] while positive actions are those motivated by beneficial attitudes such as compassion, love, nonattachment, and wisdom.

Another way to distinguish nonvirtuous and virtuous actions is by way of their results. Buddhist scriptures define nonvirtue as that which brings suffering and virtue as that which brings happiness. Most of us lack the ability to foresee the future results of our actions, so the Buddha—who had this ability—explained ten nonvirtuous actions that cause the greatest amount of suffering: killing, stealing, unwise and unkind sexual behavior, lying, divisive speech, harsh speech, idle talk, covetousness, ill will, and wrong views. He also taught a corresponding list of ten virtuous actions that bring the greatest happiness: these involve consciously refraining from the ten nonvirtuous actions, knowing they lead to misery, and engaging in their opposites—protecting life and property, speaking honestly and kindly, and so on.

Bring to mind several negative actions you have done. Reflect that, although at the time they may not have seemed harmful, they will bring problems later if you do not purify them. If you can accept this, decide to learn and practice purification methods and try your best to avoid repeating those actions in the future. You can also commit yourself to engage in positive actions as much as possible, understanding that they are the cause of the happiness and good experiences that you wish for.

2. Karma increases.
The *Tibetan Dhammapada*, a collection of the Buddha's teachings, says:

> Even a tiny evil deed
> can cause great ruin and trouble
> in the world that lies beyond—
> like poison that has entered the body.

> Even small meritorious acts
> bring happiness to future lives,
> accomplishing a great purpose
> like seeds becoming bounteous crops.[39]

Just as a single seed planted in the right environment and conditions can bring a large tree bearing flowers and fruit every year, the karmic imprints of our actions can lead to multiple results over a long period of time. Nonvirtuous actions, if left unpurified, will bring numerous painful experiences, both in our present life and in future ones. Likewise, virtuous actions, if not opposed by a negative force such as anger, will lead to many positive experiences occurring over many lifetimes. This is true for both major, significant actions and those that seem minor or insignificant.

If this makes sense to you, resolve to do your best to avoid negative actions, even relatively light ones like killing insects, and to perform as many positive actions as possible, including those that don't require much effort, such as offering a kind smile to a stranger.

3. If we do not perform an action, we will not experience its result.
The agreeable and disagreeable experiences we encounter in life are the result of our own virtuous and nonvirtuous past actions, respectively. Other conditions such as family, environment, society, and global events play a role, but the principal cause of our happy experiences is past virtuous deeds and the principal cause of our painful experiences is past nonvirtue. Understanding this helps us take responsibility for our experiences rather than blaming others for our problems or expecting them to make us happy.

This general characteristic also means that our future experiences depend on our present actions. To attain the good experiences we naturally wish for, we must create the right causes, just as farmers who want a harvest of corn must plant seeds, water them, and care for the young shoots. Standing in a field and praying for corn to magically appear doesn't work! Likewise, to avoid the unpleasant experiences we do not want, we must refrain from their causes.

Check if you believe that your happiness and unhappiness are mainly due to external things—other people, the government, society, the environment. If so, recognize that this notion is unrealistic.

Resolve to change it and learn to accept that the main responsibility for your experiences lies with you.

4. Karma is never lost.

Our actions of body, speech, and mind leave imprints on our consciousness that do not disappear on their own. At some later point—usually in a future life—when the right conditions come together, these imprints will ripen as pleasant or painful experiences, like seeds developing into plants and trees. In the *Tibetan Dhammapada*, the Buddha said:

> Whether it was good or bad,
> the power of any action
> once performed is never lost;
> the results arise accordingly.[40]

There are exceptions to this. Negative karma can be purified with the four opponent powers: feeling regret, taking refuge, applying remedies, and resolving to not repeat the action.[41] The seeds of positive actions can be damaged by getting angry or generating certain wrong views—rejecting karma or the possibility of attaining enlightenment. Fortunately, we can protect the good karma we create by dedicating it to enlightenment for the benefit of all beings and recalling emptiness, at whatever level we understand it.

Conclusion

Review the four characteristics of karma:

- *It's definite*—negative karma brings suffering and positive karma brings happiness.
- *It increases*—even a small action can bring multiple results over many lifetimes.
- *If we don't perform an action, we won't experience its result.*
- *The results of actions are not lost,* even over many lifetimes, unless they meet with counterforces.

Make the determination to do your best to refrain from negative actions, do as many positive actions as possible, and purify the negative actions you have already done.

Dedication

Return to the practice for lamrim meditation and complete the remaining steps. Then dedicate the merit you created that all sentient beings may encounter the Dharma and follow the path, finally attaining the full enlightenment of buddhahood.

2. Specific Details of Karma

Although there are countless examples of negative and positive actions, the Buddha mentioned ten nonvirtuous actions to be avoided, as they are the principal causes of future suffering, and ten virtuous ones to be engaged in, as they are the main causes of happiness. The following meditation goes through these twenty actions in a brief way; more details can be found in lamrim texts.

The Meditation

Sit in a comfortable position for meditation and settle your thoughts by being mindful of your breathing for a few minutes. When your mind is calm, perform the practice for lamrim meditation on page 35, inserting the following meditation at the appropriate point in the practice.

Let's start with contemplating the ten nonvirtues. As you go through the list, recall any examples of these from your experience. See if you can recognize how they are the cause of problems, both in the short-term and long-term. Feel regret for having done them and resolve to do your best to avoid repeating them.

The first three actions are physical, done with our body:
1. *Killing*—intentionally destroying the life of any living being.
2. *Stealing*—taking what doesn't belong to us or not paying money that we owe, like taxes or train fares.
3. *Unwise and unkind sexual behavior*—engaging in sexual activity that causes suffering, such as being unfaithful to your spouse or partner, or forcing someone to have sex against their will.

The next four actions are done with our speech:

4. *Lying*—saying what is not true. The worst form of lying is about spiritual attainments, such as falsely claiming to have realizations. But even minor lies can be very damaging.

5. *Divisive speech*—speech that causes disharmony between two or more individuals or groups or that increases disharmony that already exists. This usually occurs due to hatred or jealousy.

6. *Harsh speech*—expressing words that are hurtful to another person motivated by one of the three main delusions: attachment, anger, or ignorance of karma.

7. *Idle talk*—speaking about unimportant topics, motivated by a delusion such as attachment. Such talk can increase disturbing emotions in the minds of ourselves and others and wastes time that could be used for more beneficial activities.

The last three actions are mental ones:

8. *Covetousness*—desiring something that belongs to another person and devising ways of procuring it.

9. *Harmful intent*—wishing to cause harm to someone and planning how to do so.

10. *Wrong views*—rejecting something that is true and important for your spiritual development, such as karma or the possibility of attaining enlightenment. Wrong view goes beyond simple doubt that wonders whether these things are true; it's when you completely close your mind to them, deciding they are not true.

On the positive side, the ten virtuous actions involve making the conscious effort to avoid the ten nonvirtues, knowing that they are harmful. For example, understanding that killing causes suffering to the victim as well as to yourself, you decide to refrain from it as much as possible. When a fly lands on your arm, you respect it as a living being who doesn't want to suffer or die and you also don't want to create the negative karma of killing—which would bring suffering to yourself in the future—so you gently brush it away. In that way you create the virtuous karma of non-killing, or refraining from killing. Simply not doing a nonvirtuous action like killing without that understanding—as would be the case for a baby or a rabbit—is not virtuous karma because they do not recognize the harmfulness of killing.

We can also create virtuous karma by doing constructive actions that are opposite to the ten nonvirtues—protecting and saving life, respecting others' possessions and being generous with our own, speaking in ways that are honest, beneficial, considerate, and compassionate, and so forth.

Conclusion

Make the determination to do your best to refrain from these ten nonvirtuous actions and to purify those you did in the past or continue to do in the present out of habit. We cannot expect to completely avoid negative actions right from the start, so it's important to be patient and compassionate with ourselves and continue trying. With further practice, we will be able to gradually decrease negative actions. Resolve to do as many positive actions as you can and rejoice in these, thus encouraging yourself to do more.

Dedication

Complete the rest of the practice for lamrim meditation and dedicate the merit of your session to enlightenment for the benefit of all living beings.

3. The Results of Karma

In Buddhist philosophy, the topic of cause and effect is considered quite important. All impermanent phenomena—which, as we saw earlier, includes our bodies and minds and everything we perceive in the world around us—are the results of causes and conditions without which they could not exist. Moreover, these results are themselves the causes and conditions for other things. A tree, for example, grew from a seed, water, warmth, and nutrients in the soil. Once it has grown, it produces more seeds as well as leaves, shade, and sometimes flowers, fruits, or nuts. These are simple facts of life that most people understand, but contemplating them in terms of our experiences is beneficial on the path to enlightenment, as it helps us gain greater clarity about how things exist and overcome misconceptions that keep us imprisoned in samsara.

Karma is sometimes called *the law of cause and effect*; our present experiences, like the tree, are mainly the result of actions we did in the past that left seeds on our mental continuum. When the appropriate conditions come together, these seeds ripen in the form of suffering and happiness. Furthermore, depending on how we experience these results, we create even more karmic seeds that will bring still more unpleasant and pleasant experiences in the future—and the cycle continues, on and on. In Buddhism, the ultimate goal is to go beyond karma altogether, but until then we need to understand how it works—which actions lead to painful and positive results. With this understanding we can attain greater control over our life and our experiences by avoiding actions that lead to suffering and problems, and engaging in those that lead to happiness and conducive conditions.

The following meditation focuses on the detailed results of our nonvirtuous and virtuous actions; reflecting on these will enhance our determination to avoid the former and engage in the latter, to the best of our ability.

The Meditation

Begin the session by sitting in a conducive posture for meditation and observing your breath for a few minutes to settle your thoughts. Do the practice for lamrim meditation on page 35, pausing after the mantra recitation to meditate on the following.

In general, negative actions bring suffering and positive actions bring happiness, but when it comes to the specifics, each action is unique. Depending on various factors, an action becomes heavier or lighter— in terms of the significance of the imprint it leaves on our mind and the intensity of its results—as well as complete or incomplete. These factors include the motivation for doing the action, the way it is done, the object of the action, and so on.[42]

As this topic can be rather complicated, a helpful way to understand it is by using examples of things we've actually done. Think of a time when you spoke harshly to someone out of anger, hurting their feelings. This is the nonvirtuous action of harsh speech. For the action to be *complete*, meaning that it brings the full set of karmic results, four factors must be present:

1. The object of the action
2. The intention, one's state of mind while doing the action, which itself has three parts: (a) recognition, (b) motivation, and (c) delusion
3. The actual action
4. The completion of the action

Examine a case of harsh speech. (1) The *object* needs to be another person who could be hurt. (2) For the *intention*, (a) the *recognition* is that you correctly identify the person you wish to hurt; (b) the *motivation* is intending to speak hurtful words; and (c) the *delusion* could be any of the three poisonous attitudes (anger, attachment, or ignorance of karma). (3) The *actual action* is speaking or writing[43] hurtful words, and (4) the *completion* is when the other person hears or reads those words, understands them, and is hurt.

If your action of harsh speech was committed with all four of these factors complete, it will bring three types of results:

1. *Ripened result.* All ten nonvirtues cause rebirth in one of the three unfortunate realms—as an animal, hungry ghost, or hell-being. Karma that ripens in the form of a rebirth is known as throwing, or projecting, karma, whereas karma that brings results in the course of a life (such as illness) is known as completing karma.
2. *Results similar to the cause.* These are of two types:
   a. *Experiences similar to the cause.* Once the karma that caused you to be born in an unfortunate realm has run its course and you take rebirth in a fortunate realm, you will have experiences similar to your original actions. As a result of harsh speech, you will be on the receiving end of others' harsh speech.
   b. *Actions similar to the cause.* When you have been born in a fortunate realm, you will have the instinctive tendency to commit the same action repeatedly—in this case, that

means you will have the tendency to use hurtful, abusive language. This is considered the worst karmic result because we continue creating negative karma, again and again.

3. *Environmental results.* When you have been born as a human being, you will experience results of your actions in the form of environmental conditions. For example, harsh speech is the cause of living in a place with sharp rocks, thorns, brambles, and other unpleasant things.[44]

If contemplating these results makes you feel uneasy or even frightened about the suffering you will experience due to speaking harshly, transform those feelings into regret for the action and the determination to purify the karma (the subject of the next meditation).

On the positive side, doing any of the ten virtuous actions with all four factors complete will bring three types of beneficial results. Let's use the example of non-killing: deliberately refraining from killing another being that we could choose to kill. Think of a time when you saw an insect in your home and felt the impulse to kill it, but refrained from doing so because you did not want to create negative karma. If that action was done with all four factors—object, intention, action, completion—it is the cause of the following results:

1. *Ripened result.* Refraining from killing (and the other nine virtuous actions) is the cause of rebirth in one of the three fortunate realms—as a human, deva, or asura.
2. *Results similar to the cause.* These are of two types:
   a. *Experiences similar to the cause.* Because you avoided killing, you will experience good health and a long life.
   b. *Actions similar to the cause.* You will have the instinctive tendency to respect and protect life.
3. *Environmental results.* You will live in a peaceful, healthy place with plentiful food, medicine, and other necessities.

By understanding the positive results of non-killing, feel a sense of joy or rejoicing that you did it, and resolve to continue behaving this way as much as possible.

Conclusion

Aware of the painful results of nonvirtuous actions and the beneficial results of virtuous actions, determine to live your life as much as possible in accordance with karma—refraining from what is negative and doing what is positive and beneficial.

Dedication

Return to the practice for lamrim meditation and complete that, then dedicate the merit you created to all beings' attainment of happiness, up to the highest happiness of enlightenment.

4. PURIFICATION WITH THE FOUR POWERS

Karma is not fate; we are not doomed to suffer as a result of our negative actions. These can be purified with the four opponent powers—regret, reliance, remedy, and resolve. These are primarily mental states we can generate anytime, anyplace. Each of the four purifies one of the four types of results: (1) the power of regret purifies the experience similar to the cause, (2) the power of reliance purifies the environmental result, (3) the power of remedy purifies the ripened result, and (4) the power of resolve purifies the action similar to the cause.

There is no nonvirtue so negative that it cannot be purified. It's a good idea to do purification practice daily, especially at the end of the day, to rectify the negative actions we committed during the day and go to sleep with a clear mind. We can also purify negative actions we did earlier in our life. The following meditation explains one way of doing a purification practice with the four powers.

THE MEDITATION

Start your session by settling your body in a comfortable, conducive position. Observe your breathing for a few minutes to settle your thoughts. When your mind is calm, do the practice for lamrim meditation on page 35, and insert the following meditation after reciting the Buddha's mantra.

1. The power of regret

Regret is an intelligent recognition that something we did was mistaken, a cause of suffering for others and/or ourselves. It is not guilt, an overly emotional reaction where we think we are permanently bad and hopeless. Regret is more rational and constructive; we feel remorse for the action because we see it as wrong, wish we had acted otherwise, and aspire to find constructive solutions. Generating regret purifies the karmic result that is similar to the cause in terms of experience—having experiences similar to those we inflicted on others.

Bring to mind actions you did recently or in the distant past that you recognize as unskillful or harmful. Reviewing the list of the ten nonvirtues could help you remember any of these you have done.

Recognize that these actions are the cause of suffering for yourself and others, both in the short-term and long-term, and generate a sincere feeling of regret that you did them. Reflect that if you do not purify these actions, the imprints they left on your mind will bring future problems and misfortune. They will also hinder your progress on the spiritual path and keep you trapped in samsara, forced to undergo continuous suffering and unable to actualize your potential for enlightenment. Recall your wish for happiness and spiritual realizations, feel that you deserve these, and resolve to purify the karma that prevents their attainment.

2. The power of reliance

For Buddhists, reliance involves renewing our refuge in the Three Jewels and our compassionate wish to benefit others and not harm them. If you do not identify as Buddhist, you can bring to mind another person or object you have faith in or the personal values you try to live by, which you transgress by performing negative actions.

Focusing on these refuge objects or personal values, humbly acknowledge your mistakes. Using your own words and speaking from your heart, make a request for forgiveness and guidance to help you avoid repeating those mistakes in the future.

To rectify your actions that harmed others, remember that everyone wishes to be happy and to not suffer, just as you do. Generate lovingkindness and compassion and a sincere wish to only benefit others and not harm them.

Remembering that the power of reliance purifies the environmental result of our negative actions—being born or living in places with unpleasant and unconducive conditions—will inspire you to practice it regularly.

3. The power of remedy

This next of the four powers means performing positive, virtuous actions to counteract the negative ones we have committed. One remedy is to recite the mantra of an enlightened being such as Shakyamuni Buddha. If you did the practice for lamrim meditation on page 35, you can focus on the visualization of the Buddha in front of you and recite his mantra twenty-one times or more while imagining light flowing from him. The light fills your entire body and mind and purifies all your negative karma and delusions.

Other recommended remedies are to recite, study, or contemplate sutras such as the *Heart Sutra*; make offerings to holy beings; recite the names of buddhas; and create images of buddhas or make donations to the building of monasteries, stupas, or holy objects.

It is said that you can use any virtuous, constructive action as the remedy to nonvirtues, so feel free to be creative—you could volunteer in a food bank or animal shelter, for example, or make donations to charities. Practicing the power of remedy purifies the ripened result of our nonvirtues—taking rebirth in an unfortunate realm in a future life.

4. The power of resolve

The power of resolve involves mentally promising to not do the same negative actions again, according to your ability. This power purifies the result similar to the cause in terms of action—having the instinctive tendency to repeat the same negative action again.

There may be some actions, such as physically harming others or selling illegal drugs, that you are confident you can completely stop, so pledge to do that. However, with more minor actions or those you are strongly habituated to, it would not be realistic to make such a promise—there's a good chance you would break it and that could damage your self-confidence. Instead, you can promise to refrain from those actions for a certain period of time—if only for one hour, or even five minutes—or simply resolve to do your best to be mindful and gradually decrease doing them.

Conclusion

At the conclusion of your purification practice, feel a sense of joy and lightness, and generate the wish that all living beings could purify their negative karma so they do not have to experience its suffering results.

Dedication

Complete the practice for lamrim meditation, then dedicate the merit you created so that all sentient beings may be free of all suffering and its causes and attain all happiness and its causes, up to the highest happiness of enlightenment.

PART 4

MEDITATIONS OF THE INTERMEDIATE LEVEL

In dependence on these, I am able to attain only the higher rebirths
of humans and gods.
Not having abandoned delusions, I will have to experience uninter-
rupted, limitless cyclic existence.
By contemplating well how cyclic existence works, may I train, day
and night, in the principal path of the three precious higher
trainings—the means of attaining liberation.
Please bless me with the potential to continuously train like this.

VAJRADHARA LOSANG JINPA, "A GLANCE MEDITATION
ON ALL THE IMPORTANT POINTS OF LAMRIM"

A Bridge between the Initial and Intermediate Levels

11

WE ARE now ready to move on to the meditations of the second section of the lamrim—the intermediate level, or medium scope. But first let's review the key points of the initial level, or small scope, meditations. This will help you understand how they lay the foundation for and connect to the intermediate-level meditations. As explained earlier, all the lamrim topics are essential practices for someone wishing to attain enlightenment, and the earlier ones must be learned and practiced prior to the later ones. Gaining insights into the initial-level topics gives us firm grounding to appreciate and realize those of the intermediate and advanced levels. They are like the steps of a ladder or staircase, or the different levels of an education system where a student must graduate from primary school before entering secondary school, and so on. It's somewhat different, however, with the lamrim because you can learn and meditate on all the topics from the beginning—familiarizing with the entire path right from the start. What you can't do is skip over any of them, thinking you don't need it.

The following review can be used as a meditation—starting as usual with the preliminary practices and concluding with a dedication—or just read through slowly and contemplatively.

THE MEDITATION

Start the session as usual by sitting in a conducive position and calming your mind with a few minutes of meditation on the breath. You may wish to do the practice of lamrim meditation on page 35, abbreviated or full, or simply generate a positive, altruistic motivation for engaging in the following meditation.

The nature of mind

Our mind is by nature pure and clear, like the sky, and has vast potential. Our greatest potential is to become enlightened: completely free of everything negative, fully developed in all positive qualities, and able to benefit all beings.

However, the pure nature of our mind is temporarily obscured, like the sky on a cloudy day. These obscurations include the delusions—ignorance, greed, hatred, and so on—as well as obscurations to omniscience—imprints of ignorance that cause things to appear incorrectly. Obscurations are not permanent aspects of our mind but can be removed, just as clouds can disappear, leaving a clear sky. However, we need help to accomplish this; it's not something we know how to do intuitively.

Long ago, the Buddha discovered a way to free his mind from all obscurations. Realizing this was possible for everyone, he explained the method in his teachings, the Dharma. These instructions have been kept alive for the last 2,500 years, transmitted by realized masters to their disciples, who in turn realize and transmit them. Among those masters and practitioners are the Sangha, arya beings who have directly perceived the true nature of things: their emptiness of inherent existence. These three—Buddha, Dharma, and Sangha—are the "Jewels" that Buddhists take refuge in and reply upon for spiritual transformation.

We live in favorable times, as there are many living masters who are qualified to explain the path to enlightenment and who are freely sharing their knowledge and experience of the path. Feel how precious it is that you can meet such teachers who can introduce you to the Three Jewels and to the nature of your mind and guide you in transforming it.

Precious human life

We are also very fortunate to have a human life with the ideal outer and inner conditions to learn and practice the path to enlightenment. Such a life is rare and valuable because with it we can create the causes for good rebirths, liberation, and enlightenment. Think of examples of those who do not have a precious human life and contemplate how fortunate you are to have one.

Death and impermanence

The precious opportunity we have to practice the Dharma in our lifetime will not last forever. Our body is impermanent—changing every moment, aging, and subject to death. It is definite that we will die but we have no way of knowing how and when—it could even happen today or tonight. Since death will separate us from our loved ones, possessions, and body, the only thing that can benefit us at that time and in future lives is the Dharma—in particular, the methods we have learned for keeping our mind positive and the virtuous karma we created during our life. Contemplate this and feel a sense of urgency: I must practice Dharma as much as possible now, purely, while I still have the chance.

Rebirth and the unfortunate realms

The importance of Dharma practice becomes even clearer when we consider what could happen after we die. Although we hope for a fortunate rebirth and positive experiences, we can't be sure we'll obtain them. We could be reborn in one of the three unfortunate realms—as an animal, a hungry ghost, or in hell—due to negative karma we created in this or a previous life. Understand that taking rebirth in one of these realms would be dreadful and generate the determination to do whatever is necessary to avoid it.

Refuge

Avoiding an unfavorable rebirth and obtaining a favorable one mainly depend on taking refuge and observing karma, the law of cause and effect. Taking refuge is an attitude arising from two causes: (1) the strong wish to avoid suffering and (2) confidence that the Three Jewels can help us, not only to avoid suffering but also to attain liberation and enlightenment. Generate this feeling of confidence, or faith, in the ability of the Three Jewels to help you. Feel the wish to rely on them and put yourself under their wise and compassionate guidance.

Karma

The principal way the Buddha helps living beings is by teaching the Dharma, the practices that free us from suffering. Buddhas are not able to magically remove problems or bestow well-being upon us because we are the creators of our experiences—whether we are happy or suffer is our own responsibility, depending on our actions. So our first task is to learn about karma, understand which actions lead to suffering and which lead to happiness, and live according to this natural law. Generate a sense of certainty that your actions are the causes of your future experiences—later in this life as well as in future lives—and resolve to do your best to create virtue and avoid nonvirtue.

Connecting to the intermediate level
By integrating the initial-level insights into our mind and living in accordance with karma, we can be assured of taking rebirth in one of the three fortunate realms: human, asura, or deva.

But this is just a temporary solution. There will be problems and unsatisfactory experiences in those lives as well, they will eventually come to an end, and once again we will take rebirth without choice or control. This is the story of samsara: the wheel of life, death, and rebirth. It can be compared to an endlessly spinning Ferris wheel on which beings are trapped and forced to die, be reborn, and experience unwanted problems again and again, ceaselessly.

If we want to be free forever from suffering and its causes, we need to liberate ourselves from samsara. That is the focus of the meditations of the intermediate level, or medium scope. They involve recognizing the faults of samsara, generating the determination to be free from it, and engaging in the practices that will bring that about.

Conclusion
The initial-level meditations provide an essential foundation for Dharma practice, but we need to build on that with the intermediate-level meditations. These lead us to become disenchanted with samsara and aspire to be free from it. They also lay the foundation for the advanced-level meditations, where we develop bodhichitta, the aspiration to help all beings become free of samsara. Generate enthusiasm to learn and practice those meditations, for your own benefit and that of all others.

Dedication

If you started with the practice for lamrim meditation, complete the remaining steps of that, then dedicate the merit you created to all beings' attainment of happiness, up to the highest happiness of enlightenment.

The Truth of Suffering 12

Violently tossed amidst waves of karma and delusions,
plagued by the many sea monsters of the three kinds of sufferings,
I seek your blessings to develop an intense longing to be liberated
from this infinite and frightening great ocean of existence.
FIRST PANCHEN LAMA, *Guru Puja*

THE ESSENCE of the intermediate-level section of the lamrim is developing the wish to be free of samsara, known as *renunciation* or *the determination to be free*. Both terms have the same meaning and are used interchangeably, but for some people, determination to be free has a more positive and inviting connotation than renunciation. This attitude is an essential prerequisite for the compassion and bodhichitta cultivated in the advanced level, or great scope, where we generate the aspiration to free not only ourselves but all other beings from samsara.

One way to generate renunciation is by contemplating the four noble truths:[45]

1. The truth of suffering, or true sufferings: all beings in samsara undergo various types of painful or unsatisfactory experiences.

2. The truth of origins, or true origins: the origins or causes of suffering are karma and delusions, mainly ignorance, attachment, and hatred.

3. The truth of cessation, or true cessations: it is possible to become completely free of all suffering and its causes and attain the state of liberation, or *nirvana*.

4. The truth of the path, or true paths: liberation is attained by developing the wisdom that realizes the true nature of things, the emptiness of inherent existence. This wisdom is the

antidote to ignorance and the other factors that keep us in samsara.

More details about these four truths and meditations on them are provided in the later chapters of this section.[46]

Regarding the first truth, the Sanskrit term *duhkha* is usually translated as "suffering," but a more appropriate term is "unsatisfactoriness." It refers to any experience that is unpleasant, unwanted, or simply unsatisfying. This chapter contains three separate meditations—on various types of suffering explained by the Buddha and Buddhist masters—that guide us to deeper insights into the reality of *duhkha* in our lives and in samsara.

While doing these meditations, if you experience resistance, depression, fear, or other troubling feelings, remember that suffering is impermanent. Suffering depends on causes and conditions, and by eliminating those you can become free from all forms of *duhkha* and help others do likewise. Also, there are methods you can use to alleviate your problems, as well as an ultimate solution—the Dharma—with which you can become utterly free of all suffering, forever.[47] So keep your mind balanced by recalling your good fortune to have a precious human life with all the ideal conditions to practice the Dharma.

1. The Eight Kinds of Suffering

Eight types of *duhkha* were mentioned by the Buddha in the first teaching he gave after his enlightenment, when he explained the four noble truths:

> Birth is suffering, aging is suffering, illness is suffering, death is suffering; union with what is displeasing is suffering; separation from what is pleasing is suffering; not to get what one wants is suffering; in brief, the five aggregates subject to clinging are suffering.[48]

We human beings encounter most, if not all, of these eight experiences as we go through life; they are also experienced by the majority

of other samsaric beings. Contemplating them gives rise to renunciation, the determination to become free of samsara. This attitude could
also be called "self-compassion." Renunciation is the highest form
of compassion for oneself because it involves wishing to be free not
merely from short-term problems like illness, depression, or loneliness, but from all problems and their causes, forever.

Depending on your level of energy and the length of your meditation session, you can reflect on all eight types of suffering at once or
focus on just one or two per session. In that way you can explore each
one deeply, think of examples from your own and others' lives, and
generate a strong aspiration to be free of these sufferings.

THE MEDITATION

Sit comfortably and relax. Generate a positive motivation for doing the
meditation, such as wishing to better understand suffering in order
to free everyone—yourself and others—from all problems, pain, and
unhappiness. Then do the practice for lamrim meditation on page 35,
and at the appropriate point, pause to contemplate the following.

1. Birth

Although we aspire to be born in favorable situations in our future
lives to continue our Dharma practice and eventually attain enlightenment, we need to recognize the painful aspects of birth in order to
overcome attachment to samsara.

Some Westerners have romantic ideas about being in a womb, thinking it's a warm and cozy place, but Buddhist texts say it's quite unpleasant. To get a sense of that, imagine that after this life ends, your mind
enters a tiny, fertilized egg in the womb of your mother in your next
life. You remain there for around ten months as the egg develops into
an embryo and then a fetus. You are alone with no one to talk to and
nothing to do, it's always hot and dark, and you are affected by your
mother's movements, activities, and diet—including drugs, alcohol,
caffeine, and certain foods that can be harmful to an unborn child.
Does that situation sound like something to look forward to?

It is well-known that the birth process is painful for mothers, but
not everyone realizes that it is painful for babies as well—Buddhist
texts say the pressure in the birth canal can feel like being squeezed

between boulders. Also, there may be complications during birth that lead to injuries, or even death, to the baby and/or the mother.

Even if the birth goes well, it can be frightening to suddenly find oneself in a completely new environment surrounded by strangers and bright lights.

Following birth we are quite helpless for the first few years of our life, dependent on others for our survival and basic needs and having to learn everything from the start: how to walk, talk, dress and feed ourselves, read, write, and so on. There's no guarantee that the people around us will be consistently loving and considerate; sadly, we see reports in the news reports of infants and small children being abused in various ways.

2. Aging

According to Buddhism, aging begins right after we are born because our body changes and disintegrates every moment. But the real sufferings of aging start later, especially in our fifties and sixties. Among the problems are losing the attractiveness, energy, and health of our youth; the deterioration of our cognitive faculties (hearing, eyesight, memory, and so forth); and being neglected or disrespected by younger people and society. Contemplate these sufferings, making examples from your own experience and that of others.

3. Illness

Most people experience illness as they go through life, sometimes for extended periods of time. The sufferings of illness can include physical pain and discomfort; loss of appetite, strength, and physical energy; mental unhappiness and worry; unpleasant or even painful medical procedures; and so on. Think of your past experiences of being seriously ill, noting the various layers of mental and physical pain that were involved, and contemplate that there is a good chance you will encounter these again in the future.

4. Death

Some people may manage to go through life with little or no difficulties related to aging and illness, but no one can escape death. The main sufferings of death include parting from loved ones; leaving behind possessions and enjoyments; having to separate from your body; physical pain and discomfort; and mental pain such as fear, sadness, and the wish to not part from everyone and everything. Imagining what we will experience as we die is uncomfortable, but it's important to prepare ourselves for this inevitable event. Death is also a powerful reminder of the painful nature of samsara.

5. Having to separate from what is pleasant

This can include people or belongings you love and cherish, as well as your home, abilities, status, and so forth. The separation could be temporary—when you or the other person are studying or working overseas, for instance—or it could be permanent, such as when a loved one dies, or you lose a job. Bring to mind examples of this from your own life, such as living far away from people you love or the death of someone you were close to. Recognize how painful these experiences are and understand that as long as we are in samsara, we will encounter them again and again.

6. Having to meet with the unpleasant

This can involve encountering people you don't like or who are difficult to deal with; unwanted experiences such as accidents, injuries, flight delays, or getting stuck in a long boring meeting; having to do work you don't really want to do; and so on. Think of examples of this from your experience and remind yourself that as long as we are in samsara, we do not have complete control over what happens to us and cannot always avoid unwanted events.

7. Not getting what we want

We think that if only we had the right partner, job, living situation, body, clothes, food, and so forth, everything would be perfect, and we would be forever happy and satisfied. The reality is that we are not always able to get what we want, and even when we do, it may turn out to be less wonderful and satisfying than we imagined. Make examples of this in your life, or in the lives of others you know. Understand that it's the nature of samsara to encounter such experiences again and again.

8. The suffering of having contaminated aggregates

The *aggregates* refer to our body and mind, the components we are made of: form, feelings, discriminations, compositional factors, and consciousness. They are *contaminated* because they arise mainly from faulty causes: karma and delusions, especially ignorance.[49] Karma and delusions continue to be constant companions throughout our life—as long as we are in samsara, our mind is never completely free of them. They are like chains that bind us, causing us to experience one problem after another.

In addition, the delusions in our mind impel us to create new karma that will bring further suffering in the future. Therefore, our aggregates of body and mind *themselves* are in the nature of suffering; they are like a magnet for mental and physical pain. Check to see if this is true or not in your experience.

It may be difficult to recognize the suffering nature of your body and mind when things are going well in your life. But good times never last; they always end and are replaced by problems.

See if you can get a sense of how unpleasant samsara is, and then generate the wish to become free from it. This is the meaning of renunciation, the determination to be free from samsara. Keep your mind focused on this feeling for several minutes or more.

Conclusion
Understand that as long as we remain in samsara, we will encounter these eight types of suffering again and again; generate the wish to free yourself from this situation so you can then help others to also become free.

Dedication
If you did the practice for lamrim meditation at the beginning of your session, return to that and dissolve the visualization of the Buddha. Then dedicate the merit you created to all beings' attainment of happiness, up to the highest happiness of enlightenment.

2. The Six Kinds of Suffering

The renowned Indian master Nagarjuna explained six types of samsaric faults, or sufferings, in his *Letter to a Friend*.[50] They are related to impermanence—the changing, transitory nature of things—and are experienced all throughout samsara. As you go through these, think of examples from your own experience as well as stories from friends, the news, and so on. Remember that the purpose of contemplating these is to generate the determination to free yourself from this unsatisfactory situation that is samsara.

THE MEDITATION

Sit comfortably and relax your body and mind. Let go of thoughts of the past and future, other places and people; resolve to keep your mind focused on the present, on your meditation.

Generate a positive motivation, such as "I am doing this meditation to become more aware of suffering and more determined to free not only myself but all other beings as well." Then do the practice for lam-rim meditation on page 35, inserting the following meditation after the mantra recitation.

1. Uncertainty

We like stability and predictability and hope for success in all our activities, plans, projects, and relationships. However, things don't always turn out the way we want or expect. Relationships may start off well but eventually (or quickly!) turn sour. Our plans for an outing or holiday may be disrupted. Our attempts to get a degree or start a business may fail. Since everything in samsara is subject to change and beyond our control, there is no enduring certainty or stability.

2. Dissatisfaction

The Buddha said that following desire is like drinking saltwater—our thirst is not quenched but only increases. When we get something we want, we may feel happy for a while but eventually become dissatisfied and want more or better. This can happen with relationships, jobs, homes, clothes, food, and so on. There is no genuine, lasting happiness or satisfaction to be found anywhere in samsara, so we need to relinquish our attachment to remaining in this situation.

3. Having to die and leave your body again and again

The Buddha said that we've had countless lives before this one and have been born in every possible type of body, place, and situation. But each life came to an end; we had to die and leave everything behind. Contemplate how painful it is to die—both physically and emotionally—and understand that as long as we are in samsara, we will have to go through the experience of dying and separating from all that we cherish, again and again.

4. Being born again and again

We have also been born countless times and had to undergo the sufferings of birth, as described earlier. The knowledge and experience we gain in each life are lost when we die and take birth in the next one, so we must relearn everything from the beginning. Also, we have no choice over the place of our birth, our parents, the type of body we have, and the experiences we will encounter—these are determined by our karma, which sometimes propels us into nightmarish situations.

5. Going from high to low, over and over again

As we circle in samsara, we sometimes find ourselves in exalted states, enjoying wealth, power, fame, respect, and so on. As always, things change and we fall from these situations to lower ones, becoming impoverished, weak, outcast, and the like. This can happen from one lifetime to the next or even within one life. Bring to mind examples of this from your own experience or from society—prominent figures who were disgraced, top athletes or entertainers who had to retire due to illness or injuries, tycoons who lost their fortunes. Understand that as long as we are in samsara, we will experience such downfalls, again and again.

6. Being alone

We come into this world alone and die alone—even if family and friends are at our bedside, they cannot come with us. During our life, we grow close to many people—relatives, friends, teachers, neighbors—but none of these relationships last. Inevitably, one of us will die first, leaving the other behind to grieve. We are also alone in our beautiful and painful experiences; when we try to tell our dear ones how we feel, they are unable to truly understand or share those experiences with us.

Conclusion

As long as we remain in samsara, we will encounter these six faults—uncertainty, dissatisfaction, dying, being reborn, falling from high positions to low ones, and being alone—again and again, unceasingly.

Clearly seeing the unpleasantness of samsara—the cycle of birth, death, and suffering—generate the wish to become free from it, for your own sake and for the benefit of others.

Dedication

Conclude the practice for lamrim meditation and dedicate the merit you created during the session to your attainment of enlightenment so you can free all beings from samsara and lead them to enlightenment as well.

3. THE THREE KINDS OF SUFFERING

This list of three sufferings is the most comprehensive way of gaining insight into the unsatisfactory nature of samsara. The Buddha mentioned them in the *Dukkhatā Sutta*;[51] they are also explained in many other Buddhist scriptures. They include all the other types of suffering and are experienced throughout samsara.

THE MEDITATION

Sit comfortably and relax. Spend some time focusing on the breath to calm your mind and center it in the present. Then generate a positive motivation, for example, "I am doing this meditation not just for myself, but for others as well, to have greater awareness of their suffering and be inspired to attain enlightenment in order to help them become free from all suffering and its causes." Follow the practice for lamrim meditation on page 35 and insert the following meditation after the mantra recitation.

1. The suffering of suffering

This is suffering that is obvious and easy to identify, such as the horrific experiences that occur due to war, natural disasters, violent crime, poverty, injustice, disease, and so on. It also includes our nor-mal, everyday problems: physical discomfort such as aches and pains, heat and cold, hunger and thirst, as well as mental difficulties like loneliness, depression, grief, frustration, anxiety, confusion, and so on. Bring to mind examples of these from your own experience, past and present. Contemplate that as long as you remain in samsara, you will continue to encounter these again and again.

2. *The suffering of change*
This is more subtle than the first; it refers to the experiences we usu-ally consider to be pleasure or happiness. Because these experiences are transitory—they last only a short time—and are not fully satisfying, they are considered another type of suffering, or *duhkha.*

Eating is a good example. Most of us enjoy eating, but if it was truly pleasurable, the pleasure should increase the more we eat. Instead, we end up with a bloated belly and indigestion. Even if we eat just the right amount to satisfy our hunger, a short time later we again become hungry and need to eat. For these reasons, eating is not fully satisfying.

Another example is the posture of our body. After being on our feet for a while our legs start to ache, so we sit down. At first that feels good but eventually sitting becomes uncomfortable, so we stand up and enjoy stretching our legs. But soon our legs again start to ache so again we sit down. This pattern continues all day. Even while we are sit-ting, standing, or lying down we don't remain still for long but almost constantly shift our position to find a more comfortable one. Observe what you do with your body throughout the day, or even for an hour, to check if this is true. If any posture was truly pleasurable it would remain so without changing, but however we place our body, it eventu-ally becomes unpleasant or even painful.

Another problem with pleasure is that we usually get attached to it and to the objects we find pleasant. We want them to remain forever and never change, but this is impossible. It is simply the nature of sam-sara that pleasure, people, and things change moment by moment, disintegrate, and eventually cease to exist. If we do not recognize or accept this reality but want things to be otherwise, we are setting our-selves up for suffering and perpetuating attachment, one of the fac-tors binding us to samsara.

This does not mean there is no pleasure or beauty in samsara. These *do* exist, but they are ephemeral, like rainbows: here one moment, gone the next. Only in the state of nirvana, beyond samsara, is there genuine, lasting happiness, satisfaction, and peace.

Think of some pleasant experiences you have had. How long did the pleasure last before it vanished or turned into something else, even suffering?

3. The pervasive suffering of conditionality

This is even more subtle and difficult to recognize than the suffering of change. It refers to our very existence in samsara, under the control of karma and delusions. Although our mind's nature is clear and has the potential to experience the peace of liberation and enlightenment, this pure buddha nature is obscured by delusions such as ignorance, anger, and attachment. These delusions, which arise uncontrollably in our minds, motivate us to create the karma that causes rebirth in samsara, again and again, as well as its myriad miseries.

To get a sense of this, consider how difficult it is to keep your mind free of negative thoughts and feelings for a day, an hour, or even a few minutes. And although you want only pleasant experiences, you are unable to have them 24/7; without choice or control unwanted problems occur.

This is the meaning of pervasive suffering. It's called "pervasive" because it pervades every realm of samsara, even the god realms. The gods, or *devas*, have extremely long lives with little or no suffering and fantastic enjoyments that are far better than ours. But they are not free of karma and delusions; when their karma to live in those realms runs out, they die and are born somewhere else, often in the lower realms.

Being in samsara is like being in a prison; our karma and delusions are like the walls, bars, and guards that prevent us from escaping. The three types of suffering can be compared to the different experiences one has in prison. Terrible experiences such as being attacked by another prisoner are like the suffering of suffering. Pleasant experiences such as getting a visit from a loved one or having a nice Christmas dinner are like the suffering of change. And simply being confined in prison, not free to leave that undesirable situation, is like pervasive suffering.

Samsara is not an external place, like planet earth, with nirvana somewhere up in space. Samsara is our very body-mind complex that is under the control of karma and delusions. So it is right here, with us all the time. However, it is not a permanent situation. We *do* have the ability to escape from it, by freeing ourselves from the causes of samsara.

Conclusion

Review the main points of this meditation: that as long as we remain trapped in the prison of samsara we will be condemned to experience

- the suffering of suffering—painful physical and mental experiences;
- the suffering of change—pleasant experiences that last only a short while then vanish, often leaving us disappointed and frustrated; and
- pervasive suffering—having a body-mind complex that is not free but controlled by karma and delusions.

Understand that there is no genuine peace or happiness anywhere in samsara and generate renunciation—the compassionate wish to free yourself from samsara with all its sufferings. Resolve to use your precious human life to create the causes to bring this about, not only for yourself but for all beings.

Dedication

If you did the practice for lamrim meditation at the beginning of your session, return to that and dissolve the visualization of the Buddha. Then dedicate the merit you created so that you and all other beings will become free of samsara with all its myriad sufferings, and that you will all swiftly attain enlightenment.

The Truth of the Origins of Suffering

13

Since beginningless time, the great demon of self-grasping,
thinking "I, I," has dwelt in my heart's recesses;
marking self off from other, it generates greed and hatred;
with these, karma's heaped up; through karma I spin in samsara.
YESHE TSONDRU, IN *The Essential Nectar*

THE BUDDHA realized through his own experience that the origins, or causes, of all the various types of samsaric suffering are twofold: karma and delusions. These are the things we need to eliminate if we wish to be free of suffering and samsara, and fortunately it is possible to do this.

Of the two causes, the main one is delusions, or mental afflictions, because they are the factors motivating the actions that lead to suffering. For instance, if we did not have anger in our mind, we would not act in harmful ways that cause problems for others and ourselves, now and in future lives.

There are numerous delusions that come and go in our mind, such as the *three poisons* mentioned earlier: ignorance of karma, anger or hatred, and attachment or craving. These three are included in the six root delusions explained below. In addition to these, there is a list of twenty secondary delusions explained in texts on mind and mental factors (Tibetan: *lorig*).[52]

This chapter includes meditations on identifying the six root delusions, understanding their faults, and applying antidotes to them. The main delusion to eliminate is ignorance—specifically, the ignorance that grasps self and all other phenomena as inherently existent. Also known as the root of samsara, its antidote is the wisdom realizing emptiness. Because it sees things as they really are—that is, empty of

inherent existence—this wisdom is the complete opposite to ignorance. That is why it can eliminate ignorance and all other delusions.

It takes time and effort to cultivate this wisdom, so it's worthwhile
learning other antidotes with which we can manage and decrease our
delusions. Included here are meditations for dealing with anger and
attachment, two disturbing emotions that create extensive havoc in
our lives.[53] This chapter also includes a meditation on six factors that
cause delusions to arise in our minds, and one on how we die and take
rebirth.[54]

Some people feel shame, guilt, or even self-hatred when they recognize delusions in their minds. Such reactions are not helpful and only
serve to exacerbate our problems rather than relieve them. It is also
unreasonable to react in these ways because delusions are transitory—
they come and go in our mind. They are not who we are, so it's unwise
to identify with them, yet most people have a habit of doing this.
When anger arises in our mind, for instance, we automatically think,
"I am angry" as if "I" and "anger" are one and the same. This is clearly
mistaken: if I and anger were one, I should be angry all the time, 24/7,
but no one is like that! Since delusions are impermanent, we can use
antidotes to diminish and eventually overcome them completely such
that they will never arise again. But that won't happen overnight; it
takes time and consistent effort.

Remember these points if you become upset and self-critical when
noticing delusions in yourself. Learn to identify with your buddha
nature rather than your delusions. Have compassion and patience
toward yourself for being under the control of delusions; that will also
make it easier for you to feel compassion and patience toward other
beings in samsara, realizing they are in the same predicament.

1. Delusions: The Main Cause of Suffering

Delusions are afflictive mental factors that, when they arise, make
the mind disturbed and unpeaceful. This is especially obvious with
anger—when we get angry, our mind becomes agitated, we have trouble thinking clearly, and even our body is restless, unable to sit still.

Delusions are also unrealistic; they cause us to see people and things in distorted ways. When we're angry at someone, we see that person as permanently, 100 percent bad, devoid of any good qualities. But no one is that bad; everyone has positive qualities, and their negative traits are transitory. Conversely, attachment involves seeing a person or object as 100 percent wonderful and able to bring us eternal happiness, but this too is unrealistic—as we eventually discover!

The following meditation goes through the six root delusions. Contemplate each one to understand its particular features and identify it in your experience. Try as well to recognize the problems they cause in your life, in society, and the world.

THE MEDITATION

Sit comfortably and relax completely. Take time to calm and concentrate your thoughts by mindfully observing the breath.

Generate a positive motivation for doing the meditation, such as "I am doing this meditation to understand the delusions in my mind that cause suffering. May this inspire me to work on overcoming them so I can eventually become enlightened and guide all other beings to do the same." Then do the practice for lamrim meditation on page 35, and insert this meditation after the mantra recitation.

1. Ignorance

In Buddhism, ignorance does not mean being uneducated. A person can be highly educated but still ignorant. In general, ignorance is a lack of understanding about how things exist, and it can manifest in different ways. One type that is particularly problematic is ignorance of karma; this is the ignorance included in the three poisonous attitudes: ignorance, anger, and attachment. People who have this are unaware of which actions bring suffering and which ones bring happiness; as a result, they may act contrary to karma and thus contrary to what they wish for. Can you identify this type of ignorance in yourself?

In the context of lamrim practice, the main type of ignorance we need to recognize and deal with is seeing things in a way that is opposite to reality. For example, this is the ignorance that believes in an "I" or self that is solid, inherently existent, and independent of everything else.[55] In reality, there is no such self; our "I" is merely what is designated in relation to our body and mind. Ignorance fails to understand this and clings to a false notion of "I"; it also sees all other beings and things in the same mistaken way. Regarding this false "I" as the center of the universe, we then experience other delusions such as attachment to people who help us, aversion to those who harm us, and so on. Therefore, this ignorance is the root of samsara, the source of all other delusions as well as the karmic actions that keep us circling in samsara. Do you think you have this type of ignorance in your mind, or do you think you know your self correctly?

2. Attachment

Attachment arises toward objects we find attractive and pleasing. The object could be external, such as a person, food, or music; or internal, like knowledge or experiences. There is an element of exaggeration involved—the mind views the object as more wonderful than it really is and may even project qualities that aren't there. This leads us to crave the object, seeing it as essential for our happiness and wanting to not be separated from it. Our mind usually fabricates stories and fantasies about the object and our relationship to it, deepening the attachment. The teachings say that attachment is like an oil stain that has soaked into cloth and is thus quite difficult to overcome. Think of some examples of people and things you are attached to and check: Do you think you view them correctly or in an unrealistic way?

3. Anger

Anger, or hatred, is a delusion that arises toward a person or object that we dislike or that has caused suffering, either to oneself or someone we care about. When we are angry, we do not see the object of our anger in a realistic way—the mind exaggerates its unlikeable features and superimposes other qualities that are not there. When we get angry, we feel antagonistic and sometimes inflict harm on the object of our anger. But there are also low-level forms of anger—irritation, impatience, frustration, or just dislike—that might not incite us to violence but nevertheless disturb our peace of mind.

Buddhist teachings list nine objects of anger: (1–3) someone who harmed me in the past, is harming me now, or will harm me in the future; (4–6) someone who harmed my friend in the past, is harming them now, or will harm them in the future; and (7–9) someone who

THE TRUTH OF THE ORIGINS OF SUFFERING   141

helped my enemy (or simply a person I dislike) in the past, is helping them now, or will help them in the future. Think of some instances where you felt angry at someone and see if they fall into one of these nine categories.

4. Arrogance

Based on the false notion of our "I" explained above under igno- rance, arrogance or pride is an inflated sense of self, seeing ourselves as superior to others in terms of social standing, intelligence, educa- tion, wealth, abilities, physical traits, and so on. Bring to mind some experiences where you felt superior to others or just one other per- son. Is that a wholesome mental state you would like to perpetuate?

5. Deluded doubt

This involves strongly doubting aspects of the Dharma that are impor- tant for our spiritual practice, such as karma, rebirth, and the possi- bility of attaining enlightenment. Although we are encouraged to question and investigate the teachings rather than blindly believe them, if our doubt is leaning toward an incorrect conclusion (for example, "There's probably no such thing as enlightenment") it becomes an obstacle to our practice. How can we feel enthusias- tic about attaining something that we don't really believe in? See if you can recall ever having this type of doubt and, if so, check how it affected your practice.

6. Deluded views

These are incorrect views that lead us to believe things exist opposite to the way they do. One example is *the view of the transitory collection*: belief in a real, independent "I."[56] Another is *extreme views*: based on that false notion of an "I," either believing it to be an eternal, unchanging soul, or believing that it becomes nonexistent when we die (and thus there is no rebirth). Do you think your views or beliefs about your self, your life, the world, what happens when we die, and so on are correct and accurate, or might be faulty, affected by ignorance and other delusions?

There are also secondary, or auxiliary, delusions that derive from one or more of the three poisons. Among them are resentment, cruelty, jealousy, miserliness, pretension, lethargy, and laziness. These too disturb our mind and create problems in our lives.[57]

Conclusion

Review the six principal delusions: attachment, anger, ignorance, arrogance, deluded doubt, and deluded views. Resolve to learn their characteristics and develop mindfulness and introspective awareness so you can recognize them when they arise in your mind. In that way you will be able to avoid coming under their influence and acting them out, which would lead to problems for yourself and others.

Dedication

Complete the practice for lamrim meditation, then dedicate the merit you created so that all sentient beings will overcome the delusions in their minds, which is the main cause of suffering, and will swiftly attain the highest happiness of enlightenment.

2. Disadvantages of Delusions

Some people believe that emotions like anger and attachment are natural parts of human nature that we need to survive and flourish. There is also the notion that the brain is hardwired to experience them and thus they cannot be eradicated. According to Buddhism, not only do we not need these emotions, we are better off without them—they are obstacles to our well-being, happiness, and spiritual attainments—and they *can* be eradicated. It takes time and effort to do that, but understanding their disadvantages—how they cause problems for ourselves and others, both now and in the future—will give us the enthusiasm we need to work on vanquishing them.

Chapter 4 of Shantideva's *A Guide to the Bodhisattva's Way of Life* contains numerous verses on the faults of delusions, which he refers to as enemies:

Although enemies such as hatred and craving
Have neither any arms nor legs,

And are neither courageous nor wise,
How have I been used like a slave by them?[58]

This and a selection of other verses by Shantideva on the disadvantages of delusions are in appendix 6 of this book and can be used to supplement your meditation.

THE MEDITATION

Sit comfortably and relax. Contemplate a positive, beneficial motivation for doing the meditation, then do the practice for lamrim meditation on page 35. If you wish, spend some time concentrating on your breath until the mind is quiet, clear, and more focused.

Think of delusions that frequently disturb you, and check whether the following points are true:
- When delusions arise in our mind, they cause it to be disturbed and unpeaceful.
- Delusions see things in distorted, unrealistic ways.
- They can lead to other problems in this life: at work, in our relationships, with our physical and mental health, and so on.
- They leave seeds in our mind that cause the same delusion to arise again and again, without choice or control.
- They motivate actions that are negative, and sometimes illegal, leading to suffering in this and future lives.
- They are the source of many tragic events in the world such as wars, conflicts, terrorism, violence, injustice, abuse, and corruption.

In addition to those disadvantages that can be directly experienced, Buddhist texts mention other faults of delusions that are less obvious:
- They keep us trapped in samsara, forced to die and be reborn repeatedly without choice and to undergo myriad types of suffering.
- They hinder the development of positive qualities such as compassion and wisdom and cause the good qualities we already have to degenerate.

- They are obstacles to attaining the realizations of the path and the supremely blissful states of liberation and enlightenment.

Conclusion

Understanding that delusions are the real enemy that must be overcome to be free of suffering, make the determination to recognize them when they arise and apply antidotes to them. But keep in mind that this takes time, so you need patience, persistence, and self-compassion.

Dedication

Complete the remaining parts of the practice for lamrim meditation, dissolving the visualization of the Buddha and so on. Then dedicate the merit so that you and all other beings will free yourselves from delusions and all the suffering they cause and will quickly attain liberation from samsara and full enlightenment.

3. ANTIDOTES TO ANGER

> While the enemy of your own anger is unsubdued,
> though you conquer external foes, they will only increase.
> Therefore with the militia of love and compassion
> subdue your own mind—
> this is the practice of bodhisattvas.
> TOGME SANGPO, *The Thirty-Seven Practices of Bodhisattvas*

The main antidotes to anger and hatred are their opposites—patience, loving-kindness, compassion, and forgiveness—so cultivating these positive qualities will lessen our anger.[59] However, when anger arises suddenly and strongly, it may be difficult to immediately switch to a more positive state of mind. Here are several other methods we can use to halt the proliferation of angry thoughts, take a different perspective on the situation, and make space in our mind for more constructive thoughts.

The Meditation

Begin each session as usual, by calming yourself and generating a positive motivation, then do the practice for lamrim meditation on page 35. When you are ready to start the actual meditation below, think of an incident when you were angry and contemplate one or more of the following.

1. Recognize the shortcomings of anger.

It is important to understand that anger is harmful rather than helpful. Recalling your experience of anger as clearly as possible, check how it affected your body—did you feel calm and relaxed or tense? Did it make your mind peaceful and happy or disturbed and unhappy?

How were other people affected by your anger, both when you acted it out and when you suppressed it? If you did act out your anger, what kind of karma did you create, and what effects will that karma bring later?

According to Buddha's teachings, not only does anger lead to painful experiences, it can also damage or even destroy much of the good karma that we work so hard to create. It is a major obstacle to cultivating positive qualities like love and compassion, and to making progress on the path to liberation and enlightenment.

Recognize that anger is harmful—to yourself and to others, both now and in the future—and generate the determination to work on overcoming it.

2. Understand the other person.

If you felt angry at someone who was behaving destructively, put yourself in their shoes and try to understand how they felt, why they were acting that way. There may have been problems in their life causing their mind to be agitated and imbalanced. Or they might simply have been under the control of karma and delusions.

Like you, they want to be happy and not suffer, but as a samsaric being, they don't have complete control over their mind and behavior. Understand that their mind is probably not peaceful and happy, but is confused, unhappy, and uncontrolled. And if they are behaving in harmful ways, they are creating the causes to experience even more suffering in the future. Generate the compassionate wish to help the person rather than harm them.

3. Reflect on karma.

According to Buddhism, any misfortune we experience, such as being harmed by someone, is the result of negative actions we created in this or a previous life. See if you can remember doing something that may have upset this person. If not, you might recall harming someone else earlier in your life. If you can't remember creating such karma in this life, you may have done so in past lives, and that karma is ripening now. Buddhist texts say we've done every kind of action in our past lives, positive and negative, and the karmic imprints of those actions travel with our mind, life to life, until they ripen or are purified.

If karma makes sense to you, see if you can let go of anger and blame and accept responsibility for the situation. You can also reflect that getting angry and retaliating will just bring more problems in the future. A more intelligent response is to practice patience with those who harm and be careful about the karma we create.[60]

4. People are mirrors.

A Buddhist teaching says that we would not see faults in others if we did not have them ourselves. Other people are therefore like mirrors, reflecting faults and mistakes that we have and need to work on.

Think of someone you find annoying. Check exactly what it is that you dislike about them—is it something they do, or some attitude they have? Then look into yourself and try to find the same thing, or something similar. It may be obvious; you might easily remember doing the same thing yourself, or realize you have the same attitude.

But in some cases, you may need to look deeper—it could be something you deny and suppress, seeing it as unacceptable. That's where the problem lies: because you dislike and don't accept that part of yourself, you get angry when you observe it in others.

The solution is to learn to accept that behavior or quality in yourself. *Accepting* doesn't mean condoning it and thinking you can behave that way as much as you want. It means being honest and acknowledging the existence of that fault, while knowing you can work on decreasing and eventually overcoming it. Being more accepting and compassionate about our own shortcomings will enable us to be more accepting and compassionate toward others.

Conclusion

Conclude the meditation by making the determination to continue working on anger. Resolve to be mindful as much as possible and, when you notice anger or aversion in your mind, to see it as a trouble-maker rather than a friend. Try to avoid getting caught up in it and instead apply antidotes to transform your mind into a more positive state.

Dedication

Do the concluding parts of the practice for lamrim meditation, then dedicate the merit to the happiness and freedom from suffering of all living beings, and for everyone to swiftly attain enlightenment.

4. ANTIDOTES TO ATTACHMENT

> Sensual pleasures are like saltwater:
> the more you indulge, the more thirst increases.
> Abandon at once those things which breed
> clinging attachment—
> this is the practice of bodhisattvas.
> TOGME SANGPO, *The Thirty-Seven Practices of Bodhisattvas*

It's relatively easy to recognize the disadvantages of anger because it is so painful, but that's harder to do with attachment, since it seems to bring us what we wish for. Many people even believe it is necessary for happiness, success, and healthy relationships. It is common to equate attachment with love, but according to Buddhism they are very different. Attachment is self-centered—you see the other person as necessary for *your* happiness—whereas genuine love is altruistic, concerned for another's happiness. If we had more love and less attachment in our relationships, we would have fewer problems.

Some people think that without attachment they would have no ambition, no motivation to do anything, but this too is a misunderstanding. We can exert ourselves for other reasons like compassion and altruism—wanting to take care of our family, for instance, or to benefit society and the world. Work done with those motivations—rather than self-centered attachment—will probably be more satisfying and beneficial both for oneself and others.

The following remedies to attachment help us to understand its disadvantages and present alternative ways of viewing things that are wiser, more skillful, and more likely to bring the results we wish for.

The Meditation

Sit comfortably and relax. Contemplate a positive, beneficial motivation for doing the meditation, then do the practice for lamrim meditation on page 35 and pause after the mantra recitation. To begin the actual meditation on working with attachment, think of something or someone you are attached to and contemplate one or more of the following points.

1. Recognize the shortcomings of attachment.
Investigate how attachment affects you. Is your mind calm and clear, or overly excited and full of expectations? Were you ever excited about getting something or going somewhere but the actual experience was less wonderful than what you expected?

Attachment leads to suffering when we don't get something we want, but even when we *do* get it, we may be disappointed or quickly bored. Recall some experiences of this.

We may feel content with some of our relationships and possessions, but attachment wants them to last forever. This is a recipe for suffering, because people and things are impermanent, subject to change, and disappear. The stronger our attachment to someone or something, the greater our pain will be when we have to separate.

In addition to those obvious disadvantages of attachment, there are also subtler ones. Attachment lies behind many nonvirtuous actions like stealing, lying, or killing, which create problems both now and in the future. It is also a hindrance to spiritual practice—since it causes our mind to be repeatedly distracted, we are unable to develop concentration and the other realizations needed to reach liberation and enlightenment.

2. Reflect on impermanence.

If you are convinced of the faults of attachment and wish to decrease it, one of the most effective remedies is to contemplate impermanence. The people and things we're attached to are not permanent but change every moment and will eventually perish. Considering this, does it make sense to cling, wishing the object to be there forever?

Even before the object disappears, it will gradually age and become less attractive and desirable. Imagine how the object of your attachment will look after a year . . . five years . . . ten years . . . fifty years . . . a hundred years. Does that impact your feelings toward it?

The pleasure you experience with the object is also impermanent. It may last a few seconds, minutes, or hours, but eventually it fades. Also, if the object was truly pleasurable, you should always enjoy it. Is that the case, or are there times when you feel bored or annoyed with it?

Overcoming attachment does not mean we must distance ourselves from people, give away our belongings, and never allow ourselves to experience pleasure. We can still enjoy these things, but without the unrealistic clinging and expectations that attachment brings. In fact, without attachment we'll probably enjoy them even more. Also, by decreasing attachment to people and increasing loving-kindness, compassion, and patience, our relationships with them will be healthier and more satisfying.

3. Cultivate a balanced view.

Since attachment is based on an exaggerated view of an object— seeing it as 100 percent wonderful, without any faults—it can be helpful to deliberately bring to mind unpleasant or negative aspects of the object. For example, you might think, "If I owned a BMW, I would be so happy!" But once you consider the expenses, maintenance, and worries involved in owning such a car, your ideas will become more realistic. Or you might feel attraction for someone and think, "If I could have a relationship with that person, it would be so wonderful!" Reflecting that the person may have hidden faults or that you might run into conflicts later will help you gain a more balanced view. But be careful—using this remedy is not meant to lead to aversion for the person or object. If you notice that happening, focus on their positive traits and cultivate loving-kindness and compassion, wishing them to be happy and free of suffering. Understand that the point of this remedy to attachment is to develop a realistic, balanced view that sees both the good and bad sides of the object.

Conclusion

Conclude the meditation by generating the determination to look out for attachment in your mind and, when you notice it, remind yourself of its drawbacks and apply one or more of these antidotes.

Dedication

If you did the practice for lamrim meditation, complete the remaining parts of that. Then dedicate the merit you created for yourself and everyone else to become free of attachment and the other delusions keeping you stuck in samsara and to swiftly attain enlightenment.

5. Six Factors That Cause Delusions to Arise

No one chooses to experience anger, greed, and other delusions, and they clearly cause problems in our life, so why do we have them? Tibetan lamas say that following delusions is as easy as rolling a boulder down a hill, whereas having positive attitudes is as hard as pushing a boulder up a hill. This is mainly due to habitual tendencies built up over lifetimes. But we can transform our mind. By learning to counteract delusions and becoming familiar with positive qualities, deluded thoughts will gradually become weaker and constructive ones will increase in frequency and strength.

Like all other impermanent phenomena, delusions come into existence due to causes and conditions. Buddhist scriptures explain six factors that are the main causes and conditions for delusions arising in our mind. By skillfully working with these factors, we can diminish the strength and frequency of disturbing mental states and enjoy greater peace of mind.

THE MEDITATION

Sit comfortably and relax your body and mind. Generate a positive, altruistic motivation such as "I am doing this meditation to understand the causes and conditions giving rise to delusions in my mind so I can work on decreasing them and having more positive mental states. May this meditation also help me get closer to enlightenment for the benefit of all beings." Then do the practice for lamrim meditation on page 35 and insert the following meditation after reciting the Buddha's mantra.

1. Seeds

The first factor that causes delusions to arise are the *seeds* or *propensities* of delusions that were in our mind in previous lifetimes and travel with the mind from life to life, so we have these from birth. For instance, even when we do not feel angry, its seed abides at an unconscious level of our mind; when we encounter an object that triggers it, the seed ripens into manifest anger. The same is true for attachment, arrogance, and the other delusions. These seeds are eliminated only by directly realizing emptiness; until then, we can avoid getting caught up in and acting out delusions by applying antidotes to them when they arise. It's also helpful to do regular purification practices, as these can reduce the strength of our delusions.

2. Objects

The second factor is the *object*—there is always an object we get attached to or angry at. It could be a person, a sound, a car, a pizza, and so on. Think of a delusion you often have trouble with, and investigate which objects trigger it to arise in your mind. It's helpful to avoid those objects, if possible, in the same way a recovering alcoholic should avoid going to bars. When that isn't possible, you can maintain mindfulness and introspective awareness when the triggering objects are nearby so that you can notice and deal skillfully with whatever delusion arises.

3. Company

The third factor, *company*, refers to friends or people we associate with. We are easily influenced by others, so if we spend time with people who have excessive attachment or anger, for example, those delusions will increase in our own mind. If you find this to be true in your experience, resolve to spend less time with such people, to be careful with your mind when you *are* with them, and to spend more time with people who influence you in positive ways.

4. Information

The fourth factor, *information*, can include conversations; watching TV and movies; reading books, newspapers, or magazines; spending time on the internet and social media; listening to lectures; and so forth. Information from these sources can trigger our attachment, anger, or other delusions and cause them to increase. Bring to mind some examples of this in your experience. Resolve to be careful about the kind of information you expose yourself to.

5. Familiarity

The fifth factor is *familiarity* or habit. We are creatures of habit—the thoughts and impulses we make a habit of are the ones that will arise in our mind most easily and spontaneously. Mentally criticizing others, for instance, can become so frequent and persistent that we stop noticing it—it becomes our default mode! Observe your thoughts and recognize the ones that are most habitual and problematic. Resolve to pay particular attention to these and to work on overcoming or at least reducing them.

6. Inappropriate attention

The sixth factor is *inappropriate attention*. When we are angry at, unhappy about, or attached to an object, our mind continues thinking about it again and again, obsessively. It's like a negative form of meditation that causes our mind to become increasingly unpeaceful and deluded. Find an example of this in your experience and recognize its disadvantages. Resolve to be mindful as much as you can, and when you notice your mind getting obsessed about something in a negative way, switch your attention to something positive, or at least neutral.

Conclusion

Review the six factors that can cause delusions to arise in your mind: seeds, objects, company, information, familiarity, and inappropriate attention. Understand that if we decrease their influence in our life, our mind will be more peaceful and positive, free of the disturbance and harm caused by delusions. Resolve to become more aware of these six factors and explore ways of working with them skillfully to the best of your ability, for the benefit of yourself and everyone else.

Dedication

Complete the remaining parts of the practice for lamrim meditation. Dedicate the merit you created in this session to peace, happiness, and freedom from suffering and its causes for all beings, and so that everyone will attain enlightenment as quickly as possible.

6. How We Die and Take Rebirth

The nine-point meditation on death in the initial section of the lamrim is practiced to overcome unrealistic attitudes about death— denying it, for example, or thinking it's a long way off—and to recognize the need for spiritual practice to prepare for death and the next life. That motivates us to take refuge and live ethically, in accordance with karma.

You might wonder what happens as we die and how the mind connects with the next life. Tibetan Buddhism contains a detailed explanation of eight stages of the death process, which we pass through as our life comes to an end. This teaching comes from the Vajrayana tradition and is not usually included in lamrim texts, but several contemporary teachers, including the Dalai Lama, explain it openly. Understanding what will happen to us as we die can help us be better prepared and alleviate some of the fear of death, since we tend to be fearful of the unknown. It is also helpful when we are present with friends or relatives who are dying.

Previous chapters contained information on karma and delusions— the main origins of suffering—and it's also important to understand the role they play in the process of death and rebirth. Ignorance and other delusions motivate us to act and thus create karma. Some of our karmic actions are virtuous, such as living ethically and helping others; others are nonvirtuous, like lying or hurting others. As we saw in the chapter on karma, when these actions are done in a complete way with all four factors they have the power to project another rebirth, which may be fortunate or unfortunate, depending on whether the karma is virtuous or nonvirtuous.

By the end of our life, our mind will contain numerous karmic seeds accumulated during this and previous lives. Our final conscious thoughts as we die will determine which of these karmic seeds will ripen and cause the next life. If we die with a negative state of mind— attached to loved ones or belongings, for example, or angry at the doctors for not saving our life—seeds of nonvirtuous karma will ripen and lead to an unfortunate rebirth. On the other hand, if our mind is positive—taking refuge in the Three Jewels, for instance, or feeling compassion for others—seeds of virtuous karma will ripen and bring a fortunate rebirth. This is one reason it is crucial to familiarize ourselves with positive states of mind and learn how to counteract and transform negative mental states.

The eight stages occur as the body gradually loses its ability to support various levels of consciousness and as the mind becomes increasingly subtle. The amount of time it takes to go through these stages is not definite but depends on various factors, such as the cause of death and the dying person's level of spiritual training. It could be a matter of minutes, in the case of sudden death due to an accident, or several hours, in the case of death by natural causes. At the eighth stage, the mind is in its subtlest state, known as clear light; this is the actual moment of death. Some highly accomplished meditators can pause the dying process and remain in this stage for days or even weeks, meditating in the clear light.

The following meditation is a brief description of what a person experiences while going through each of the eight stages. It is most effective to imagine yourself dying and experiencing these stages.[61] However, if you find it overly challenging to contemplate your own death, you might want to skip this meditation for now and come back to it later when your mind has become more at ease with the idea of dying. Alternatively, you can simply read through the meditation to become more familiar with how Tibetan Buddhism explains the dying process.

THE MEDITATION

Begin as usual with the preparatory practices—settling your body and mind, generating an altruistic motivation, and performing the practice for lamrim meditation on page 35. When your mind is calm and focused, imagine the following experiences.

Over the first four stages, the four elements that make up the body (earth, water, fire, and wind) dissolve;[62] the first four aggregates (form, feelings, discriminations, and compositional factors) become weaker; and coarse levels of mind (the five sense consciousnesses and coarse thoughts) gradually cease to function. Each stage is also accompanied by an inner vision perceived only by the dying person.

On the first stage, the earth element dissolves, the form aggregate (our body) becomes weak, and the visual sense diminishes. Our body feels heavy and as if sinking, our eyesight becomes unclear, and we have an inner vision of a shimmering appearance, like a mirage.

On the second stage, the water element dissolves, the feeling aggregate weakens, and the sense of hearing declines. Our mouth and nose become dry, and we stop having feelings—pleasant, unpleasant, or neutral. We can no longer hear external sounds, and there is an inner vision of smoke.

On the third stage, the fire element dissolves, the aggregate of discriminations becomes weaker, and the sense of smell ceases. Our body becomes cold and no longer able to digest food. We forget the things of this life, such as peoples' names; our breathing starts to become more difficult; and we have an inner vision of sparks flying through space.

On the fourth stage, the wind element dissolves, the aggregate of compositional factors weakens, and our taste and tactile senses cease. Our breathing becomes more and more difficult, and then stops altogether. Our last thoughts fade, and we have an inner vision of a flame about to go out.

It is at this point that a person is considered dead according to conventional understanding. However, according to Buddhism we are not yet dead because consciousness still resides within the body; it leaves only after the eighth stage, the clear light. By the end of the fourth stage, coarse levels of mind have ceased, and over the final four stages the mind will gradually become more subtle. The factors dissolving on these stages are the aggregate of consciousness, the mental faculty, and the energy-winds that serve as the mount of consciousness.

On the fifth stage, there is the dissolution of eighty indicative conceptions along with the winds that serve as their mount, and a subtle mind, known as white appearance, dawns. The inner vision is of clarity and vacuity, like a night sky in autumn pervaded by the white light of the full moon.

On the sixth stage, there is the dissolution of the mind of white appearance and the wind that serves as its mount, and the mind of red increase dawns. The inner vision is like that of a clear, empty autumn sky filled with orange-red light, like a sunset.

On the seventh stage, the mind of red increase and the wind that serves as its mount dissolve, and the mind of black near-attainment dawns. The inner vision is of radiant black vacuity, like thick darkness pervading an autumn sky at night.

On the eighth and final stage, the mind of black near-attainment and the wind that serves as its mount dissolve, and the very subtle mind of clear light dawns. This is the subtlest level of mind, a part of our mind that has existed since beginningless time mostly in a non-manifest state. The inner vision is like the natural color of an autumn sky at dawn, completely pure and free of dualistic appearances.

This appearance is similar to that of a mind in meditative equipoise directly realizing emptiness, the true nature of all phenomena. Practitioners who are familiar with emptiness and have trained in specific practices during their life are able to recognize the clear light mind and use it to meditate on emptiness; they even look forward to this precious opportunity to progress along the path at the time of death. However, ordinary beings who are not familiar with the clear light or with emptiness are unable to utilize this experience and usually pass through it quickly.

When the clear light of death ceases, our consciousness briefly passes back through the eight stages in reverse order—the minds of black near-attainment, red increase, and so on. As soon as this reverse process begins, we enter the *bardo*, or intermediate state, with a subtle body that can travel instantly to any place we think of as we search for our next rebirth. The form of our bardo body is that of our next rebirth, and the maximum amount of time we spend in the bardo is forty-nine days; we will definitely find our next place of birth during this period of time. And then we start all over again: another lifetime in samsara.

Conclusion

Understand that as long as we are in samsara, we are not free. We have no choice or control over where we are born or what experiences we have; all of those are determined by our karma and delusions. Feel the strong wish to free yourself from this situation and resolve to do whatever is necessary to accomplish this.

Dedication

Return to the practice for lamrim meditation and complete the remaining parts, then dedicate the merit you created so that you and all other beings will become free of samsara, the cycle of death and rebirth, and will quickly reach full enlightenment, buddhahood.

True Cessations and True Paths 14

Therefore, if this self-grasping is not expelled,
I cannot be free from samsara.
It has to be expelled by the wisdom that realizes selflessness.
Therefore, I must develop the training relating to wisdom.
YESHE TSONDRU, IN *The Essential Nectar*

THE FIRST two truths—suffering and its causes—are things to be
abandoned or eliminated, whereas the last two truths—cessations
and paths—are things to be attained. This chapter contains meditations for gaining a better understanding of true cessations and true
paths and how to start creating the causes to attain them.

Be aware that these two truths are not easy to comprehend—you
need to study, reflect, and meditate on them for quite some time
before they start to make sense. Here they are explained in a simplified way, but to understand them fully, it is best to study Buddhist philosophy in greater depth.

1. TRUE CESSATIONS

The third noble truth tells us that suffering and its causes can be
ceased forever. Every being is able to accomplish true cessation by
developing the wisdom that directly realizes emptiness, the true
nature of all things. This wisdom—the antidote that eliminates ignorance and all other delusions—is the fourth truth, true paths. Other
qualities that supplement wisdom—mindfulness, ethical conduct,
concentration, patience, compassion, and so on—also need to be
developed.

Cessation of ignorance and the other delusions occurs gradually, not all at once. Coarse levels of delusion (those we acquire through learning) are eliminated when one first attains a direct realization of emptiness, and subtler levels (those that have existed in our mind from beginningless time, innately) are gradually eliminated as one continues to meditate on this wisdom. Each time we eliminate a delusion, even partially, we attain a true cessation, thus there are multiple true cessations. The final true cessation occurs when all delusions and their seeds have been utterly vanquished such that they will never arise again. That is nirvana, complete liberation.

This may sound abstract, so a simple example might help. Let's say you have a disease that causes you a lot of suffering. Your doctor prescribes medicine, which you take for a while until the disease is cured. When that happens, you experience the absence of the disease and the problems that resulted from it. This is like a true cessation, and the medicine is like the true path. Once ignorance and the other delusions have ceased to exist in our mind, we are free forever from the suffering they cause.

The Meditation

Sit comfortably and relax your body and mind. Put aside thoughts of the past and future, other places and people, and resolve to keep your mind focused on the meditation.

Generate a positive motivation for doing the meditation, such as wanting to understand true cessations so you can begin creating their causes for the benefit of yourself and others. Then do the practice for lamrim meditation on page 35 and reflect on the following points to get a sense of how it is possible to cease, or eliminate, suffering and its causes.

1. Delusions and suffering are impermanent.
You can see this in your own experience—sometimes you feel angry or jealous, but often you do not. Remember a time—even just for a moment or two—when your mind was free of disturbing thoughts and emotions, and you felt completely peaceful and at ease. This is like a tiny taste of cessation, or nirvana.

2. There are antidotes you can use to overcome the delusions.

For example, meditating on loving-kindness overcomes anger; contemplating impermanence decreases attachment; rejoicing in another's happiness counteracts jealousy. However, most antidotes only subdue delusions temporarily; they do not eliminate them from the root. As long as their root, ignorance, remains in our mind, the other delusions will again arise. This is similar to the way noxious weeds will continue to grow as long as their roots remain in the ground. That is why you need to learn and meditate on wisdom, the ultimate antidote, which eliminates all delusions from their source.

3. You have access to those antidotes.

The Buddha found a way to eliminate the delusions in his mind and taught it so others could do the same. You are very fortunate to have a chance to learn his teachings, such as those contained in the lamrim.

4. You are able to apply these antidotes.

Even if you have limited time to meditate, some antidotes are relatively easy to learn and practice in your daily life, so you can at least start to use them to reduce the strength and frequency of the delusions in your mind.

Conclusion

Open your mind to the possibility that you can eradicate delusions, the cause of suffering, just as the Buddha and many of his followers have done. Once you have accomplished this, you will never again have to undergo any suffering. Imagine how wonderful that would be and generate the determination to begin practicing the path to attain it.

Dedication

Conclude the practice for lamrim meditation and dedicate the merit you created during this session so that you and all other beings will quickly attain the true cessation of all delusions, the causes of suffering, and will attain the genuine peace and happiness of enlightenment.

2. TRUE PATHS

For those who wish to attain liberation—or nirvana, a state of genuine peace that is free of suffering and its causes—there is a way to do this: true paths. A path is a realization, a higher state of consciousness. The main true path is the wisdom that directly realizes emptiness, but other realizations informed by this wisdom are also true paths.

When this wisdom is developed with the aim of attaining liberation, it is included in three practices known as the three higher trainings: ethics, concentration, and wisdom.[63] The term "higher training" means that one engages in these practices with the motivation of renunciation: wishing to be free of samsara and to attain liberation.

THE MEDITATION

Sit comfortably and relax. Generate a positive motivation for doing the meditation, such as wishing to better understand true paths—the principal antidote to the causes of suffering—in order to free yourself and others from all problems, pain, and unhappiness. Before beginning the actual meditation, do the practice for lamrim meditation on page 35.

Reflect on the following explanation of the three higher trainings to understand how they are essential causes of liberation:

1. *The higher training in ethics* involves refraining from harmful, nonvirtuous actions and doing what is virtuous. It also includes keeping whatever precepts we have taken, such as lay precepts, monastic precepts, and bodhisattva precepts.

2. *The higher training in concentration* involves learning to keep our mind focused single-pointedly on our chosen object of meditation without distraction, dullness, and other hindrances.

3. *The higher training in wisdom* involves learning to see things correctly, as they really are. The principal wisdom to be developed is the direct realization of emptiness, the actual antidote to ignorance and the other delusions that keep us imprisoned in samsara.

Now contemplate how these three are connected. The higher training in wisdom is the most important of the three, but cultivating it is not easy. We need to keep our mind still and focused during meditation to penetrate the veils of incorrect perceptions that prevent us from seeing the true nature of things. Therefore, training in concentration is an essential prerequisite for developing wisdom. A simple example that illustrates this is preparing for an exam—if you can't keep your mind concentrated, you won't be able to understand and retain the material you are studying.

But learning to concentrate—which, in Buddhism, means training our mind to remain focused on a chosen object with a virtuous motivation—is also difficult because our normal state of mind is highly distracted, constantly bouncing from one thought, memory, or fantasy to another. One cause of this is carelessness about our behavior during daily life. Getting caught up in delusions like attachment or anger and then acting them out in unwholesome ways leads to disturbances in our mind when we meditate. We remember those unwise actions, re-experience the anger or attachment, and feel regret, guilt, anxiety, and so on. On the other hand, if we try our best to avoid unwholesome actions and to engage in wholesome ones, when we sit down to meditate our mind will be more settled, clearer, and easier to stay concentrated. Therefore, ethical conduct is an essential foundation for concentration.

The three higher trainings are presented according to the order they are to be developed because ethics facilitates concentration, and concentration facilitates wisdom. But that doesn't mean we must first perfect the earlier ones before starting to work on the later ones; we can practice all three from the start.

Conclusion
Generate the strong determination to do your best to cultivate ethics, concentration, and wisdom in order to attain the complete cessation of all sufferings and their causes and be able to help others do the same.

Dedication
Conclude the practice for lamrim meditation and dedicate the merit you created in this session so that you and all other beings will quickly

attain the true paths leading to complete liberation from suffering and to the full enlightenment of buddhahood.

3. THE BENEFITS OF ETHICS

Lamrim texts usually explain the last two trainings—concentration and wisdom—in the context of the advanced level, the great scope, and elaborate on the training in ethics during the medium scope. In line with that approach, two meditations—on the benefits of ethics and how to practice it—are presented next; meditations on concentration and wisdom will come later, in part 5.

The essence of Buddhist ethics, or ethical conduct, is refraining from harming others. For our first meditation, we focus on understanding the benefits of ethical conduct (the pros) and the drawbacks of neglecting it (the cons), which will inspire us to practice it.

THE MEDITATION

Sit comfortably with your back straight and relax your body. Relax your mind by staying in the present, letting go of thoughts of the past, the future, other places, people, and so forth. Paying attention to the breath for several minutes will help your mind to settle in the here and now.

When your mind is calmer, generate a positive, altruistic motivation for doing the meditation. You can think, for example, "I am doing this meditation to gain a better understanding of ethics so my actions will be solely beneficial and not harmful to others." Then do the practice for lamrim meditation on page 35 and after the mantra recitation, spend some time reflecting on the following benefits of upholding ethical conduct and drawbacks of unethical behavior drawn from Buddhist scriptures.

- Just as the earth is the foundation of all the animate and inanimate things that abide on it, ethics is the foundation of all good qualities and realizations. Based on a stable practice of ethical conduct, we will be able to cultivate compassion, loving-kindness, calm abiding, special insight, liberation, and all the realizations of the bodhisattva path up to full enlightenment. On the other hand, if we do not safeguard our ethical conduct, we will be unable to attain any of these.

- The Buddha said that ethics is like a beautiful ornament. A person with good ethics acts and speaks in a gentle, nonharmful way, and their mind is calm and subdued. Others feel safe, relaxed, and happy around such a person and want to be close to them. But someone who lacks good ethics is the opposite: their behavior is reckless and harmful; people and even animals mistrust and avoid such a person.

- Ethics gives rise to happiness. It is the cause of favorable rebirths and good experiences in our future lives, and also brings happiness in this life: better relations with others, greater peace of mind, and so on. On the other hand, faulty ethics is the cause of unfortunate rebirths and suffering in future lives, as well as many unwanted problems in our present life.

How do we practice ethics? Start by studying karma; learn to avoid the ten nonvirtues and practice the ten virtues as much as you can. Keep in mind the "golden rule": don't do to others what you wouldn't want them to do to you and treat others the way you wish to be treated.

If you decide to take refuge and commit yourself to the Buddhist path, you can also take any number of the five lay precepts: refraining from killing, stealing, unwise and unkind sexual behavior, lying, and taking intoxicants. In addition, there are several levels of monastic precepts for those serious about dedicating their lives to Dharma practice. Taking and keeping precepts is more powerful and virtuous than simply avoiding those actions without precepts.

Conclusion

Review the key points of the meditation:

- Ethical conduct brings many benefits, both now and in the future, both for yourself and for others.
- Being careless about ethics or neglecting it altogether leads to numerous problems for yourself and others, in the short-term and long-term.

If you feel so inspired, set the determination to practice ethics as best you can by avoiding the ten nonvirtues, practicing the ten virtues, and perhaps even taking some of the five lay precepts.

Remember that with good ethics, your mind will be more calm, subdued, and able to concentrate. With good concentration you can attain the wisdom realizing emptiness and eliminate ignorance, the root of samsara, thus freeing yourself from all suffering, forever.

Dedication

Return to the practice for lamrim meditation and do the concluding parts. Finally, dedicate the merit you created so that you and all other beings will wear the ornament of pure ethical conduct, thus acting in ways that are only beneficial and never harmful to anyone. In this way, may everyone quickly become free of suffering and its causes and reach the sublime state of enlightenment.

4. Four Doors to Downfalls in the Practice of Ethics

When practicing ethics, there are four factors we need to watch out for and counteract. These are known as the four doors leading to downfalls—broken precepts and negative behavior.

The Meditation

Settle into the meditation posture and calm your mind by focusing on the inhalation and exhalation of the breath for a few minutes. Determine to put aside all other thoughts and activities for now—you can attend to them after the session.

Then generate a positive, altruistic motivation for doing the meditation. You can think, for example, "I am going to do this meditation to better understand where I get tripped up in my efforts to live ethically. That way, I have a better chance of avoiding those mistakes in the future." Then do the practice for lamrim meditation on page 35, and at the appropriate time after the mantra recitation, consider these four doors to downfalls, making examples from your own life and that of others.

1. Not knowing

The first door is *not knowing*. If you don't know how to differentiate virtuous and nonvirtuous actions or if you take precepts but aren't sure how to keep them, you might unknowingly create nonvirtue and break these precepts. To avoid this problem, study teachings on karma and your precepts. You can also ask your teachers questions to clarify any doubts you might have and make sure your understanding is correct.

2. Carelessness

The second door is *carelessness*. Even if you know about karma and how to keep your precepts, you might not really care about avoiding nonvirtue and creating virtue—this is the meaning of carelessness. Its opposite is conscientiousness, a mental factor that is concerned about virtue and wants to protect the mind from delusions. Cultivating the following four factors will help you be more careful and conscientious:

1. Mindfulness: keeping in mind what is wholesome and unwholesome and which precepts you have taken.
2. Introspective awareness: watching your mind and behavior to make sure you avoid nonvirtue.
3. Personal integrity: refraining from negative actions out of a sense of self-respect—for example, "It wouldn't be right for me to do that."
4. Consideration for others: refraining from negative actions out of concern for others, such as not wanting to upset them or be a bad influence.

3. Lack of respect

The third door is *lack of respect* for the Buddha and his teachings, as well as for your teachers and spiritual friends. For example, if you are not happy about some of the advice you receive from your teacher and think, "My teacher is so strict and controlling; I'm not going to do what he says," you will become careless about your behavior and even break precepts. To counteract this problem, cultivate respect for the Buddha, the Dharma, your spiritual teachers and companions by contemplating their good qualities and how they help you.

4. Strong delusions

The fourth door is *strong delusions*. These can take over our mind, inciting us to act destructively and break precepts, so we need to apply antidotes to them. It's difficult to work on all of them at once, so start with whichever delusion is strongest and most problematic. Once that delusion has been subdued to a certain extent, you can then work on the next strongest, and so on. It is vital to familiarize yourself with the antidotes so you can swiftly bring them to mind when delusions arise.

Conclusion

Resolve to look out for the four factors that lead to downfalls—not knowing, carelessness, lack of respect, and delusions—and to cultivate the factors that protect you from these—study, mindfulness and introspective awareness, respect, and applying antidotes to delusions. Encourage yourself to live ethically, recalling the benefit it brings not only to yourself but to all other living beings.

Dedication

Conclude the practice for lamrim meditation and dedicate the merit you created to the peace, happiness, liberation, and enlightenment of all sentient beings.

PART 5

MEDITATIONS OF THE ADVANCED LEVEL: CULTIVATING BODHICHITTA

In dependence on these [practices of the initial and intermediate
    levels],
I am able to attain only self-liberation.
As there is not one sentient being in all the six realms
who has not been my mother or father,
I will turn away from this lower happiness
and generate the wish to fulfil their ultimate purposes.
By contemplating the path of equalizing and exchanging self
    for others,
I will generate the precious bodhichitta
and engage in the bodhisattva's actions of the six perfections.
Please bless me with the potential to train in this way.

VAJRADHARA LOSANG JINPA, "A GLANCE MEDITATION ON ALL
THE IMPORTANT POINTS OF LAMRIM"

Introduction to Bodhichitta and Its Benefits

15

WITH the advanced level, or the great scope, we reach the heart of the lamrim: cultivating bodhichitta, the aspiration to attain enlightenment for the benefit of all sentient beings, and practicing the six perfections, which are the main causes for attaining enlightenment. A person who has worked on cultivating bodhichitta over a long period of time and has reached the point where it arises effortlessly and spontaneously is a bodhisattva. Everyone can develop bodhichitta and become a bodhisattva; the advanced-level meditations show us how to do that.

Just as the upper levels of a house will be solid and stable only if the lower levels are well built, for our practice of bodhichitta and the six perfections to be strong and stable, we must train well in the meditations of the initial and medium levels. In the initial-level meditations, we realize that our current situation is precarious: our life will end at some point, but we do not know when. What happens to us after death depends on how we live our life, the kind of karma we create. If we are not careful to refrain from nonvirtuous karma, we could find ourselves being reborn in an unfortunate situation where we would encounter unbearable sufferings and lack the necessary conditions to continue following a spiritual path. To avoid such a predicament, we rely on the Buddha and his teachings to understand the difference between nonvirtuous and virtuous karma so that we can refrain from the former and create the latter, and thus take rebirth in a favorable situation.

The intermediate-level meditations pick up from there, revealing that there are problems even in fortunate states of rebirth. As long as we remain in samsara, we are never completely free of suffering and its causes. Clearly recognizing this, we develop renunciation—the determination to free ourselves from samsara—and the wish to attain nirvana.

Renunciation can also be called self-compassion. Compassion is the wish for sentient beings—in this case, ourselves—to be free of suffering and its causes. If we really care about ourselves, it's not enough to merely wish that we avoid problems like sickness or depression in this life; ideally, we take a wider perspective and wish ourselves to be free of problems in all future lives as well. That is renunciation. Renunciation sees that samsaric existence involves one painful situation after another and that we deserve better—we have the right to be free of suffering and to experience the lasting peace and happiness of nirvana. Such understanding motivates us to start practicing the methods to become free: the three higher trainings of ethics, concentration, and wisdom.

A person who has followed this path and attained nirvana—the cessation of all delusions such that they will never arise again—is known as an *arhat*, or "foe destroyer," one who has destroyed the foe of the delusions. This is an excellent achievement, but is not the fulfillment of our highest potential. There are still subtle obscurations in the mind preventing it from being fully enlightened, like a buddha's mind, and one's ability to help others is limited. Therefore, some practitioners aspire to attain perfect, complete enlightenment—the state the Buddha reached—because only then will they have the fully developed ability to help all other sentient beings become free of samsara. Nevertheless, even those who wish to become a buddha must familiarize themselves with the intermediate-level meditations in order to clearly recognize the faults of samsara and generate the wish to free all sentient beings who are trapped in it.

This chapter contains two meditations: one on the connection between the intermediate level and the advanced level, and the second on the benefits of cultivating the extraordinary attitude of bodhichitta.

1. THE ROOTS OF BODHICHITTA

THE MEDITATION

Begin by sitting in a comfortable posture for meditation and settling your thoughts. When your mind is calm, do the practice for lamrim meditation on page 35, in either a long or abbreviated way, pausing after the mantra recitation to insert the following meditation.

Recall what you learned about samsara, cyclic existence—that it is a situation in which we are under the control of karma and delusions and therefore are not free to experience genuine, enduring peace and happiness. Our main delusion is ignorance, which is not just a lack of knowledge but a misconception about how things exist through which we see things in mistaken ways. We can recognize this with our own sense of self or "I," our notion of how we exist. We all have an innate sense of a solid, real "I" that seems to exist on its own, somewhere inside of us. Most people never question this sense of "I," asking, "What is it? Does it exist the way it appears?" Rather, they blindly believe in it and follow its orders, even when it tells us to act destructively.

We are also strongly preoccupied with our sense of self, feeling as though we are the most important person in the world, the center of the universe. Everything revolves around *me*; everything has to be done *my* way; no one should ever disagree with *me* or go against *me*. With such attitudes at the core of our being, we feel justified in being possessively attached to whoever and whatever pleases us and making sure they remain within our reach. And for the people and things that seem to interfere with our happiness, we feel aversion and hatred and think there's nothing wrong with complaining about or harming them.

This is how attachment and aversion develop based on ignorance about our own self or "I." These three harmful attitudes—ignorance, attachment, and aversion—exist in our mind right from the beginning of our life, carried over from past lives. You can see a rudimentary form of them in small children: they get attached to the people and things they find attractive, react with anger or fear toward people and things they find unattractive or frightening, and have a strong sense of "I"—"*I* want this, *I* don't want that."

With our mind overpowered by these delusions we act and create karma. Some of our actions are negative: stealing, lying, insulting, using our sexuality in harmful ways. Any of these actions that are complete with all four factors leave seeds in our mind that could cause unfortunate rebirths if they are not purified. Even our virtuous actions, if done under the influence of ignorance, will merely plant seeds for fortunate rebirths, and thus keep us circling in samsara. This is the mechanism that perpetuates samsara, and for most beings it happens without full awareness or control, as though we are driving on automatic.

In the course of each life we might accumulate millions of karmic seeds that travel with our consciousness into future lives. When we come to the end of one life, if we have not yet freed ourselves from samsara by eliminating its root, ignorance, one of those seeds will ripen and propel us into another rebirth. We don't get to choose where we are born, the family we are born into, or the experiences we have as we go through life. As the Buddha said in a discourse found in the Pali canon, these are determined by our karma:

> Beings are the owners of their karma, heirs of their karma;
> they originate from their karma, are bound to their karma,
> have their karma as their refuge. It is karma that distin-
> guishes beings as inferior and superior.[64]

See if you can get a sense of how you are bound by your karma, like someone tied up or handcuffed, not free to go where you want, do what you want, or have the experiences you wish for.

If the thought arises "But samsara isn't all bad; there are beautiful and enjoyable things," this is true; Buddhism does not deny beauty and pleasure but reminds us of their transience. Even a long, enjoyable, trouble-free life inevitably comes to an end and then we are like the ball on a roulette wheel, uncertain where we will land—it could be in one of the three unfortunate realms, or in a miserable situation in the human world. As long as we are in samsara, we are never completely free of suffering.

Recognize that samsara is a dreadful situation, like a prison. Imagine being taken from your home and brought to such a place. You probably wouldn't feel delighted and wish to stay there but would do everything possible to get out. Renunciation is similar to this state of mind: clearly seeing the faults and disadvantages of samsara, you have no wish to remain in it but are constantly focused on how to become free. Generating such a mind is the purpose of the intermediate-level meditations.

But what about everyone else? You're in samsara along with many other beings. Would it be right to just free yourself and then remain in a state of peaceful bliss, forgetting those other beings? What about your family and friends and people who have helped you in your life? If you and your family were imprisoned and you found a way out, would it be right to walk away and not try to help them escape as well? Thoughts such as these form the connection between the intermediate-level meditations and those of the advanced level. There we generate compassion for the other beings trapped in samsara and search for a way to help them escape. Realizing that only a fully enlightened buddha is able to provide such help, we generate bodhichitta—the aspiration to become enlightened for the purpose of helping all other sentient beings in the most effective, skillful way.

Conclusion

Compare the two aspirations: wishing to be free of samsara and attain nirvana for oneself alone, and wishing to become a buddha who can help all sentient beings become free of samsara. Which do you feel more attracted to? If you are uncertain, resolve to spend more time learning and thinking about them.

Dedication

Complete the remaining parts of the practice for lamrim meditation and dedicate the merit of your session so that all beings will quickly develop the altruistic intention of bodhichitta and will thereby attain the peace and happiness of enlightenment.

2. THE BENEFITS OF BODHICHITTA

Just like the lotus among flowers
is bodhichitta supreme among all virtuous thoughts.
Since having it brings immediate and final happiness,
one should make every effort to produce it.
KHUNU RINPOCHE, *Vast as the Heavens, Deep as the Sea*

We are all capable of developing bodhichitta and becoming a bodhi-sattva, but doing so requires a great deal of energy over a long period of time; it won't happen just by wishing for it. We need to meditate again and again on the various methods for cultivating this sublime mental state. Enthusiasm for this endeavor can be generated by con-templating the benefits of having bodhichitta in our mind.

The Meditation

Begin as usual by settling body and mind, then doing the practice for lamrim meditation on page 35, in full or abbreviated form, inserting the following meditation after reciting the Buddha's mantra.

One benefit of cultivating bodhichitta mentioned in lamrim texts is that we will enter the Mahayana, the Great or Universal Vehicle that takes us to enlightenment. Strictly speaking, it is only bodhisattvas—those whose bodhichitta arises naturally, spontaneously—who have entered the Mahayana. Having spontaneous bodhichitta is similar to having an air ticket to board a flight and travel to its destination. Likewise, only those with bodhichitta actually enter the Mahayana and travel on this path that culminates in buddhahood. Initially our bodhichitta is contrived, but with continued practice, it transforms into the spontaneous, uncontrived form and we become full-fledged bodhisattvas.

Other benefits include the ability to quickly accumulate extensive merit, purify a vast amount of negativities, and become a source of peace, happiness, and benefit for all living beings. Pause and contem-plate each of these advantages to get a sense of how helpful it would be to gain them.

The Dalai Lama has taught additional benefits of bodhichitta that we can experience here and now:

- Happiness and peace. Bodhichitta will make us less prone to critical, judgmental attitudes toward others; without these neg-ative thoughts in our minds, we will naturally feel better.
- Good health and improved relationships with family and friends.
- Having more hope, courage, confidence, and self-esteem.
- Being better able to deal with difficult people and other prob-lems we encounter in our life. This is because we understand

that suffering arises from causes and conditions and that these can be overcome.

- Having more care for the environment and living beings. Cultivating bodhichitta makes us aware that this planet is the home for many living beings, and because we care for them, we want to look after our planet.
- Dying with a peaceful mind and no regrets. Having lived with kindness, compassion, patience, ethics, and so on, our mind will be at ease as we die, knowing we lived a good life.
- Enriching our practices of the initial and intermediate levels. For example, we will be more motivated to refrain from actions that bring harm and suffering to others, as well as to oneself.
- Everything we do that is motivated by bodhichitta becomes a cause of enlightenment. Practicing meditation or reciting mantras without bodhichitta are beneficial but do not lead to enlightenment. On the other hand, they *do* become causes of enlightenment when done with bodhichitta. Having the bodhichitta motivation transforms even ordinary actions like eating, sleeping, working, or exercising into causes of enlightenment, bringing us closer to that state.[65]

Conclusion

After contemplating these benefits, if you feel inspired to start cultivating bodhichitta, keep your mind focused on that feeling as long as possible. If you find the idea of becoming a buddha daunting or wonder how you could possibly work for the benefit of *all* beings, resolve to keep learning about bodhichitta. The advanced-level meditations and the teachings they are based on flesh out how the beautiful aspiration of bodhichitta is not only possible, but a reflection of our own and others' highest potential.

Dedication

Complete the remaining parts of the practice for lamrim meditation and dedicate the merit of your session so that all beings will quickly develop the altruistic intention of bodhichitta and will thereby attain peace and happiness in all their lives up to the highest bliss of enlightenment.

The Sevenfold Cause-and-Effect Instruction 16

Having considered how all these miserable beings have been my mothers
and have raised me with kindness again and again,
I seek your blessings to develop effortless compassion
like that of a loving mother for her precious child.
FIRST PANCHEN LAMA, *Guru Puja*

THERE ARE two main methods for cultivating bodhichitta that
developed in the Sanskrit tradition. The first of these, the sevenfold cause-and-effect instruction, involves contemplating how others
have been kind and helpful to us as a basis for generating gratitude,
loving-kindness, compassion, and ultimately bodhichitta. We thus
aspire to attain enlightenment in order to repay their kindness in the
most sublime way. The other method, equalizing and exchanging self
and others, is presented in the next chapter.

The sevenfold cause-and-effect instruction actually comprises eight
steps, because initially one should meditate on equanimity, an even-
minded attitude toward all beings, if one has not already cultivated
that quality. That is followed by seven steps; the first four are *causes* of
the fifth step, compassion, and the last two are *effects* of compassion.[66]
This is the reason for calling it a "cause and effect" instruction. The
seven are as follows:

1. Seeing all beings as having been our mother
2. Recalling their kindness
3. Repaying their kindness
4. Love
5. Compassion
6. The great resolve
7. Bodhichitta

Initially, it's best to meditate on one step per session to get a deeper experience of it. Later, when you are more familiar with all the steps, you can combine two or more per session, or even do a quick scan of all seven to keep them fresh in your mind.

THE PRELUDE: EQUANIMITY

Equanimity is an even-minded attitude that regards all beings as equally deserving of our respect and concern. We need to develop this attitude as a basis for cultivating loving-kindness and compassion in the same way that it is necessary to make the ground smooth and level before constructing a building on it. Without equanimity, our love and compassion may be partial, reserved only for select people such as our family and friends.

In this meditation we will examine our usual way of relating to others: liking some people, disliking others, and being indifferent to the rest. Why are we so biased? Is that the ideal way of treating people? If not, is there a way to change it?

It is important to accept that we *can* change our attitudes. To share a personal example: I once felt a lot of anger for George W. Bush because of the wars he started. Then I heard the Dalai Lama say in a public talk that he liked George Bush—he didn't like his politics, but he liked him as a person because he was very down-to-earth. That got me thinking that maybe he wasn't such a bad person—he was probably kind and loving to his family, friends, and pets, and most likely had other good qualities as well. I also found it helpful to reflect that his presidential decisions were not entirely his making but resulted from numerous causes and conditions that in turn came from different places and people. My mind began to soften toward him. Later I heard that he likes to paint. Looking at some of his paintings online— including a portrait of the Dalai Lama and one of his little white dog—helped me see him as just another human being trying to find happiness and avoid suffering. When I heard that his mother passed away in 2018, I spontaneously felt compassion and the wish to reach out and comfort him. This was a powerful experience of how the mind can change!

Feeling compassion for a person who has perpetrated harm, however, does not mean we condone their actions. We can regard destructive behavior as wrong while keeping our heart open to the person. If we feel angry, we can use antidotes—such as those explained in chapters 13 and 20, or other methods we find effective—to manage our feelings, and work on cultivating opposite states of mind such as compassion, forgiveness, and love for everyone involved. Another helpful strategy is to mentally separate the person and their behavior—they are not one and the same—and then do what we can to stop the harmful behavior, or at least express our disagreement with it, while extending compassion to the person. Contemplating impermanence is also helpful, to recognize that no one acts harmfully 100 percent of the time; everyone has some good qualities and sometimes engages in positive behavior.

THE MEDITATION

Begin by sitting comfortably and settling your thoughts. When your mind is calm, do the practice for lamrim meditation on page 35, in full or abbreviated form, pausing at the designated place to insert the following meditation.

Start by visualizing in front of you someone you like, such as a close relative or friend. Check your reasons for liking this person. Is it partly because they are nice to *you* and behave in ways *you* approve of? If so, are those good reasons for liking someone and wanting to be close to them?

Next to your friend, visualize someone you dislike. Check your reasons for feeling that dislike for this person. If it's because they are nasty to *you* or *you* don't approve of the way they behave, are those good reasons for disliking someone and treating them badly or wishing that they suffer?

Then visualize beside the other two someone you feel indifferent toward, like a supermarket cashier or a stranger you pass in the street. Why do you feel this way, neither liking nor disliking them? Is it partly because this person has not done anything helpful or harmful to *you*?

Holding the visualization of these three in front of you, check if it feels right to have such different emotions and ways of behaving toward them. Reflect that buddhas and bodhisattvas are not biased; they have equal love and compassion for all beings without exception, like the feelings parents have for their children. If you wish to follow in their footsteps, develop bodhichitta, and attain enlightenment, you also need to open your heart to every living being. Equalizing your feelings toward others is an essential first step.

You can start by contemplating that relationships are not permanent. We tend to believe that a friend will always be a friend, an enemy will always be an enemy, and we will never get close to a stranger. Think again: Did you ever have the experience of a friend becoming an enemy? Or an enemy becoming a friend? Or a total stranger becoming one of your best friends?

Relationships are contingent upon causes, conditions, and circumstances, and since these change, relationships can also change. Focus on the person you like and imagine this person doing something hurtful or unacceptable. Would your feelings toward this person change?

Then, turn your attention to the one you dislike; imagine this person doing something kind or helpful, such as praising you for something you did, or helping you with your work. Does this cause you to open up to the person and view them differently? Have you ever had the experience of getting to know someone you didn't like at first, and gradually becoming more friendly with them? This can happen again, so is it right to cling to the idea that this person is an "enemy" and will be like that forever?

Now focus on the person you are indifferent to. This relationship could turn either positive or negative, but since we are trying to develop positive feelings, imagine the person doing something helpful, such as giving you the right directions when you are lost or returning your wallet after you dropped it absentmindedly. How would this affect your feelings toward this person?

If you are open to the notion of rebirth, you can contemplate what the Buddha taught: that you have known all these people before, in past lives—and not just once, but many times, in every type of relationship. Consider that the friend of this lifetime was your enemy in another lifetime. Your present enemy was someone very dear to you: a parent or sibling, or even your child. And the present stranger has been both friend and enemy. See how this affects your feelings toward these three people.

Another way to balance your feelings for others is to contemplate that just as you want happiness and not suffering, so does everyone else. Focus on each of the three people in front of you, one at a time, and think: "This person wants happiness and good experiences just as I do. And just as I do not want suffering or bad experiences, so do they." Then gradually extend this awareness to other people and beings. From this perspective, does it make sense to discriminate and care about some but not others?

Developing equanimity doesn't mean denying that there are friends and enemies. Some people are easy to get along with, while others are not, and some are even hostile to us. But with the understanding that these relationships are temporary and contingent, we see no reason to close our hearts to certain individuals simply due to present circumstances that will inevitably change.

The purpose of developing equanimity is to overcome strong attachment, aversion, and close-minded indifference and cultivate an open heart and a caring attitude toward everyone, where we are ready to do what we can to relieve their suffering and bring them happiness. Focus on whatever sense of balanced, open care you have generated through this meditation to help it stick in your mind postmeditation.

Conclusion

As you may have noticed, regarding others as friends, enemies, and strangers is largely a function of self-centeredness—how have others affected *me*? This is a narrow view, ignoring how changeable relationships are: friends become enemies, strangers become the best of friends. Seeing this, resolve to cultivate equanimity toward others, like the attitude of a good, responsible doctor who—recognizing that all beings want happiness and to be free from the slightest pain—treats all patients with equal respect and concern.

Dedication

Complete the remaining parts of the practice for lamrim meditation and dedicate the merit of your session so that all beings will overcome their biased attitudes toward others, will cultivate equanimity, and will quickly attain peace, happiness, and enlightenment.

1. SEEING ALL BEINGS AS HAVING BEEN OUR MOTHER

This is the first of the seven steps and is said to be one of the most difficult meditations in the entire lamrim. It is based on the concept that we have had beginningless previous lives and have been in every possible relationship with every being. The Buddha spoke about this in a discourse found in the Pali canon:

> Bhikkhus, this samsara is without discoverable beginning. A first point is not discerned of beings roaming and wandering on, hindered by ignorance and fettered by craving. . . . It is not easy, bhikkhus, to find a being who in this long course has not previously been your mother . . . your father . . . your brother . . . your sister . . . your son . . . your daughter.[67]

Since, as the Buddha said, we and other beings have been in various types of relationships, why focus on that of mother and child? This becomes clear in the following meditation, on the kindness of mothers. Some people have no trouble recognizing and appreciating their mother's kindness, but others have experienced difficulties in their relationship with their mother and for them just thinking or hearing the word "mother" can trigger anger or tears. For such people it may be more effective to meditate on the second point of this method—the kindness of mothers—before the first, because they may never have thought about what their mother did for them and only remember the bad times. One man I met had been physically and emotionally abused by his mother when he was a child. He severed all ties with her when he left home. Twenty years on, he heard his mother was ill and had no one to take care of her—her severe anger had alienated all other family members. He felt the compassionate wish to help her but was still hurt and angered by his childhood experiences. When he learned the meditation on the kindness of mothers, he thought this could help him heal the wounds and be able reach out to her. Likewise, if your relationship with your mother brings up painful or negative feelings, you might try meditating on her kindness before contemplating that all beings have been your mother—otherwise that might lead you to feel angry at everyone! If you were raised by some-one other than your mother—such as your father, a grandparent, an aunt or uncle—simply replace "mother" in the meditation with who-ever was your primary caregiver.

Some Tibetan prayers contain the phrase "mother sentient beings" (Tibetan: *ma sem chen*)—for example, "I will free all mother sentient beings from suffering and place them in the great bliss of buddha-hood." Most Tibetans seem to readily accept this notion that every sentient being has once been their mother. Repeating such phrases multiple times on a daily basis can profoundly affect the way we view and relate to others.

THE MEDITATION

Begin by sitting in a comfortable posture for meditation and settling your thoughts. When your mind is calm, do the practice for lamrim meditation on page 35, pausing at the appropriate place to insert the following meditation.

Start by examining your thoughts about rebirth. Do you accept that you had another life before this one, and another life before that, and so on? Buddhism teaches that our mind is a continuum, an ever-flowing stream of thoughts and experiences. This moment's mind is the continuation of the previous moment's mind, just as today's mind is the continuation of yesterday's mind, and so on, back to conception. The mind at the moment of conception is the continuation of the mind of the previous life. When that person died their mind left their body and connected with the fertilized egg in our mother's womb. And before that life there was another life, and before that another one, and so on.

Some people do not accept previous lives because they cannot remember them. If you think that way, ask yourself if you can remem-ber being born, being a baby, taking your first steps, or speaking your first words? Most of us do not remember early childhood experiences but that doesn't mean they didn't happen. We can forget something we did this morning or yesterday, but we *did* do those things. There-fore, not remembering past lives does not prove they do not exist. And there *are* people who remember past lives and their memories can sometimes be verified. When our mind becomes clearer through practicing meditation, we will also remember our past lives. There is actually no proof that past lives do *not* exist, therefore it is possible that they do exist. See if you can put aside your doubts for now and think, "Maybe it's true; maybe I *have* had past lives."

Now let's look at the idea that we have been in every possible relationship with every other living being. Bring to mind a friend, someone you care about. Visualize that person in front of you and contemplate what the Buddha said: that you have known this person before, in previous lives. You have been in various kinds of relationships with them, including as mother and child. See if you can accept that this person was once your mother, who gave birth to you and brought you up with loving-kindness.

Now think of a person you know but are not so close to, like a neighbor or someone at work. Visualize that person in front of you, next to your friend, and again contemplate that you have known this person before in other lives—this person was your friend, your brother, your sister, your father, and also your mother. If doubts come up in your mind, ask yourself if you can prove that it's *not* true—can you be 100 percent certain that this person was *not* your mother in a previous life? If you can't disprove it, that means it's possible. See if you can accept this.

Now bring to mind someone you don't like—a person you find irritating or just unlikeable. Visualize them in front of you, next to the other two, and contemplate: "I have known this person before, in other lives—this person has been my friend, my brother, my sister. This person has also been my father and my mother." Even if you can't feel 100 percent certain that it's true, try to accept that it *could* be true—it can't be disproven!

Conclusion

If you are open to the idea of every being having been your mother, resolve to keep that in mind and reflect on it when you see or meet others: "This person was my mother in a previous life." Alternatively, if you find this idea difficult to accept, don't reject it but keep your mind open and resolve to explore it further.

Dedication

Complete the remaining parts of the practice for lamrim meditation and dedicate the merit of your session so that all beings will cultivate universal love, compassion, and bodhichitta and will quickly attain the sublime peace, happiness, and fulfillment of enlightenment.

2. RECALLING THEIR KINDNESS

The second step in the sevenfold practice is to contemplate the kindness of others when they were our mother. Although we have had every possible relationship with every being—we've even been enemies and killed each other—the focus here is on mothers because the aim is to cultivate positive attitudes for everyone, and one of the best ways to do this is to recognize how helpful they have been to us. Of all the people in our life, our mother has probably been the kindest; contemplating that naturally awakens our love and compassion. Then, when we can accept that every being has been our mother, we easily understand their kindness and feel gratitude, love, and compassion toward them as well.

The following meditation involves reflecting on the kindness of your mother of this life. If you did not receive much (or any) kindness from your mother, or if your mother was not your primary caregiver, you can do the meditation by recalling another person—your father, grandmother, or other caregiver—who treated you with compassion and kindness.

To increase awareness of motherly kindness, it's helpful to observe mothers with small children or animal mothers with their offspring. Notice what is involved in taking care of little ones and how mothers usually act with patience and unselfish dedication, sometimes even risking their lives in order to protect their young.

THE MEDITATION

Start by settling your body and mind, then doing the practice for lamrim meditation on page 35, inserting the following meditation at the appropriate point.

With a calm mind, become aware of your body. Contemplate that although it is fully developed, or perhaps nearly so, and you are able to take care of yourself and perform many other tasks, your body was not always as it is now. At the beginning of your life it was small and vulnerable and you were completely dependent on others just to survive. Imagine yourself as a baby and realize that if people had not looked after you then, you would not be alive today. And the person who cared for you the most at that time was probably your mother.

Bring to mind a mental picture of your mother and reflect on whichever of the following points are applicable; generate a deep sense of appreciation and gratitude for what she contributed to your life and well-being.

- She carried you in her womb for around ten months as your body developed from a microscopic zygote to a fetus and then a fully formed baby. During the pregnancy she experienced discomfort, even pain, and adjusted her lifestyle out of concern for you—giving up certain activities, avoiding foods she liked, eating things she didn't like.

- She endured the pain of childbirth, and may also have experienced anxiety at that time, worried that a mishap might endanger the health of her baby.

- After the birth, looking after you was a full-time job, twenty-four hours a day, week after week. Imagine yourself at that time, tiny and unable to do anything for yourself. It was probably your mother who did most of the work in those early weeks and months—feeding you every few hours, changing your dirty diapers, bathing and dressing you, and affectionately holding and talking to you.

- She was also the first teacher from whom you learned the most basic skills: how to feed yourself, drink from a cup, crawl, walk, talk, get dressed, use the toilet, brush your teeth, and so on.

- When you were older, she took you to school and picked you up afterward; helped you with your homework; took you to friends' houses, sports practices, or music lessons; prepared your meals; washed your clothes; and so on ad infinitum. She did not get paid for any of this—it was a labor of love.

- When you were older and more independent, she was still there to help you with emotional crises, relationship problems, or financial difficulties. There may have been times when she was the only person in the world you could turn to and trust.

If you have memories of your mother being unkind—getting angry or punishing you unjustly—or if you feel she didn't raise you well, contemplate how she is just an ordinary human being, not a buddha. Understand that being a mother is difficult and it's only natural that mothers sometimes experience anger, frustration, and sadness. It's also helpful to reflect that your mother was not always an adult: she was once a child, too, and went through difficulties with her parents, at school, as a teenager, and so on. Seeing her as a human being with her own problems and limitations can help you find forgiveness.

By contemplating these points, if a feeling of gratitude and the wish to repay your mother's kindness arises in your mind, pause and stay focused on that feeling as long as you can.

Then recall the Buddha's statement about being unable to find anyone who has not been your mother. Think of other important people in your life—such as your father, siblings, grandparents, teachers, friends, neighbors, people you work with—and consider that each of them was your mother in previous lives and took care of you with kindness. If it's difficult to really believe they have been your mother, at least try to accept that it could be true; you can't be completely certain that it's not true.

Conclusion

Feel grateful for the help and kindness you have received from your mother of this life. Resolve to gradually extend this awareness to others who were your mothers in past lives.

Dedication

Complete the remaining parts of the practice for lamrim meditation and dedicate the merit of your session so that all beings will cultivate universal love, compassion, and bodhichitta and will quickly attain the sublime peace, happiness, and fulfillment of enlightenment.

3. REPAYING THEIR KINDNESS

Step three involves cultivating the wish to repay the kindness of mother sentient beings. If our meditation on step two has gone well and we are able to recognize their kindness and truly feel grateful, wishing to repay their kindness should arise spontaneously. If it does not, don't feel discouraged; you may need to repeat step two several times before that wish arises.

It is also beneficial to contemplate other ways we receive help and kindness from people—our teachers, those who produce our food and clothing, those who build our houses and schools, and so on. This meditation begins with some of these examples of kindness, then looks at how we can repay it.

THE MEDITATION

Relax your body and settle your mind in the present moment. When your mind is calm, do the practice for lamrim meditation on page 35, in long or abbreviated form, pausing at the right place to insert the following meditation.

In addition to your mother who brought you into the world and took care of you when you were small, many other people have helped you in your life:

- Your father, grandparents, aunts and uncles, older siblings, and so on who helped with your care and education as you were growing up.
- Teachers who taught you the knowledge and skills you needed to function in the world, support yourself, travel, and so on.
- Farmers and the many other people involved in producing the food you need to stay alive.
- All the people who provide the clothes you wear, the house or apartment you live in, the furniture and appliances you use, electricity, gas, water, the internet, public transportation, and so on.

If, when recalling the last two groups, the thought arises "But I pay for those things, so I am helping *them*," check again. How did you get your money? You likely either inherited it from relatives or received it for work you did; either way, you depend on others. We can't earn money without teachers from whom we learn the necessary skills, an employer who hires and pays us, or clients who support our business if we are self-employed. So without others we would have no money to buy food, clothing, a car, books, and so on. In short, we depend on others for everything we own, use, and enjoy, as well as our knowledge and skills. Imagine what your life would be like if all those people were to disappear from the world.

We also depend on others to learn the Dharma—our teachers, the people who run Dharma centers and organize courses, those who write Dharma books, and so on. In addition, we need others to be able to practice the Dharma and create the causes for favorable rebirths, liberation, and enlightenment. For example, we cannot practice giving without others who are in need. We cannot practice ethics without other beings that we could harm but choose not to. Even difficult people are beneficial for us—they provide opportunities for us to increase our patience, compassion, forgiveness, and love. In short, without others it would be difficult to create virtue or good karma, and enlightenment would be impossible.

If we contemplate these points well, we will feel grateful to others for what they do for us, the important roles they play in our life. Recognizing and feeling grateful for others' kindness arouses the wish to repay their kindness.

There are various ways to repay their kindness. We can start with what the Dalai Lama advises: help others as much as you can, and if you can't help them, at least do not harm them.

Helping others with their present needs such as food and money is excellent, but as long as they remain in samsara they will continue to suffer and will be bereft of genuine, lasting happiness. Most beings are unaware of the methods to become free of samsara, or even to create virtue, which is the cause of future happiness. So the best way to repay their kindness is to help them learn the Dharma, the path that leads to good experiences in the future, liberation from samsara, and full enlightenment.

That doesn't mean we should push people to listen to Dharma teachings or read Dharma books if they are not interested. There are other ways to share the Dharma, and among the most beneficial ways is living in accordance with it—being kind, ethical, honest, and so on—and being a positive example for others to follow. We can also offer skillful advice to those who are going through difficulties, using everyday language rather than Buddhist terminology.

Another way to share the Dharma is to visualize ourselves surrounded by all mother sentient beings when we meditate or recite prayers, mantras, and sutras. Even though this is imaginary, it nonetheless enhances our compassion and love and creates the cause for us to one day enact the buddhas' activity of teaching Dharma to all beings.

Conclusion

We are entirely dependent on others in every aspect of our lives. The kindness we have received from them is immense. Resolve to remember this, generate a feeling of gratitude, and practice repaying it as much as you can.

Dedication

Complete the remaining parts of the practice for lamrim meditation and dedicate the merit of your session that all beings will cultivate universal love, compassion, and bodhichitta and will quickly attain every type of peace and happiness up to enlightenment.

4. LOVE

The fourth step of the seven-point cause-and-effect instruction is meditating on love, or what Buddhist texts often call loving-kindness. There are different types of love. One type, known as endearing or heartwarming love (Tibetan: *yi ong gi jampa*), arises naturally when we meditate on the first three steps: seeing sentient beings as our mother, remembering their kindness, and wishing to repay their kindness. This love is like that which parents have for their children: cherishing them with feelings of closeness and affection.

Another type of love is wishing sentient beings to have happiness and its causes. To attain bodhichitta, we need to cultivate this kind of love for all living beings without exception. We already have its seed in our mind; it just needs to be nurtured through meditation and in our interactions with others.

Not all happiness is the same. Buddhism explains different types of happiness that are progressively more sublime and satisfying. The most basic type occurs when we have essentials like food and shelter and from enjoying beautiful sights, sounds, and so on. This kind of happiness is valuable but not completely satisfying or reliable because it is contingent on external conditions that we can't always control. It can quickly vanish like a rainbow in the sky.

A deeper and more reliable type of happiness is that which arises from positive mental states such as contentment, unselfish love, compassion, and altruism, and from doing actions motivated by these states—helping others in need, being generous, and so on. Knowing how to generate this kind of happiness enables us to experience it anytime, even in difficult situations.

There are even more sublime and satisfying types of happiness we can experience by transforming our mind through meditation. These include the bliss of concentration and the peace arising from developing the wisdom that eliminates our disturbing thoughts and emotions. The highest happiness of all is experienced at enlightenment—when the mind is utterly free from delusions and other obscurations, it abides in inexpressible peace and bliss.

When we meditate on love, we wish sentient beings to have these different kinds of happiness and to create their causes: virtuous states of mind, good karma, and spiritual practice. If you have difficulty understanding or even accepting the higher types of happiness, you can begin with the simpler types—wishing that everyone has food, clothing, shelter, access to health care, and so on, as well as emotional stability and peace.

The Buddha's teachings explain many benefits of cultivating lovingkindness. Some of these can be experienced here and now: enjoying greater health and happiness, sleeping well at night, being liked by others, being able to concentrate, and so on. The long-term benefits include fortunate rebirths, happiness in future lives, and, ultimately, enlightenment.

It is recommended that we start by cultivating love for our near and dear ones. As we gain greater familiarity with the practice, we can gradually extend our love to those who are more distant, those we find difficult, and finally to all beings.

Don't worry if you are unable to actually generate a feeling of love during this meditation. This is a common problem, so there's no need to think something is wrong with you or that the practice is useless. For some people, it takes time for that feeling to arise. I heard one meditation teacher say that it took him five years of practicing loving-kindness before he was able to feel it! Know that it's enough just to do the practice and *try* to feel love, but don't expect that you will. As you become more familiar with the practice, the feeling of loving-kindness will slowly grow in your heart.

Loving-kindness can also be practiced in daily life. When we're walking around, riding on a bus or train, working in an office, or shopping, we can occasionally pause and wish the people and beings around us to be happy, even silently reciting the loving-kindness phrases mentioned below. This is especially helpful with someone we feel uneasy about—it can soften and transform our heart and lighten the energy around us, making it easier to relate to that person as a fellow human being.

The Meditation

Begin by observing your breathing for a few minutes to calm and settle your mind. Then generate an altruistic motivation for doing the meditation and do the practice for lamrim meditation on page 35, pausing after the mantra recitation to meditate on the following.

Go into your heart and get in touch with the feeling of love. One way to do this is to think of someone you love, such as a parent or grandparent, a child, or a pet. It's preferable to not think of someone you love in a romantic or lustful way, as that kind of love is often mixed with ego, attachment, and expectations.

If it is difficult to get a sense of love in this way, you could think of a time when someone showed love either to you or to another person, such as a mother caring for her child or a caregiver helping an elderly person. Observing acts of love and kindness can trigger those feelings in our own mind.

Once you're in touch with the feeling of love, bring to mind a number of people you are close to—family members, friends, neighbors, and so on. Imagine this group in front of you; let feelings of warmth and care arise in your heart. Then focus on one individual at a time and reflect that this person, just like you, wants to be happy. Feel how wonderful it would be if they could be happy. To enhance this feeling, you can silently repeat phrases such as the following:

> May you be well. May you be happy. May you have all that you
> need. May all your experiences be positive and beneficial,
> and may you grow spiritually on the path to enlightenment.

Feel free to alter these phrases or compose your own. It's important to use words and phrases that resonate with you.

Think of the various forms of happiness mentioned above, as well as their causes, and sincerely wish the person to have these. You can also imagine giving them gifts and watching their face light up with joy. If you find your heart is moved by a sense of truly wishing others to be happy, pause and focus on this feeling as long as you can. You can then continue meditating on love for the same person, generate it for another person you're close to, or bring the session to a close.

When you are more familiar with meditating on love for people you already know and care about, start generating it for people you don't know well or are not close to, like distant relatives, your bus driver, the person who delivers your mail, a stranger in the supermarket, and so on. Focus on one person at a time, contemplate their desire for happiness, and generate the wish for them to be happy. You can repeat the phrases mentioned above or create your own, using whatever words help you feel loving-kindness. Imagine giving them little gifts, or just greeting them and bringing a smile to their faces.

When you feel ready to start generating love for difficult people, do the same practice as above, beginning with those you mildly dislike and gradually including more challenging ones. If you feel resistant to the idea of loving such people, reflect that it's not necessary to like everything about a person in order to feel love for them. We can disagree with a person's political views or some of their habits but still wish them to have happiness; we can see them as another human being like ourselves who is just trying to be happy and avoid suffering. In fact, if we wish to influence someone in a positive way, there's a better chance of doing that if we show them genuine love and compassion rather than judgment.

In this way, gradually extend your feeling of loving-kindness to more and more people and beings, and eventually to all living beings without exception.

What about love for oneself? This is not mentioned in traditional lamrim texts but contemporary teachers include it, since many people nowadays have negative feelings toward themselves. Sometimes we treat ourselves worse than we treat others. This is not correct and is even an obstacle to really loving others. If you find self-love challenging, it's a good idea to include yourself in this meditation—at the beginning, middle, or end, whichever way is most effective. Focus on yourself, repeat the phrases, and do your best to generate feelings of loving-kindness for yourself.

Conclusion
Recall that generating love is beneficial for yourself and others and resolve to do your best to cultivate loving-kindness, especially for the people you interact with every day—family, neighbors, friends, and those you work and study with. Sincerely wish them to be happy: to have physical and mental comfort and ease in this life, as well as the stable and lasting peace and happiness of full enlightenment.

Dedication
Complete the remaining parts of the practice for lamrim meditation and dedicate the merit of your session so that all beings will cultivate universal love, compassion, and bodhichitta and will quickly attain every type of peace and happiness, up to the sublime bliss of enlightenment.

5. Compassion

The fifth step is meditating on compassion, the wish for sentient beings to be free of suffering and its causes. Compassion is a natural quality in everyone's mind, so we already have it—we feel it when someone we care about is suffering. We can gradually learn to feel it for more people and living beings, eventually extending it to all beings.

Since compassion is the wish for beings to be free of suffering, we can start by contemplating obvious physical and mental suffering. This is the first of the three types of suffering explained in the intermediate level. As our practice develops, we can also contemplate the two subtler types of suffering: the suffering of change—those pleasant experiences that are transitory and thus not really satisfying—and pervasive suffering—that is, being imprisoned in samsara, having to die and take rebirth again and again under the control of delusions and karma. Realizing that all beings in samsara encounter these sufferings repeatedly, life after life, enables our compassion to grow ever stronger and deeper.

We can also contemplate the causes of suffering. These are not merely external events like war, natural disasters, climate change, or others' abusive behavior. As explained in the intermediate level, the main causes of suffering lie within our minds: delusions such as ignorance and hatred, and karma created under their influence. For sentient beings to be free of suffering, they must eliminate these causes by learning and practicing the Dharma.

As with the meditation on love, we are advised to begin cultivating compassion for those we already care about, followed by strangers, and then difficult people. We also need to have compassion for ourselves. This is already cultivated in the intermediate level—wishing ourselves to be free of samsara with all its suffering and causes of suffering— but we can continue to contemplate self-compassion while cultivating compassion for all sentient beings.

You can do this meditation with the three types of people—friends, strangers, and difficult people—in one session or in separate ones.

The Meditation

Begin the meditation with a few minutes of observing your breathing to calm your mind. After cultivating a positive motivation, perform the practice for lamrim meditation on page 35, pausing at the designated point to insert the following meditation.

Get in touch with the feeling of compassion. An easy way to do this is to think of a small child who is crying or a puppy or kitten that is lost and distressed. Imagine that being as clearly as you can and allow your heart to soften and open with concern and the wish to free them from their sorrow. That is the feeling of compassion. Alternatively, you can think of a time when someone acted compassionately toward you—for example, you needed help and someone was there for you, treating you with kindness and concern. Observing people's facial expression, body language, and ways of acting when they feel compassion can cause it to arise in our own mind or heart.

Don't worry if you are unable to get in touch with compassion at the beginning of the session. It might arise later as you continue with the practice. It may even take several sessions of this meditation before you can actually feel compassion.

Now think of someone you care about. Imagine them in front of you, and reflect on some of their problems, physical and mental. Understand that, just as you do not want even the slightest suffering, neither does this person. Wish them to be free of all suffering of body and mind as well as the causes of suffering, especially delusions and negative karma. You can silently repeat a phrase expressing this, such as "May you be free of all suffering and its causes." Feel free to use your own words. Let yourself rejoice in imagining them free of suffering and its causes.

Then bring to mind other people you care about and do the same contemplation with each one. You might like to incorporate in your meditation some of the other forms of suffering explained in the medium scope—the eight, six, and three types of suffering. A more expansive awareness of suffering and the unsatisfactory nature of samsara will enrich and deepen your compassion.

If your heart is moved by a sense of truly wishing others to be free from suffering and its causes, pause and focus on this feeling as long as you can. You can then continue your meditation focusing on the same person, or generate compassion for another person you're close to, or bring the session to a close.

When you are accustomed to cultivating compassion for people you know and care about, begin cultivating it for strangers—those you feel neutral toward, like people you see on TV, construction workers on their jobsites, fellow shoppers in the store, and so on. As before, have a mental picture of them and imagine the kinds of physical and mental sufferings they encounter. Understand that they wish to be free of all this suffering just as you and your loved ones do, and that they deserve to be free. Then generate compassion, wishing them to be free of all suffering and its causes. If you find it helpful, recite the phrase above or use your own.

When you are more familiar with the practice, move on to enemies and difficult people. Bring to mind someone you dislike or who has acted in harmful ways toward yourself or others. Imagine the person in front of you and contemplate that they wish to be free of suffering, just like you and everyone else. The things they do that are annoying or destructive are probably attempts to find happiness and avoid suffering. Due to confusion they don't realize they are actually creating more suffering for themselves and others.

Put yourself in their shoes and try to understand what is happening in their mind. Is it calm, clear, and positive, or disturbed and negative? Can you remember times when you were caught up in delusions and acted destructively like that? What was that experience like?

If you can understand that this person is suffering now and is creating the cause for more misery in the future, your mind will soften and open with compassion for them. It is also helpful to mentally separate the person from their delusions and harmful behavior and to feel compassion for the person while deploring the delusions and misbehavior.

Generate the compassionate wish for the person to be free of suffering and its causes. Mentally repeat the phrase "May you be free of all suffering and its causes," or another phrase you prefer.

Finally, extend compassion to all sentient beings. Although they wish to be free of suffering, as long as they are in samsara they encounter problems, pain, and unwanted experiences. Feel how wonderful it would be if they could be free of suffering and wish this to happen: "May everyone be free of all suffering and its causes."

Conclusion

Compassion is a logical and natural response when observing or hearing of others' pain because it's clear that no one wants even the slightest unhappiness or discomfort. Even when people act in horrendous ways that harm others, it makes sense to extend compassion toward them—they wouldn't act that way unless they themselves were miserable. Make the determination to do your best to keep compassion in your heart when you meet others and to be as kind and helpful to them as possible.

Dedication

Complete the remaining parts of the practice for lamrim meditation and dedicate the merit of your session so that all beings will cultivate universal love, compassion, and bodhichitta and will quickly attain the sublime state of enlightenment.

6. The Great Resolve

With continued practice of the previous steps in the sevenfold instruction, our love and compassion will grow ever stronger and will eventually become *great love*—wishing happiness for all beings without exception—and *great compassion*—wishing to free all beings from their suffering. The best example of these two attitudes is that of parents toward their children: a spontaneous, heartfelt wish to do everything they can to ensure the children are happy and free of suffering. When great love and great compassion are cultivated even further, they become the *great resolve*. Here one decides to take on the responsibility to ensure that sentient beings experience only happiness and freedom from suffering, as in the thought, "I myself will do whatever it takes to give happiness to all sentient beings and free them from suffering." This is the sixth step in the process.

The following meditation reviews the previous steps from equanimity to compassion that lead to the great resolve. You are asked to imagine all sentient beings sitting around you, as this will enhance your awareness that the practice is to benefit everyone without exception. If doing this makes you uneasy, imagine as many beings as you can comfortably and simply think that the rest are there, all around you.

THE MEDITATION

Start with a few minutes of observing your breathing to bring your mind to a peaceful, calm state. Perform the practice for lamrim meditation on page 35, and at the appropriate place do the following meditation.

Visualize your mother and other female relatives sitting beside you on your left; your father and other male relatives are on your right. Your friends are behind you, and people you dislike are in front of you. (If you are surprised by this arrangement, the purpose is to ensure that you keep your "enemies" in view so you can overcome any negative feelings you may have toward them.) Finally, imagine all other sentient beings sitting around you in all directions. Don't worry if you are unable to visualize all details clearly; it's enough to simply imagine that they are there.

Check if your feelings toward these different people are biased. Do you have warm, positive feelings toward family and friends, aversion toward enemies, and indifference toward everyone else? If so, recognize that this is an obstacle to bodhichitta; it will also lead to problems now and in future lives. Generate the wish to be free of partiality and to have greater equanimity. Contemplate that your relationships with others are not fixed and permanent: friends can become enemies, enemies can become friends, and strangers can become either friends or enemies, depending on changing circumstances. You have already experienced this in the past and it will happen again in the future. Therefore, it doesn't make sense to cling to your present feelings of liking, disliking, and indifference. Having an attitude of equal

concern for every living being makes more sense and is highly beneficial for everyone.

In addition, everyone has been your mother in one or more of your
previous lives. They gave birth to you, looked after you when you were
small and helpless, and devoted themselves to ensure your well-being
and happiness. They have also helped you at other times and in other
ways: growing the food you need to stay alive, making the clothes that
keep you warm, building the house you live in, and so on. In fact,
everything we own, use, and enjoy is provided by other beings.

Contemplating this naturally arouses the wish to repay their kindness by doing whatever we can to bring them happiness and alleviate
their suffering. Reflect on some ways you can show your gratitude to
others.

Appreciation and gratitude also give rise to heartwarming love, seeing others with warmth and affection. Spend some time generating
great love for all sentient beings, sincerely wishing them to have the
happiness they long for as well as its causes: positive states of mind and
virtuous karma.

Genuine love is the basis for compassion: wishing all sentient beings
to be free from suffering and its causes. Ideally, this includes not
just obvious suffering like sickness and pain, but even subtler forms
of suffering—the suffering of change and pervasive suffering, being
trapped in samsara because of the delusions and karma within their
minds. Contemplating this to whatever extent you can, cultivate compassion for all beings.

After meditating on these points repeatedly for a long time, our
love and compassion become stronger and more stable and gradually give rise to a greater sense of responsibility. We realize that it's not
enough to simply *wish* others to be happy and free from suffering; we
need to go further and decide to do everything possible to make that
happen. This is the sixth point in the practice: the great resolve. It is
the same attitude loving parents have for the child they brought into
the world: feeling responsible to ensure that their child has whatever
she needs to be happy, comfortable, safe, and free of pain and suffering. On the Mahayana path, we cultivate this feeling for every living
being without exception. See if you can generate such a feeling toward
the beings visualized around you by thinking, "I myself will ensure that
all these beings have every type of happiness and will liberate them

from all suffering." Whatever slight feeling you are able to generate, even if it is merely a thought, be content with that and keep your mind focused on it as long as possible.

Conclusion

Resolve to keep in mind whatever insights and positive feelings you experienced during the meditation, and to continue nourishing them so that they will transform your mind and your life in beneficial ways.

Dedication

Complete the remaining parts of the practice for lamrim meditation and dedicate the merit of your session so that all beings will cultivate universal love, compassion, and bodhichitta and will quickly attain the sublime peace and happiness of enlightenment.

7. Bodhichitta

The seventh and final step, bodhichitta, is the resulting culmination of the previous six steps, especially the great resolve. When we investigate how we can fulfill the sense of responsibility to free all beings from suffering and bring them all to happiness and peace, we realize the only way to do so is by becoming a buddha. This is because only a buddha has removed all obscurations—both those preventing liberation and those preventing full enlightenment—from their mind and has perfected all positive, beneficial qualities, and is thus in the best position to help others do the same. You can refer back to the qualities of a buddha explained in the meditation on refuge (page 91) to refresh your memory of these. In this way, the aspiration to become a fully enlightened buddha in order to help all beings arises in one's mind.

THE MEDITATION

Start with a few minutes of observing your breathing to bring your mind to a peaceful, calm state. Perform the practice for lamrim meditation on page 35, and at the appropriate place do the following meditation.

Begin as in the meditation on the great resolve: visualize yourself surrounded by all sentient beings, or as many as you can imagine, comfortably. Then reflect on the previous steps of this method, spending as much time as possible on each one so that you can generate a sincere feeling: equanimity; seeing all beings as your mother; remembering their kindness; repaying their kindness; great love; great compassion; and the great resolve. Then contemplate, "I have received immeasurable kindness from every living being and will continue to be benefited by them far into the future. Therefore, it is only right that I repay their kindness in the best way possible, by taking on the responsibility to ensure that they have every type of happiness and are completely free from all suffering."

It is wonderful to have such a wish, but we need to be practical and realistic. In our present state, we have a hard time even keeping ourselves truly happy and free from suffering, much less doing this for all other beings. But it's not impossible. We have the potential to reach enlightenment, or buddhahood, and once we attain that state, we *will* be able to help everyone.

To understand this better, contemplate the qualities of a buddha that enable him or her to benefit others: pure, unconditional love and compassion for all living beings without exception and an unwavering commitment to help them attain enlightenment. Buddhas also have perfect wisdom that sees the true nature of all phenomena and thus are free of all imperfections, especially the deluded obscurations that prevent liberation and the obscurations to knowledge that prevent enlightenment. They have perfect skillful means that knows the best way to help each being, based on perceiving their individual karma, inclinations, personalities, and so forth. Buddhas also have special abilities, such as emanating many different forms at the same time, to help numerous beings throughout the universe.

It's also helpful to contemplate that buddhas are free of all personal needs and desires. They never become tired or discouraged, never need to take a holiday or even a coffee break, and thus they can work for sentient beings every moment, 24/7.

See if you can generate, from the bottom of your heart, the wish to become a buddha in order to have all these excellent qualities and abilities with which you can bring happiness and freedom from suffering to all kind mother sentient beings. This is the meaning of bodhichitta. Focus your mind as long as possible on whatever experience of it you can generate, even a tiny spark.

Conclusion

Wishing to be of the greatest benefit to all kind mother sentient beings without exception, determine to become a buddha with all the qualities necessary to lead others to a lasting state of happiness and peace. This is the beautiful attitude of bodhichitta. Resolve to keep in mind whatever positive thoughts and experiences you were able to generate during the meditation and to continue cultivating them so that eventually bodhichitta will arise within you naturally and spontaneously.

Dedication

Complete the remaining parts of the practice for lamrim meditation and dedicate the merit of your session so that all beings will cultivate universal love, compassion, and bodhichitta and will quickly attain the sublime peace and happiness of enlightenment.

Equalizing and Exchanging Self and Others

All suffering comes from the wish for your own happiness.
Perfect Buddhas are born from the thought to help others.
Therefore exchange your own happiness
for the suffering of others—
this is the practice of bodhisattvas.
TOGME SANGPO, *The Thirty-Seven Practices of Bodhisattvas*

THE SECOND method for cultivating bodhichitta is known as equalizing and exchanging self and others, which has five points. This method is considered more challenging than the sevenfold method because it targets two deeply held mental states: grasping at a solid, independent self or "I"—known as self-grasping ignorance—and the self-centered attitude that feels "I am the center of the universe; my needs and wishes are more important than everyone else's." This attitude afflicts everyone in samsara and is one of the main obstacles to cultivating bodhichitta and attaining enlightenment. Self-grasping ignorance will be explained later, under the perfection of wisdom, while self-centeredness will be the focus of this chapter.

Traditional lamrim texts refer to the self-centered attitude as *self-cherishing*, but that term can lead to misconceptions. When these texts say we need to eliminate self-cherishing, we might think that means we should not care about ourselves or even that we should disparage ourselves, but that is not correct. The Dalai Lama was once asked if self-compassion can help us generate bodhichitta, and in his reply he said that just as we cherish ourselves, we should cherish all other sentient beings. Cherishing ourselves should not be abandoned, because we ourselves need to attain buddhahood. He said that although some Buddhist texts will say things like "hold others dear and abandon yourself," this doesn't mean literally that we should not work for ourselves.

The Buddha meditated for six years for his own enlightenment as well. The Dalai Lama advised that what we need to get rid of is this extreme self-centered attitude; the reasonable cherishing of self is not something we need to abandon.

Thus we need to differentiate a healthy attitude of cherishing oneself—having love and compassion for oneself—from unhealthy self-centeredness. The former helps us become free of suffering and attain buddhahood, whereas the latter causes nothing but problems and is an obstacle to genuine happiness and enlightenment.[68]

This method of developing bodhichitta begins with a meditation on equalizing feelings for oneself and others by reflecting that we all equally wish to be happy and to not suffer. Following that are two meditations in which we compare two opposing attitudes—self-centeredness and altruism, traditionally known as *cherishing others*—in order to recognize the drawbacks of the former and benefits of the latter. This recognition leads to the fourth meditation, in which we resolve to overcome our usual tendency to regard ourselves as more important than others and replace it with altruism. That's the meaning of the phrase *exchanging self and others*. The final meditation is a practice for bringing about this change of heart: *tonglen*, or taking and giving.

1. Equalizing Oneself with Others

> There is no difference between myself and others:
> none of us wishes for even the slightest of sufferings
> or is ever content with the happiness we have.
> Realizing this, I seek your blessings that I may generate joy
>   for the happiness of others.
> FIRST PANCHEN LAMA, *Guru Puja*

This meditation involves contemplating that all beings—oneself and everyone else—have the same natural, spontaneous wish to enjoy happiness and avoid suffering. We encountered this idea earlier, in the meditation on equanimity. The emphasis there was to overcome attachment, aversion, and indifference, respectively, for the three types of people—friends, enemies, and strangers—and cultivate equal concern for them. This equanimity is an essential basis for developing universal love and compassion. Here the emphasis is on recognizing that everyone is basically "just like me" in wanting to be happy and not miserable. With this awareness we can easily understand that to regard ourselves as more important than others is unreasonable.

Included here are two versions of the meditation: a brief, simple one you can use when you have limited time to meditate and a more extensive one with nine points you can use when you have time to go more in depth.

THE MEDITATION

Begin as usual by relaxing and settling your body and calming your thoughts. Then do the practice for lamrim meditation on page 35, in either a long or abbreviated way, pausing at the right place to insert the following meditation.

Brief Version
Start by going into your heart and getting in touch with your own wish to be happy and not suffer. This is like a little voice deep inside that says, "I just want to be happy, and I don't want anything bad to happen to me." This wish motivates most of your actions and choices, such as what you eat and drink, where you go, who you spend time with, and so on. It's natural, instinctive—even animals have it. And there's nothing wrong with feeling this way. According to Buddhism, we all deserve to be happy and no one should have to suffer. It's only because of our delusions and karma that we have pain and problems instead of happiness. The whole point of Dharma practice is to eliminate the causes of suffering and create the causes of genuine, lasting happiness. So do not be afraid to acknowledge your wish to be happy; accept that you are worthy of happiness.

Then bring to mind various people and beings, one at a time, and reflect that each of them, just like you, wants to be happy and does not want to suffer. You could start with those you are closest to, and then gradually widen the circle to include neighbors, other people in your community, town or city, state or province, and so on, depending on how much time and energy you have.

Alternatively, you could start with the people you knew early in life and then gradually move forward in time: your parents and siblings, playmates, teachers and classmates, people you worked with, and so on. As above, focus on one person at a time and reflect, "This person is basically just like me; they want to be happy and to not have even the slightest problem or pain." Feel free to experiment and find a way of doing the meditation that works best for you.

Spend as much time as you wish contemplating this in formal meditation and bring it into your daily life, reflecting on it with respect to the people you see and interact with.

Extensive Version

A more elaborate way to meditate on the topic of equalizing oneself and others—taught by Trijang Rinpoche, the Dalai Lama's junior tutor—involves contemplating nine points.[69] Contemplate as many of these as you have time for in each session.

The first three points contain reasons related to others:
1. Every being has the same wish to be happy and free from suffering, so is it right to discriminate among them and wish only some of them to be happy and pain-free, but not others?
2. If you were volunteering in a food bank and there were ten hungry people standing in front of you, would it be right to give food only to some of them and not to the others?
3. Imagine you are a doctor with ten people in your waiting room who are all suffering from the flu. Would it be right to take care of some of them and not the others?

The next three points contain reasons related to oneself:
4. Since everything we have and enjoy—our body, food, clothing, car, house, knowledge, skills, and so on—comes from others, is it right to ignore them and focus only on our own happiness? As we saw in the meditations on the kindness of others (pages 187 and 190), we have received immeasurable kindness from every being and will continue receiving it in the future until we are enlightened. Considering this, shouldn't we feel grateful and try to repay their kindness?
5. We might object, thinking, "But they have also harmed me." This is true—we have been harmed by others in this life and past lives, and we have also harmed them—but their kind-

ness outweighs the harm they have done. Most interactions between people and other beings on our planet are friendly, or at least nonharmful. Violence and harm exist, of course, but they are the exception rather than the norm. And since our aim is to cultivate positive states of mind and eventually attain enlightenment for the benefit of all beings, it is more productive to focus on their kindness.

6. Since we are all impermanent and subject to death, is there any point in discriminating against anyone or clinging to old resentments? Imagine yourself in an airplane that encounters strong turbulence and you worry that it might crash. Would it make sense to pick fights with your fellow passengers over small things, or fret about the person who didn't pay you back the $10 they borrowed? What state of mind would be most desirable and constructive at the point of death: animosity or altruism?

The above six reasons are from the point of view of conventional truth, our everyday world of people, things, and events. The last three are from the viewpoint of ultimate truth, how things are empty of inherent existence:

7. There are no inherently existing friends or enemies—no one who is a friend or enemy from their own side. If there were, the buddhas would perceive them as such, but they see no one as an enemy. Buddhas love everyone equally, just as a mother loves all her children.

8. If there were permanent, inherently existing friends, enemies, and strangers, they would be like that forever and would never change. But people *do* change, and relationships change. A friend can become our enemy, an enemy can become a friend, and a stranger can become either. This happens from one life to another and even within one life, due to changes in circumstances and in the ways our mind perceives and labels people.

9. Clinging to permanent, inherently existing friends and enemies is like having fixed ideas of "this side" and "that side." For example, when we're standing on one side of a road we refer to it as "this side" and call the opposite side "that side," but when we cross the road, "that side" becomes "this side"

and "this side" becomes "that side." Such labels depend on our perspective from where we stand. The same happens with people: someone who has similar political views as oneself is on "this side," but a person who has opposing views is on "that side." These labels are not fixed and permanent because any of us might change our views at any time. Similarly, we label "I" in relation to our own body and mind and label "others" in relation to other sets of body and mind. But from their point of view, their body-mind complex is "I" and our body-mind complex is "other." Therefore, "I" and other, as well as friend, enemy, and stranger, are just labels that depend on shifting circumstances and concepts; they do not exist from their own side, inherently.

Conclusion

If you experience a sense of the equality between yourself and others, even to a slight degree, focus on it single-pointedly for as long as possible without thinking of other things. Then resolve to keep this in mind as you go about your daily activities when you see and interact with others: "These people want happiness and do not want suffering just as much as I do."

Dedication

Complete the remaining parts of the practice for lamrim meditation and dedicate the merit of your session so that you and everyone else will learn to have equal concern and respect for all other beings, and will quickly attain the peace, happiness, and fulfillment of enlightenment.

2. DISADVANTAGES OF SELF-CENTEREDNESS

This chronic disease of cherishing myself
is the cause giving rise to my unsought suffering.
Perceiving this, I seek your blessings to blame, begrudge,
and destroy the monstrous demon of selfishness.
FIRST PANCHEN LAMA, *Guru Puja*

Although it is fairly easy to understand that everyone equally wishes to be happy and to not suffer, our instinctive tendency is to feel that we are more important; that one's own needs and wishes take precedence over those of others. That attitude drives much of our behavior: pushing our way to the head of the line in a supermarket, making sure we get the biggest and best, worrying incessantly about our own problems that are minuscule compared to those of others, manipulating others to achieve our own aims, and even causing harm to others.

We may believe this attitude is necessary to survive and fulfill our needs, but in reality it's the source of problems. As Shantideva wrote, "Whatever worldly suffering there is arises from wishing for your own happiness."[70] In this meditation we will look at why this is so.

THE MEDITATION

Sit in a comfortable, conducive posture for meditation and settle your thoughts. When your mind is calm, do the practice for lamrim meditation on page 35, in either a long or abbreviated way, pausing at the right place to insert the following meditation.

Start by thinking of some human-made misfortunes happening in the world today, such as the climate crisis, violent crime, wars and conflicts, corruption, injustice, abuse, and other harmful behavior. Imagine you can read the minds of the perpetrators of these problems and check: Are they acting selfishly, putting their own wishes and aims before those of others?

Next bring to mind a few incidents in your own life where you acted selfishly. What was the outcome? Looking back, how do you feel now about your behavior?

We can also recognize the problems caused by selfishness by reflecting on karma. When bad things happen to us, we tend to blame others, whether that means parents, partners, kids, the government, neighbors, or our boss. It may be true that these people are acting negatively and thus creating conditions for our suffering, but the Buddha's teachings say that the chief cause of our problems is our own karma, mainly from previous lives. Some examples of this:

- Sickness and poor health are the result of killing and harming others.
- Financial problems and lack of success are due to stealing and miserliness.
- Fears and phobias are the result of harmful intent.
- Difficulties in finding stable, healthy relationships are the result of sexual misconduct.
- Being verbally abused is due to verbally abusing others.[71]

Contemplate: If you have done any of these negative actions in this life, what motivated you to do so? Can you recognize thoughts of self-centeredness, in which you considered yourself more important than others?

Selfishness usually leads to delusions like anger and attachment, which in turn motivate negative actions such as lying, stealing, or harming others. As a result of this karma, we experience problems and suffering in this and future lives. If you can accept this, learn to put the blame for your problems on the selfish attitude that incited you to create the cause for them in the first place, and resolve to overcome this attitude. Keep your mind focused on this thought as long as you can.

Even without considering karma and past lives, we can see many harmful effects of selfishness in our present life. Relationship problems usually involve a certain amount of ego and selfishness. We feel that *my* happiness is more important than the other person's, therefore I must have my way, I must win the argument, I must be in charge. Think of some difficulties you have experienced in relationships and try to recognize the role self-centeredness played.

Self-preoccupation also lies behind our automatic tendency to compare ourselves with others in terms of social status, physical traits, level of education, abilities, and so on. We then experience one of three delusions: envy or jealousy toward those who seem better than us, arrogance toward those who seem inferior, and competitiveness toward those who are roughly equal. We may also feel shame or self-loathing, which are other forms of self-preoccupation, with thoughts such as "I am so awful; I'm the worst person in the world." All these attitudes are unhealthy, disturbing our happiness and peace of mind, and lead to unwise behavior.

Self-centeredness can also corrupt our positive actions and Dharma practice. When we help someone in need, is our motivation purely altruistic, or is it mixed with the wish to appear generous in order to win respect or receive something in return? Is our interest in learning and practicing Dharma truly to benefit others and relieve their misery, or to impress them with how much we know and how well we can sit in meditation? If you recognize such ulterior motives in yourself, it doesn't help to feel guilty or dismayed. Understand that it takes time—a very long time!—to overcome selfishness because it is such a deeply ingrained habit. Resolve to watch out for it, remember its faults, and avoid it like the plague.

Can you think of any benefits of being selfish? You might think, "Yes, it helps me get what I want." Check again: If you act selfishly to get what you want—being inconsiderate, pushing people out of the way, even hurting them—do you really feel happy and satisfied in the end? Couldn't you strive for your goals without being self-centered?

If we carry on being self-centered, we will continue creating negative karma, which will only cause further suffering and problems in future lives. That includes being born in unfortunate circumstances with almost no chance of following the path to enlightenment.

Selfishness is also a major hindrance to cultivating genuine love, compassion, and bodhichitta, and to progressing on the path to enlightenment. The Buddha was once like us—imprisoned in samsara, full of delusions and suffering—but he became enlightened long ago, while we are still stuck in samsara. Why? It's because the Buddha decided to stop being selfish and instead to cherish others, but we have not.

Conclusion

Selfishness is the root of all problems, from the personal to the global level. All forms of inconsiderate behavior, relationship problems, competition, jealousy, arrogance, and insincere Dharma practice are fueled by self-centeredness and self-preoccupation. Focus your mind for a few moments or more on whatever understanding or feeling you reached as a result of this meditation. Resolve to look out for self-centeredness in your daily life and do your best to avoid acting on it.

Dedication
Complete the remaining parts of the practice for lamrim meditation and dedicate the merit of your session so that all beings will overcome self-centeredness and develop altruism, and will quickly attain genuine peace, happiness, and enlightenment.

3. BENEFITS OF CHERISHING OTHERS

The mind that cherishes mothers and places them in bliss
is the gateway leading to infinite qualities.
Seeing this, I seek your blessings to cherish these transmigratory beings
more than my life, even should they rise up as my enemies.
FIRST PANCHEN LAMA, *Guru Puja*

Opposite to self-centeredness is altruism, also known as *cherishing others*. There are many benefits of this attitude for ourselves and for others. Shantideva said, "Whatever worldly joy there is arises from wishing for others' happiness."[72] Let's look at why this is so.

THE MEDITATION

After settling your body in a comfortable posture, calm your mind with a few minutes of meditation on the breath. Perform the practice for lamrim meditation on page 35, pausing after the mantra recitation to do the following meditation.

The Mahayana Buddhist teachings say that cherishing others—that is, viewing them with compassion and love and doing what we can to help them—is the source of all good and happiness. Think of some acts of kindness and compassion you have observed or heard about, such as people helping those who are hungry, homeless, sick, dying, frightened, and so on. These acts arise from altruism and a willingness even to forgo one's own comfort and needs in order to alleviate others' suffering and bring them happiness. What would the world be like if no one was altruistic, if no one stepped up to assist the victims of wars, natural disasters, or famine?

It is also helpful to think of the people you most admire and check why you feel that way: What qualities do you see in them that attract and inspire you? Are they self-centered and greedy or altruistic and compassionate? This reflection can help us to identify the ideal qualities to cultivate in ourselves.

We can also recognize the benefits of altruism by contemplating karma and its results. Good things that happen in our lives are the result of virtuous karma we created in the past, motivated at least partially by an altruistic cherishing of others. For example:

- Good health and a long life are the result of nonviolence toward others and protecting lives.
- Having resources like food, clothing, and shelter and being successful in our endeavors are due to refraining from stealing and practicing generosity.
- Being physically attractive is the result of practicing patience.
- Enjoying stable, healthy relationships is due to using sexuality wisely and refraining from harmful sexual behavior.
- Being respected by others is the result of humility and treating others with respect.[73]

These examples from the Buddhist teachings demonstrate that in our past lives altruism—caring about others, wanting them to be happy and to not suffer—motivated us to avoid harmful actions and do what was beneficial and virtuous. We are currently enjoying the fruit of that good karma. If we wish to enjoy similar experiences in the future, we need to act altruistically now.

Look for positive results of altruism in your life. For example, recall some experiences in relationships where you learned that being less selfish and more concerned for the other person led to greater harmony, peace, and happiness. Also, compare how you feel when you do things motivated by concern for others versus doing things just for yourself.

The attitude of cherishing others is also an essential ingredient of the path to enlightenment. We need it to cultivate unconditional love, compassion, and bodhichitta and to practice generosity, ethics, patience, and the other perfections. By cultivating these positive mental states and practices, not only do we create the causes to become enlightened—and thereby able to benefit others in unimaginable ways—we will also experience greater happiness now and in future lives.

Conclusion

If you recognize that cherishing others is a more beneficial attitude than self-centeredness, resolve to be less selfish and more concerned for others, and focus your mind on that resolution as long as possible. Close the meditation by identifying one or two ways that you can incorporate cherishing others into your day, in acts of body, speech, or mind.

Dedication

Complete the remaining parts of the practice for lamrim meditation and dedicate the merit of your session so that all beings will overcome self-centeredness and develop altruism, and will quickly attain the peace and happiness of enlightenment.

4. EXCHANGING SELF AND OTHERS

> Cherishing myself is the doorway to all loss,
> while cherishing my mothers is the foundation of all qualities.
> Hence I seek your blessings to make my heart practice
> the yoga of exchanging myself for others.
> FIRST PANCHEN LAMA, *Guru Puja*

Having compared the consequences of selfishness and altruism in the previous two meditations, it should be clear that cherishing others is far more beneficial for everyone, oneself included. At some point, you will feel ready to commit yourself to changing your attitude from being mainly focused on yourself and your needs to being attentive to the needs and wishes of others and helping them as much as possible. Continuing to cultivate love, compassion, and altruism, your focus shifts even further away from self-centeredness and you come to regard others as *more* important than yourself. This is the meaning of the fourth point in this method for cultivating bodhichitta: exchanging self and others. Here, we are exchanging the self-centered attitude for the attitude of cherishing others.

Some people naturally care more for others than themselves, even without training in these methods: parents who are more concerned about their children's well-being than their own; doctors and nurses who work long hours, even through the night, to relieve the suffering of their patients; and rescue workers who sometimes risk their own lives to save others. With familiarity we can become like this as well.

The Dalai Lama says that an effective way to recognize the need to become more concerned for others is to imagine in the space in front of you yourself on one side and all other beings on the other side. You then ask yourself who is more important: that one person, me, or all those other beings, who are innumerable?

Keep in mind that self-centeredness is just a transitory state of mind based on ignorance; it is not permanent, and not who you are. It's best to avoid identifying with it, as that can lead to self-denigration when engaging in these meditations.

Learning to be less self-centered and more altruistic may be easy for some but challenging for others. We need to practice at our own pace and not try to force ourselves to change. As we become increasingly familiar with the meditations for cultivating bodhichitta—particularly equanimity, loving-kindness, compassion, the faults of self-centeredness, and the benefits of altruism—we will notice a gradual shift in our mind: we've become a little less selfish and more concerned for others. The practice of taking and giving, the fifth step in this method, is another excellent way to transform ourselves.

The Meditation

Sit in a comfortable, conducive posture for meditation and settle your thoughts. When your mind is calm, do the practice for lamrim meditation on page 35, inserting the following meditation after the mantra recitation.

Start the meditation by briefly reviewing the previous three points:
- Everyone wants to be happy and avoid suffering. In that sense, there is no difference between yourself and everyone else; we are all equal.
- Self-centeredness is the cause of numerous problems in this and future lives and is one of the greatest obstacles to achieving spiritual goals, especially enlightenment.

- Cherishing others, on the other hand, is the source of all good and happiness and an essential component of the spiritual path. In fact, it is impossible to generate bodhichitta and attain enlightenment without being genuinely concerned for others and committed to helping them.

After contemplating these points, do your best to generate the firm determination to bring about a change in your mind. You can think, for example, "I will work on my mind to decrease my self-centered attitude and to increase my concern for others. I will change my priorities and learn to put others before myself."

You might encounter internal resistance to the idea of cherishing others. Below are several objections that could arise in your mind, and some suggested ways of dealing with these.

1. "I have been so selfish all my life; I can't possibly change."

It's true that selfishness is not easy to get rid of, but it's not impossible. Remember that the mind is impermanent and clear in nature, like a cloudless sky. Selfishness and other unskillful habits are not permanent but are like clouds that come and go in the sky. We *can* change them by applying effort over a long period of time. Shantideva says: "There is nothing whatsoever that is not made easier through acquaintance."[74] Find examples of this in your experience, such as a person, activity, or object you initially disliked but later came to accept or even like due to familiarity.

2. "Why should I help others? Their suffering doesn't harm me and their happiness doesn't benefit me."

Think again: Can you really be happy when someone nearby is in pain? And hasn't someone else's joy made you happy? We human beings are social animals; we need others to find meaning and joy in life. And as we saw earlier, we are dependent on others for everything from food and water to knowledge and livelihood. Is it reasonable to think that others' well-being does not affect us?[75]

3. "If I cherish others, what will happen to me? Who will take care of me?"

Cherishing others does not mean we have to neglect ourselves. We continue looking after ourselves, but with a new outlook. At mealtimes, for example, we can think, "I am eating this food to have energy to continue practicing Dharma, work for enlightenment, and make my life beneficial for others." We can have similar thoughts when sleeping, working, playing, seeking medical help, and so on. Also, if we truly dedicate our lives to spiritual practice and to helping others, they will cherish us and make sure we don't starve!

Conclusion

Based on what you have realized in this meditation, resolve to avoid following self-centeredness and to act instead for the welfare of others. If you are not entirely convinced that altruism is preferable to selfishness, you could reflect: "I've been following self-centeredness all my life, and where has it gotten me? Maybe I should try being more altruistic and see what happens!"

Dedication

Complete the remaining parts of the practice for lamrim meditation and dedicate the merit of your session so that all beings will overcome self-centeredness and develop altruism and will quickly attain the sublime happiness of enlightenment.

5. Taking and Giving (Tonglen)

> May I be beloved of beings,
> and may they be more beloved to me than myself.
> May I bear the results of their negativity
> and may they have the results of all my virtue.
> NAGARJUNA, *Precious Garland*

The fifth point in this method of developing bodhichitta is the practice of taking and giving, or *tonglen* in Tibetan. We imagine *taking* on the suffering of others with compassion and *giving* them our happiness with love. Some people are comfortable doing this right from the start, but others find it difficult or even frightening. For such people, it is advised to start doing the practice with oneself—learning to take on one's own problems. Therefore, this section contains two variations of tonglen, one in which we imagine taking on our own future suffering—a step helpful for beginners—and one that involves taking on the suffering of others, for those who are ready to do this. Feel free to try both.

The Meditation

Whichever version of the tonglen practice you do, start the session by settling your body and mind, then doing either the full or brief practice for lamrim meditation on page 35, pausing at the right place to insert the following meditation.

Begin by spending a few minutes contemplating the reasons and benefits for practicing tonglen. Recall that you and everyone else instinctively wish to be happy and free from pain. There's nothing wrong with feeling this way; we deserve to be happy and shouldn't have to suffer. Where we often go wrong is in putting ourselves before others in order to achieve our goals. This self-centered attitude can lead to greed, hatred, arrogance, and other delusions, and under their influence we may act unwisely: being deceitful, manipulative, or even harming others. These attitudes and actions are the cause of suffering, not happiness. Find examples of this in your own experience.

On the other hand, when we put aside self-interest and act out of genuine concern for others—treating them with respect and kindness, benefiting them as much as we can, and not harming them—we create the cause of real happiness. Again, check if this is true according to your own experience.

If you accept those ideas, feel determined to work on changing your attitude to be less self-centered and more other-focused. Tonglen is a powerful technique for bringing about this change. Practicing it brings many other benefits, such as greater peace and happiness, fewer problems in our relationships, the purification of negative karma and obscurations, the accumulation of a vast amount of merit, and quickly attaining enlightenment. Generate the motivation to practice tonglen for the benefit of yourself and others, both now and in the future.

Tonglen for one's own suffering

Think of a problem you might experience later today, this week, this year, or later in your life: it could be illness, age-related discomfort and difficulties, the pain of separating from loved ones and cherished possessions, or anxiety about dying. It might be best to start with just one problem; when you have more experience in this practice you can bring in more problems. Also, choose only a minor problem if you feel resistance or fear when thinking about major ones. But remember that such feelings are transient, not permanent. With greater familiarity over time, you can become more courageous and resilient when facing life's problems in tonglen.

Next, generate self-compassion, wishing your future self to be free of this difficulty. It can help to repeat a phrase such as "How wonderful if my future self could be free of this problem and all other miseries." Then decide to take on this problem now so that your future self does not have to experience it. Due to that, imagine that suffering in the form of dark smoke and draw it into yourself, either with your breath or another way that you are comfortable with. At your heart, visualize your self-centered attitude as a dark ball or lump. When the smoke of suffering enters you, it transforms into a shaft of lightning that strikes the lump of self-centeredness, smashing it into smithereens. Feel that all your self-centered thoughts and concerns vanish, becoming nonexistent. Let your mind rest for a few moments in the peacefulness that brings.

Then imagine giving your future self what it needs to flourish and be happy. Visualize all you have that is positive—good qualities, virtuous karmic seeds, a healthy body, possessions, and enjoyments—in the form of a brightly shining light at your heart. Rays of light emanate from this and transform into whatever will bring happiness to your future self, such as nourishing food, a comfortable living space, good medical care, pleasant encounters with others, and positive inner qualities like courage, optimism, and resilience. Imagine your future self receiving these and looking happy, calm, and content. Since the principal cause of happiness is Dharma, give your future self whatever they need to continue practicing Dharma: staying connected with spiritual teachers and friends; confidence and joyous effort to keep practicing right up to the end of life; the steady growth of positive qualities like compassion, loving-kindness, wisdom, patience; and so on.

There is also a simple tonglen practice you can use with the problems of daily life, such as depression, a headache, being stuck in a traffic jam, and so on. Focus on the problem and generate compassion for yourself. Then think of others who have the same or a similar problem and generate compassion for them as well, thinking: "All those people wish to be free of their suffering, just as I want to be free from mine. May they be free from their suffering and its causes."

Then cultivate the courageous wish to accept your own problem so those other people can be free of theirs. Let go of resistance and aversion and say to yourself, "By my accepting and experiencing this problem, may all the other people who have a similar problem be free from it." Rest in this beautiful thought as long as you can.

You can accompany these thoughts with the visualization explained above: imagine the problem transforming into a lightning bolt that smashes the dark lump of self-centeredness at your heart. Let your mind rest briefly in a state of peaceful acceptance of the problem, free of self-centered anxiety and aversion. Then think of all your positive energy—merit, good karma, good fortune, all the positive things you have in your life—and imagine these in the form of a bright light at your heart. Send this out to those other people, imagining that it transforms into whatever they need to be happy, free of suffering, and able to follow the spiritual path, ultimately attaining enlightenment.

If you wish to end your meditation here, skip to the conclusion and dedication on page 226, at the end of the second practice, tonglen for others.

Tonglen for others' suffering

Imagine in front of you someone you know and love who is experiencing difficulties. Contemplate their suffering, doing your best to empathize with what they are going through. Understand that they wish to be free of suffering, just as you do, and generate the compassionate wish for them to be released from all their pain and problems. Then generate the courageous wish to take their suffering upon yourself.

If you feel frightened by this idea, know that it's not possible to *actually* take on others' suffering—even a buddha is unable to do that. Nonetheless, the practice of tonglen is a powerful way to increase our courage and willingness to help when we can, so that we do not shrink back because it seems too difficult or inconvenient. It's also helpful to remember impermanence—that all experiences, pleasant and unpleasant, are transient, changing each moment, and do not last forever. Our thoughts also make a difference. Anticipating that an experience will be unbearable increases the likelihood that it will be, but rousing our courage and thinking, "I'll be OK; I can handle this," will enable us to go through it more easily.

Visualize that your self-centered attitude and self-grasping ignorance take the form of a dark ball or lump in your heart. Then visualize the suffering of the person in front of you leaving them in the form of dark, pollution-like smoke. As you inhale, this smoke enters you, transforms into a shaft of lightning, and strikes the lump of self-centeredness and ignorance at your heart, destroying them. Both the suffering and the lump become utterly nonexistent. Imagine being filled with peace and clarity. Feel joyful that this person is now free of his or her difficulties.

Then generate loving-kindness for this person. Think about how they want to be happy, just as you do. Wish them to have happiness and its causes. Imagine all the good things that are part of you and your life—your body, possessions, virtuous karma, happiness, and positive qualities—in the form of pure, radiant light at your heart, and send this out as you exhale. It transforms into whatever will bring joy and peace of mind to this person: basic necessities such as food and clothing, good relationships with others, and inner qualities such as love, compassion, wisdom, courage, and equanimity. Imagine that their temporal needs and wishes are fulfilled and that they gain what they need to follow the spiritual path and ultimately attain enlightenment. Let your mind rest for some time in a feeling of joyfulness that you have helped your loved one in this way.

Gradually expand the practice of tonglen to include other people you know and care about, as well as strangers and people you find difficult. Eventually you will be able to practice it with all beings—including the animals, hungry ghosts, and hell-beings of other realms.

Conclusion

Rejoice in the practice you have just done, knowing that it's beneficial for yourself and others. Resolve to continue practicing tonglen with other difficulties you encounter, your own and those of others, and thus transform them into factors that nourish compassion and altruism and diminish self-centeredness.

Dedication

Complete the remaining parts of the practice for lamrim meditation and dedicate the merit of your session so that all beings will overcome self-centeredness, develop altruism, quickly progress along the path, and attain the perfect peace and happiness of enlightenment.

⚛ PART 6 ⚛

MEDITATIONS OF THE ADVANCED LEVEL: THE SIX PERFECTIONS

In countless previous lives all living beings
have again and again been our parents and have shown us
   great kindness.
Take upon your shoulders the load of repaying them
and think only of what brings good to others. [. . .]

Break off from the mentality that holds self above others.
Generate bodhimind, which yearns
for enlightenment for the sake of all,
and have a firm will to train in the ways of the mighty
   bodhisattvas.

THE SEVENTH DALAI LAMA,
Meditations to Transform the Mind

Introduction to the Six Perfections

WE HAVE now covered the two methods for generating bodhichitta: the sevenfold cause-and-effect instructions and the method of equalizing and exchanging self and others. Some texts explain a third method that combines these two into eleven points to contemplate: (1) equanimity, (2) seeing all sentient beings as having been your mother, (3) remembering their kindness both when they were your mother and in other ways, (4) wishing to repay their kindness, (5) equalizing self and others, (6) the disadvantages of self-centeredness, (7) the benefits of cherishing others, (8) exchanging self and others, (9) taking others' suffering with compassion, (10) giving your happiness to others with love, and (11) the great resolve. These contemplations culminate in the generation of bodhichitta.

Someone who wishes to attain enlightenment needs to meditate repeatedly on these methods in order to realize bodhichitta. The bodhichitta that initially arises in one's mind from doing these meditations is *contrived*, meaning that one needs effort to generate it. After doing such meditations for an extensive period of time, bodhichitta will start to arise effortlessly and spontaneously, similar to the way thoughts of food arise in our mind when we are hungry. This is called *uncontrived* bodhichitta, and when it first arises, one becomes a bodhisattva.

There are two types of bodhichitta: wishing or aspirational bodhichitta and engaged bodhichitta. The first is comparable to wishing to go somewhere, such as India, while the second is like actually deciding to go—that's when you book your flight, apply for a visa, and pack your bags. In that way, the first type of bodhichitta is having the *wish* to become enlightened for the benefit of all sentient beings, and the second involves *engaging* in the actual practices that will transform our mind into the mind of a buddha. Those practices are summarized in the six perfections: generosity, ethics, patience, joyous effort, concentration, and wisdom.[76] What makes these actions *perfections* is doing them with the motivation of bodhichitta.[77] For example, when bodhisattvas give food to a hungry person, they are concerned not only about the being in front of them but about all living beings. Their ultimate aim is enlightenment to free all sentient beings from suffering and lead them to enlightenment as well, and they perform this act of giving to create the cause for that goal. This is quite a high level of practice, but by gradually training in the lamrim meditations in general and the meditations of the great scope in particular, we will eventually be able to practice in this way.

The bodhisattva path and the six perfections can be divided into two aspects: method and wisdom. *Method* involves helping sentient beings with compassion and love and *wisdom* involves cultivating the correct understanding of how things exist, especially the emptiness of inherent existence. These two are compared to the wings of a bird: just as a bird needs two wings to fly, a bodhisattva needs the two wings of method and wisdom to ascend the path to enlightenment. Method is the cause of the *rupakaya*, or form body of a buddha, and wisdom is the cause of the *dharmakaya*, or truth body, which includes the nature truth body and the wisdom truth body.[78]

There are different ways of dividing the six perfections between method and wisdom. In one way, the first five perfections are included in method and the sixth perfection in wisdom. Another way has the first four perfections included in method and the last two in wisdom. Either way, one definitely needs all six perfections to reach enlightenment. Method alone without wisdom will not lead out of samsara, and wisdom alone without method will lead only to self-liberation.

Although we are meant to engage in the practice of the perfections with bodhichitta, we don't have to wait until we are bodhisattvas to begin practicing them. We can generate contrived bodhichitta now, and with that as our motivation, give generously, live ethically, cultivate patience, and so on.

The Perfection of Generosity 18

With the key of generosity bold and pure
spring the lock most difficult to open—the tightness of the heart.
Train in detachment,
which gives whatever is needed.
THE SEVENTH DALAI LAMA, *Meditations to Transform the Mind*

IN THE lamrim, generosity is explained as the virtuous intention to give as well as physical and verbal acts that are motivated by that intention. When such intentions and actions are motivated by bodhichitta, they become the perfection of generosity.

Most people are generous—out of kindness and compassion we donate money to charitable organizations, give food to the hungry, care for abandoned animals, and so on. Such actions are admirable, but if they are not motivated by bodhichitta, they are ordinary acts of generosity, not the perfection of generosity. When bodhisattvas give, they do so with the intention to attain enlightenment for the benefit of all beings; that is the perfection of generosity.

This chapter contains two meditations. In the first, we contemplate the benefits of generosity to arouse enthusiasm to practice it, and in the second, we reflect on how to be generous by practicing the three ways of giving.

1. THE BENEFITS OF GIVING

THE MEDITATION

Start by settling your body in a comfortable posture and calming your mind with a few minutes of meditation on the breath. Perform the practice for lamrim meditation on page 35, pausing after the mantra recitation to insert the following meditation.

It will be easier to give if we understand the benefits of generosity and the disadvantages of the opposite state of mind: being miserly and reluctant to give. Spend some time reflecting on the following benefits of being generous:

- Effects we can experience in this life include physical and mental well-being and greater ease in our relationships and interactions with others. People will be drawn to us and feel comfortable in our presence; in that way we can benefit them with the Dharma.
- We will easily obtain resources like food, clothing, shelter, and money in the future. This is the karmic result of giving. Having what we need to survive allows us more time and freedom to help others, practice the Dharma, and continue following the path to enlightenment.
- Generosity creates the cause for enlightenment. It is impossible to attain this marvelous state of peace and happiness, with its countless ways of helping others, if we are selfishly attached to what we have and unwilling to share it. Therefore, learning to open our hearts, let go of our fears and attachments, and practice giving is an essential cause of enlightenment.

On the other hand, selfishness and strong attachment to our belongings, knowledge, and skills can make us stingy and reluctant to share them, like Scrooge in Charles Dickens's *A Christmas Carol.* The karmic result of stinginess is rebirth as a hungry ghost or an impoverished human being, situations in which it would be difficult to practice Dharma and continue on the path to enlightenment. In this life, our mind will be troubled by fear and anxiety and we will have difficulty making friends.

Think of times when you were generous and other times when you felt tight and reluctant to give. Which state of mind is more satisfying and beneficial, to yourself and others? It is also useful to check how you feel about *others* who are either generous or miserly. Which type of person do you want to emulate?

One helpful way to lessen stinginess and increase generosity is to recollect impermanence and death. Contemplate along these lines: "One day I will die and separate from my body, wealth, and possessions. I can't take any of these things with me to the next life. The only thing that will help me at the time of death is Dharma—positive states of mind such as nonattachment, love, and compassion and the good karma I created during my life by practicing generosity and the other perfections. Also, being attached to my things at the time of death is an obstacle to dying peacefully and obtaining a good rebirth. Therefore, I should stop being so miserly and try to be more generous. In that way, I will create the causes for a peaceful death, happiness in future lives, and, ultimately, enlightenment."

In case you wonder if perfecting generosity means eliminating all the poverty in the world, no, it does not. Shantideva addresses that question in *A Guide to the Bodhisattva's Way of Life*:

> If the perfection of generosity
> were the alleviation of the world's poverty,
> then since beings are still starving now,
> in what manner did the previous Buddhas perfect it?
>
> The perfection of generosity is said to be
> the thought to give all beings everything,
> together with the fruit of such a thought;
> hence it is simply a state of mind.[79]

Conclusion

Giving, especially with the motivation of bodhichitta, brings many benefits, both temporal and ultimate. There are numerous disadvantages of its opposite, miserliness—unhappiness here and now, unfavorable rebirths in future lives, and remaining imprisoned in samsara. Resolve to cultivate a generous heart and think of one or two practical ways you can extend your generosity in your present circumstances.

Dedication

Complete the remaining parts of the practice for lamrim meditation and dedicate the merit of your session so that all beings will engage in the practice of giving, overcome miserliness, and will quickly progress along the path and attain the perfect peace and happiness of enlightenment.

2. How to Give

The Meditation

Start your session as usual by settling body and mind and then doing the practice for lamrim meditation on page 35, pausing at the right place to insert the following meditation.

There are three kinds of giving explained in the lamrim: material giving, giving Dharma, and giving protection. As you reflect on each of these, think of ways you can practice them in your life.

1. Giving material things
Material generosity means giving to others things such as money, food, clothing, and medicine. Even if we are not wealthy, we can still practice this in small ways that we can afford—giving spare change to a homeless person, for instance, or even giving breadcrumbs to birds. The important thing is our state of mind, not how much we give.

Bodhisattvas are willing to give everything they have, including their body. We are advised against doing that until our bodhichitta is strong and stable, but we can start practicing it by giving blood or signing up as an organ donor.

2. Giving Dharma
This is said to be the best gift because money and food help others only temporarily, whereas the Dharma enables them to achieve genuine, long-term happiness. Even if we have not studied enough to give Dharma talks, we can share what we have learned with family and friends—practical advice on how to be more positive or to deal with disturbing emotions like anger or depression—using common language rather than Buddhist jargon. But we need to be skillful and not push our ideas on others if they are not open.

Other ways to give Dharma include visualizing sentient beings around us when we recite prayers or sutras, reciting mantras for those who are sick or dying, giving Dharma books to those who wish to learn it, and bringing someone to a Dharma teaching.

3. Giving protection

This form of generosity involves helping those who are in danger of being killed or injured—saving an insect from drowning, for example, or removing an animal from a road where it might be run over. It also includes giving comfort to those who are frightened or anxious and caring for the sick.

Ideally, our motivation for practicing generosity is bodhichitta: wishing to benefit not just the person in front of us, but *all* living beings. For example, when giving money to a homeless person, you can think: "By making this gift, may I become a buddha and be able to benefit all sentient beings." Afterward, dedicate the merit to that goal.

Conclusion

Notice the effect that just imagining being generous to others has on your mind. Focus on that positive, expansive feeling as long as you can. With an understanding of the benefits of generosity, especially when it is motivated by bodhichitta, resolve to practice the three types of giving—material things, Dharma, and protection—in your daily life, even in small ways.

Dedication

Complete the remaining parts of the practice for lamrim meditation and dedicate the merit of your session so that all beings will engage in the practice of giving, overcome miserliness, and quickly attain the sublime peace and happiness of enlightenment.

The Perfection of Ethics 19

Without ethical conduct you can't accomplish your own
  well-being,
so wanting to accomplish others' is laughable.
Therefore without worldly aspirations
safeguard your ethical conduct—
this is the practice of bodhisattvas.
TOGME SANGPO, *The Thirty-Seven Practices of Bodhisattvas*

IN GENERAL, ethics is the practice of refraining from nonvirtue, especially actions that harm others. Based on the compassionate awareness that no sentient being wants to suffer, it plays an important role on all levels of the path:

- At the initial level (small scope), ethics involves refraining from the ten nonvirtues and practicing the ten virtues mainly with the motivation of avoiding unfortunate rebirths and obtaining fortunate ones.

- At the intermediate level (medium scope), ethics is the first of the three higher trainings that are practiced to attain liberation from samsara. It is an essential basis for the other two trainings, concentration and wisdom. Here, in addition to avoiding the ten nonvirtues, practitioners usually take lifelong *pratimoksha*, or individual liberation, precepts,[80] as this enhances our commitment to living ethically and cultivating virtue.

- At the advanced level (great scope), ethics is practiced with the bodhichitta motivation: aspiring to become a buddha for the benefit of all sentient beings. This is the perfection of ethics. It also includes taking bodhisattva precepts when our aspiration to attain enlightenment is strong and stable.

Two meditations are presented here: one on the benefits of practicing ethics and the disadvantages of not doing so, and another on how to practice ethics.

1. BENEFITS AND DISADVANTAGES

THE MEDITATION

After settling your body in a comfortable posture and calming your mind, do the practice for lamrim meditation on page 35, pausing after the mantra recitation to meditate on the following.

Knowing the benefits of ethics inspires us to practice it:
- Practicing ethics leads to fortunate rebirths in our future lives. Ethical conduct is the principal cause of being born as a human being or in a pure land—the most ideal situations to engage in Dharma practice and continue following the path to enlightenment.
- Ethics is said to be the foundation of all good qualities and realizations, just as the earth is the foundation of all the animate and inanimate things abiding on it. Aspiring to attain higher states of mind and realizations with corrupt ethics is unfeasible.
- A person with good ethical conduct has behavior that is nonharmful, speech that is gentle and considerate, and a mind that is peaceful, clear, and subdued. Their mind is not troubled by strong delusions, including guilt and fear. People and animals are naturally attracted to such a person and feel at ease in their presence, making it easier to benefit them.
- Without ethics, it is impossible to attain liberation or enlightenment. Even on the way to enlightenment, if we want to help others practice ethics, we need to be a good example—to "walk our talk." If our own ethical conduct is deplorable, how can we effectively teach it to others?

On the other hand, failure to live ethically has disadvantages:

- Not safeguarding ethics can lead us to create negative karma, the cause of unfortunate rebirths in future lives.
- We may aspire to develop concentration, bodhichitta, wisdom, and other realizations of the path, but our attempts will not be successful if we lack good ethical conduct.
- Without ethics, it is impossible to attain the highest states, liberation and enlightenment. Instead, we will continue to wander in samsara, life after life, unable to benefit ourselves in any long-term way, much less others.
- Even in this life, by disregarding ethics we may commit crimes and end up in prison, separated from family and friends and facing numerous unpleasant experiences.

As ethics begins with the wish to refrain from harmful actions, we can strengthen it by reflecting on the equality of self and others: no one wants to be harmed and everyone wants to be treated with kindness and respect. It's also helpful to realize that when we harm others, we also harm ourselves. Do you really want to create more suffering for yourself?

Conclusion
Resolve to keep in mind the benefits of practicing ethics and the disadvantages of neglecting it, and to practice it to the best of your ability, for the benefit of yourself and all other beings.

Dedication
Complete the remaining parts of the practice for lamrim meditation and dedicate the merit of your session to the peace, happiness, and enlightenment of yourself and all other beings.

2. How to Practice Ethics

The Meditation

Start by sitting in a comfortable posture and calming your mind with a few minutes of meditation on the breath. Then do the practice for lamrim meditation on page 35, inserting the following meditation at the designated place.

There are three ways to practice ethics: restraining from misdeeds, creating virtue, and benefiting sentient beings. Reflect on each of these, below, taking time to recognize and rejoice in how you are currently practicing them. Identify ways you could extend your ethics to be more far-reaching and aspire to do this for the welfare of all beings.

1. Restraining from misdeeds
This is the principal way of practicing ethics, and consists of avoiding nonvirtuous actions of body, speech, and mind, starting with the ten nonvirtues explained earlier. It also includes keeping precepts, or vows—lay, monastic, and bodhisattva.

2. Creating virtue
When we practice the first type of ethics, restraining from misdeeds, we automatically practice the second, creating virtue. Other ways to create virtue include acting opposite to the ten nonvirtues, such as protecting others' lives and property; practicing the other five perfections; making prostrations and offerings to holy objects; meditating on the three principal aspects of the path: renunciation, bodhichitta, and the correct view of emptiness; listening to, contemplating, and meditating on the Dharma; teaching the Dharma; rejoicing; and so on.

3. Benefiting sentient beings
This comprises all types of Dharma practice as well as any action of body, speech, or mind that we do with the motivation to benefit others. It thus includes the first two kinds of ethics when they are practiced with bodhichitta. It also involves helping sentient beings who are in great need, like those suffering from poverty or homelessness, threatened by danger, afflicted with sorrow, and so forth—doing what is appropriate for their temporal and long-term benefit.

Having considered the various ways one may practice ethics, stay focused for a while on any feeling of inspiration to practice it that has arisen in your mind, or any resolve you've generated to maintain or extend your ethics going forward.

Conclusion

Remembering the benefits of ethical behavior and disadvantages of unethical behavior, generate the determination to use mindfulness and introspection to maintain good conduct as much as possible, for the benefit of yourself and all other beings.

Dedication

Complete the remaining parts of the practice for lamrim meditation and dedicate the merit of your session so that all beings will practice pure ethical conduct and will quickly attain every type of peace and happiness, especially the highest peace of enlightenment.

The Perfection of Patience 20

To bodhisattvas who want a wealth of virtue
those who harm are like a precious treasure.
Therefore toward all cultivate fortitude without hostility—
this is the practice of bodhisattvas.
TOGME SANGPO, *The Thirty-Seven Practices of Bodhisattvas*

IN THE context of the lamrim, patience is the ability to remain calm
and unruffled in the face of others' harmful behavior or your own
personal suffering.[81] It is not apathy or stoicism to harm or suffering,
but a virtuous mental state deliberately cultivated to counteract anger
and discouragement. When it is practiced with the bodhichitta motivation, it becomes the perfection of patience. This perfection is also
referred to as fortitude, forbearance, or tolerance.

Because of their loving-kindness, compassion, and commitment
to the welfare of all beings, bodhisattvas develop particularly strong
patience, and they are able to practice it even when they are physically harmed by someone. In one of the Buddha's previous lives, when
he was known as the bodhisattva Kshantivadin, "Teacher of Patience,"
although his limbs were severed by a cruel and jealous king, his mind
remained patient and compassionate, undisturbed by anger. Such a
high level of patience is attained not only by cultivating bodhichitta
but also by realizing emptiness, the fact that all phenomena—oneself,
others, and all things in samsara and beyond—do not exist inherently
or independently. Practicing patience at that level is not easy and takes
time, but it is not impossible if we work on the methods explained
below. Shantideva devoted the entire sixth chapter of his text *A Guide
to the Bodhisattva's Way of Life* to the cultivation of patience, and this is
an excellent and beautiful resource to inspire your practice.

This chapter includes four meditations: one on the disadvantages
of anger and benefits of patience, and one on each of the three types

of patience. These three are (1) disregarding harm—that is, not getting upset and retaliating to others' harm; (2) voluntarily accepting suffering; and (3) certainty about the Dharma.

1. THE DISADVANTAGES OF ANGER AND BENEFITS OF PATIENCE

Everyone has a certain amount of patience—for a while we can remain at ease waiting for a friend, standing in line at the bank, or listening to a crying baby. But at some point, we may lose our patience and get agitated or angry. However, with practice we can extend the limits of our patience and maintain it in increasingly difficult situations. Being motivated to work on this comes from understanding the benefits of patience and the disadvantages of anger.

THE MEDITATION

After settling your body in a comfortable posture and calming your mind, do the practice for lamrim meditation on page 35, inserting the following meditation at the appropriate point.

Begin with contemplating the disadvantages of anger. If we don't recognize these, we may think it's fine to get angry and act it out when we are bothered or slighted, or worse. Anger comes in various shades. It can range from mild dislike that we can easily hide to irritation or judgment that shows in our face and voice, all the way up to uncontrollable rage and aggression. Anger is said to be the worst delusion because of the horrific suffering it can lead to—war, murder, terrorism, and the miseries of unfortunate rebirths in future lives. It is something we all experience at different times and in different ways. Reflect on some instances when you were angry and ask yourself:

- Was my mind calm or agitated? Was it easy or difficult to concentrate on what I was doing, think clearly, and feel relaxed? Did I feel happy or unhappy?
- How did it affect the people around me? Were they comfortable with me being angry, or did it make them feel uneasy?

Did it have any adverse effects on my relationships with others, especially the people I deeply care about?
- How do I feel about myself when I get angry and say or do nasty things? What kind of person do I want to be?
- Was being angry beneficial for my health or harmful? When I'm angry, do I sleep well and have a good appetite?

In addition to the above observable effects of anger, there are more subtle and long-term consequences:
- Suffering in future lives is caused by the karma we create under its influence.
- It destroys our virtue, the positive energy we work so hard to create. This would be like throwing our hard-earned money into a fire.
- It is one of the greatest obstacles to attaining the realizations we need to progress on the path to liberation and enlightenment, such as bodhichitta, calm abiding, and the wisdom realizing emptiness.
- If we don't learn to manage our anger, it becomes habitual and increases over time.

It's also helpful to look at the world around us. Many of the tragic events we learn about in the news—war, terrorism, violent crime, racism, injustice—can be traced to anger and hatred. We may think it's appropriate to get angry in response to such events, but isn't that like fighting fire with fire? If we truly wish to remedy violence and injustice, we need a cool, calm mind that can think clearly, not one inflamed by anger.

Hopefully, when we carefully examine anger, we recognize its harmful effects and conclude that it's something from which we want to be free.

Patience, on the other hand, has numerous benefits. Remember a time when you remained patient in a situation where you would normally get angry. Then contemplate the following positive consequences of patience:
- We can remain calm and clear, even when others are agitated. Patience is a comfortable, even beautiful, state of mind that protects us from the painful effects of anger and hatred.

- Responding with patience toward a harmful person can affect others who are angry, helping them to calm down. In general, a patient person has a pacifying effect on others—people and animals feel relaxed and safe in their presence.
- Patience protects you from acting or speaking aggressively and from the negative consequences of such behavior, both immediate, such as upsetting the people around you, and long-term, such as painful experiences later in this life and in future lives.
- Since patience is a virtuous mental state, we create the karma for future happiness and positive experiences. These include being reborn in favorable situations like a precious human life; having a peaceful mind that is clear and able to concentrate; being attractive and likable; and, ultimately, attaining the sublime states of liberation and enlightenment.

Conclusion

After contemplating these points, recognize that anger causes harm and suffering, whereas patience brings far more satisfying results for yourself and others. Make the decision that you will learn to manage your anger and cultivate patience so you can respond more skillfully to harm and difficulties.

Dedication

Complete the remaining parts of the practice for lamrim meditation and dedicate the merit of your session to the peace, happiness, and enlightenment of yourself and all other beings.

2. THE PATIENCE OF DISREGARDING HARM

Three ways we can practice patience are explained in the lamrim. The first involves learning to avoid responding with anger and retaliation when someone acts in a disturbing or harmful way, either to oneself or to people we care about. There are numerous methods to counteract anger; it's best to be familiar with these *before* we encounter provoking situations so we can easily recall and use them. Some antidotes to anger were explained earlier in the meditation on true origins of suffering (page 144). Several additional methods are presented below.

THE MEDITATION

Sit in a comfortable posture and calm your thoughts, then do the practice for lamrim meditation on page 35, pausing at the right place for the following meditation.

Begin by recalling some of the adverse effects of anger and the benefits of patience that you are now familiar with. Let yourself feel convinced that you want to overcome anger and increase patience as much as possible.

While meditating on the points below, recall past experiences when you have become angry about someone's behavior. Imagine that instead of getting angry, you responded in the ways described in these points. Allow yourself to feel the mental and physical ease that arises from even just thinking about responding in a more calm and reasoned way. Contemplate as many of these methods as you have time for, checking if they could be helpful if you again find yourself in a similar situation.

1. Reflect on dependent arising.

Dependent arising means that everything depends on other things for its existence; nothing stands alone. A person's harmful behavior is due to numerous causes and conditions: the family and environment they grew up in, experiences they had earlier in life, karma and afflictions carried by their mind from past lives, things we did or said that upset them, our own karma that leads us to experience harm, problems the person encountered just prior to their destructive behavior, and so on. Think of a time when *you* behaved destructively and contemplate the various factors—many of which you had no control over—that led to that behavior. It is similar with this person—they too are helplessly controlled by causes and conditions. Understanding this point can soften and open our heart such that we feel compassion and wish to help people who do harm rather than retaliate.

2. Recognize the suffering of the one doing the harm.
Someone who harms others is similar to a person whose mind is affected by mental illness or drugs. Think of someone who has been very kind to you, such as a parent or grandparent, and imagine them becoming mentally ill and acting aggressively. Knowing that they are not in their right mind and have no control over their behavior, you would not be angry but would treat them with compassion and kindness and do everything possible to relieve their suffering. If this analogy makes sense in your situation, apply it to those who behave harmfully—after all, they are suffering from the illness of ignorance and other delusions—and understand that compassion is a more appropriate response than anger.

3. Consider whether anger erases the harm.
A verse from the great Indian philosopher Chandrakirti's *Supplement to the Middle Way* says:

> If you get angry with someone who has done you harm,
> is that harm stopped because of your resentment of him?[82]

Consider if this is true in your experience. Let's say someone insults you or damages your belongings. Does getting angry reverse their action? Whatever happened in the past—even one minute ago—is over and cannot be changed or undone. Getting angry and retaliating will only disturb your own mind and might cause further resentment in the other's mind, even leading to a feud! This does not mean we have to remain silent and do nothing in the face of harmful actions. We can try communicating with the person to resolve the problem, but such communication will be more effective if we keep our own anger out of it. Contemplating Chandrakirti's words can help with that.

4. Consider whether our anger comes from others.
We often say, "They make me so angry," as if the anger in our mind was somehow transferred from their mind, but this is not correct. The main cause of our anger is a seed or imprint left in our mind by previous experiences of anger, and the other person's behavior is like the water that causes our seed of anger to sprout. If we did not have that

seed, we would not get angry. Buddhas have extinguished all seeds of anger in their minds and thus never get angry, no matter what anyone does to them. Understanding this point helps us take responsibility for our reaction rather than blame the other person. In fact, we can actually be grateful to enemies, as they are valuable teachers—they show us the extent of our anger and the limits of our patience so that we recognize how much work we have yet to do.

5. Remember death.

Recall the points of the death meditation (page 74). We don't know when death will happen, and it's important to die with a positive mental state. If we do not learn how to manage our anger now, thoughts of aversion and resentment could overwhelm our mind at the time of death, or we could be struck by regret that we didn't forgive or seek forgiveness while we still had time. Realizing how detrimental it would be to die feeling angry is a strong incentive to quickly apply a remedy and replace anger with something positive, such as patience or compassion.

6. Mentally separate the person doing the harm and their behavior.

People sometimes think that practicing patience means being passive and unresponsive when others act destructively. This is not correct; we *should* do what we can to stop them. Only we should do so not with anger but with compassion, both for the victims and the perpetrator. It's easy to sympathize with victims, however, but not with perpetrators. One helpful strategy is to mentally separate the person and their behavior; recognize that the person is not 100 percent negative but has positive qualities and only occasionally behaves destructively. When they do, condemn the behavior and generate compassion for the person by using the suggestions above. It is also helpful to contemplate that they wouldn't act that way if they weren't suffering— which you can understand from your own experience—and that their unskillful actions are creating the causes for even more misery in the future.

Conclusion

If any of these methods help you transform your mind, resolve to continue meditating on them to be prepared for difficult situations.

Such situations are like a traffic circle in a road where we can choose between several different routes. One of these is Anger Road, which we've traveled many times and know the kind of problems it leads to. From now on, we can choose one of the other roads—Patience Lane, Compassion Boulevard, Wisdom Way—that take us in more beneficial and satisfying directions.

Dedication

Complete the remaining parts of the practice for lamrim meditation and dedicate the merit of your session so that all beings will practice patience and overcome anger and hatred, and that everyone will swiftly attain the peace, happiness, and fulfillment of enlightenment.

3. THE PATIENCE OF VOLUNTARILY ACCEPTING SUFFERING

How do you react when things don't turn out as you wish or you encounter misfortune—whether that's an accident, sickness, the loss of a friend, or even just stubbing your toe? Do you calmly accept the situation? Or do you fly into a rage and start swearing and slamming doors, or sink into emotional despair and worry? Based on your experiences and those of others you have observed, do these reactions help or make things worse?

According to Buddhism, when we experience an unpleasant feeling[83] in response to a problem, it usually leads to aversion, which can escalate into rage or depression. Although everyone wants to be free of problems and suffering and we all *deserve* to be free, we can't expect that to happen anytime soon. As long as we're in samsara we will continue to experience problems, but we can learn to notice unpleasant feelings as soon as they arise and prevent them from triggering anger, despair, anxiety, and other disturbing emotions. Such reactions are not only unhelpful—they make the situation worse, creating additional suffering for ourselves and others. The Buddha compared this to being hit with a second arrow after already being shot with one. In other words, the initial problem—like the first arrow—is painful enough, but reacting with disturbing thoughts and emotions—like the second arrow—merely exacerbates our misery instead of relieving it.[84] It doesn't have to be this way; we can learn to remain calm in the face of suffering. Better still, we can use it in our practice as fuel for spiritual growth.

The second type of patience involves managing our mind when facing difficulties—not letting it be carried away by negative emotions but keeping it positive and even bringing that suffering into the path to enlightenment. Lama Tsongkhapa stresses the importance of this practice in *The Great Treatise on the Stages of the Path*:

> As you continually experience whatever suffering is appropriate to you, you absolutely must know how to bring it into the path. Otherwise [...] you either generate hostility or you become discouraged about cultivating the path, either circumstance interfering with applying yourself to virtue.[85]

There is a genre of teachings and practices in the Tibetan tradition known as thought transformation (*lojong*) that presents a variety of methods for transforming our attitude toward problems and using them in the path to enlightenment. These methods are to be employed in our day-to-day life. Every day of our life we encounter unwanted, unpleasant circumstances that can potentially disrupt our mental peace, throw us into a bad mood, and affect our mental focus and interactions with others. Recalling any of the thought-transformation methods, such as those explained below, can reverse this process and restore our mind to a calm, clear state.

THE MEDITATION

Start your session as usual, by settling body and mind. Then perform the practice for lamrim meditation on page 35, pausing at the designated place to insert the following meditation.

Bring to mind some experiences of suffering you have had, such as physical pain, illness, injury, frustration, or disappointment. How did you react? Was that reaction helpful to you or anyone else?

Getting upset about problems is natural, but there are other ways to respond that are less painful and even help us grow spiritually.

Focusing on a present situation that is causing you difficulty, contemplate one or more of the following methods.

1. Remember the nature of samsara

Accept that problems are a natural part of samsara, as explained in the first noble truth. And if our goal is to free ourselves and all other beings from suffering, genuine freedom will take a long time to achieve. In the meantime, we will face difficulties, so it's best to accept that fact and cultivate resilience. Accepting suffering is also helpful to develop renunciation. If life was always rosy and we never encountered problems, it would be difficult to become disenchanted with samsara, wish to be free from it, and be motivated to follow the path to liberation and enlightenment.

2. Reflect on impermanence

All conditioned things change every moment. Since suffering is a conditioned phenomenon—that is, it arises from causes and conditions—it's subject to change and will not last forever. To get a sense of this, recall some problems you experienced in the past that at the time seemed permanent, as if they would last forever. They may have been in your life for a while, but eventually they either disappeared or no longer bothered you. You may even value these experiences now for what you learned from them.

3. Understand that problems are not necessarily bad

Whether something is bad depends on our perspective, how we view and utilize it. Just as a knife can be used to destroy or save a life, a problem can make us miserable or help us grow spiritually. In addition to strengthening renunciation, as explained above, problems are also ideal opportunities to enhance our compassion—how can we understand and empathize with others' suffering if we never experience it ourselves? So when you face difficulties, remind yourself that you are not alone, that everyone has problems, and some are far worse than yours. Think of some examples of these and let your heart open with compassion—just as you do not want to suffer, so does everyone else. Let that awareness blossom into the sincere wish for all beings to be free from every type of suffering, physical and mental.

4. Meditate on taking and giving

After using the previous method to generate compassion for others who are suffering, you are in the ideal frame of mind for the tonglen practice explained earlier, on page 221. You can use the simple version for one's own suffering or the longer version for others' suffering.

5. Contemplate karma

A difficult situation is also a good time to deepen your understanding of karma and your determination to follow it. Recall the third general characteristic of karma: if we don't create the karma, we won't experience its result. That means painful experiences only happen to us because we created their causes, nonvirtuous actions. Contemplating this gives rise to a strong commitment to stop creating nonvirtue, the cause of suffering, and to create instead the causes of happiness, such as the ten virtuous actions.

Bodhisattvas feel joy rather than discouragement when they face difficulties because they see them as excellent opportunities for spiritual practice and getting closer to enlightenment. Lama Zopa Rinpoche said they like problems the way we like ice cream! But it takes time to get to that point. We are advised to start practicing thought-transformation methods on small problems like annoying insects or burnt toast, and with greater familiarity we can take on larger ones. It is said in the teachings that while following the path, karma that would normally ripen as a horrific experience, such as an unfavorable rebirth, can ripen instead in this life in a much lighter form, like a headache or minor injury. Contemplating this gives us another reason to welcome difficulties!

While applying such strategies for transforming problems into the path, we can still look for practical solutions, like seeing a doctor when we're sick or acting to bring about social or political change. The purpose of these methods is to keep our mind positive, not overwhelmed by despair or anger. Shantideva said:

> Why be unhappy about something
> if it can be remedied?

And what is the use of being unhappy about something
if it cannot be remedied?[86]

In other words, if there are solutions to a problem we should at least
try them; getting stuck in unhappiness is of no use. This advice is similar to the serenity prayer used in Alcoholics Anonymous and other
twelve-step programs, a secular version of which goes like this:

May I have the serenity to accept the things I cannot change,
the courage to change the things I can,
and the wisdom to know the difference.[87]

It's worthwhile doing what we can to bring about positive changes in
ourselves, in society, and in the world, but we also need to be realistic
and accept that we cannot change everyone and everything.

Conclusion
If, during the meditation, you notice a transformation in your mind
toward how you perceive suffering and problems, stay focused on that
experience for as long as possible. And at the end, resolve to continue
this practice of bringing problems into the path by using thought-
transformation methods.

Dedication
Complete the remaining parts of the practice for lamrim meditation
and dedicate the merit of your session to the peace, happiness, and
enlightenment of yourself and all other beings.

4. THE PATIENCE OF CERTAINTY ABOUT THE DHARMA

Engaging in the Dharma can be challenging and requires fortitude.
Attaining realizations, or even gaining a sound intellectual understanding of Buddhist philosophical topics, entails a lot of time and
energy devoted to study and practice. Topics like emptiness are complex, difficult to understand, and challenge our "normal" way of think-

ing. We may feel resistant to doing certain practices like prostrations or making offerings, which are unfamiliar and have no equivalent in most Western cultures. As a result of these and other difficulties, we may sometimes have negative feelings about our practice and think of giving it up. The third type of patience—of certainty about the Dharma—is the remedy to these problems.

Geshe Lhundub Sopa explains this kind of patience as "using wisdom to see the reality of the Dharma."[88] If we lack it, we may have doubts and discomfort about specific practices and not really want to do them. He says:

In order for religious practitioners to be comfortable and inspired to practice, they must understand the causes, the nature, and the results of each practice.

He goes on to say that by cultivating this type of patience we will "hold religious practices in a positive light [. . .] admire them, like them, and become able to do them." [89]

Let's take the example of prostrations, which many newcomers to Tibetan Buddhism have resistance to; some even think, "You expect me to do that? No way!" If we take the time to learn the reasons for doing this practice, as well as its benefits—purifying our negative karma, reducing arrogance, cultivating humility and respect—we will have more enthusiasm and might even come to like it. A woman who attended a retreat I once led told me she didn't like doing prostrations, but since they were included in the schedule, she gave them a try. By the end of the one-week retreat her mind had changed— she came to understand the value of the practice and even found it enjoyable!

Mahayana scriptures explain that to develop the patience of certainty about the Dharma we need to increase our knowledge of eight objects. These include the qualities of the Three Jewels; selflessness; what is to be adopted (virtue) and abandoned (nonvirtue); the qualities of buddhahood that we wish to attain; and so on. The main points of these objects are summarized in the lamrim, so we can increase the third type of patience by learning and meditating on the lamrim topics, in their proper order. Geshe Sopa says:

> The more knowledge we integrate into the mind, the more
> stable, calm, and patient we become.[90]

Another possible cause of doubt and reluctance regarding Dharma practice is having unrealistic expectations. Lama Yeshe used to tell us to not have any expectations when we meditate, and I have heard similar advice from other teachers, but they are very hard to avoid. We expect wonderful results from just about everything we do in life and that attitude can infiltrate our Dharma practice. We would like to be blissful and concentrated every time we meditate, and to be always calm, loving, and clear, even when we're not meditating. Some people hope to attain realizations like calm abiding, the wisdom of emptiness, or even enlightenment after meditating for just a few months or years. It's excellent to have such positive aspirations, but if we are attached to seeing these results within a certain timeframe, we're setting ourselves up for disappointment. In fact, expectations create obstacles to successful meditation because they usually involve self-centered craving—an afflicted attitude that stands in the way of attaining realizations. So any time we feel discouraged about our study or practice, it's a good idea to check: What did I expect? Was that a realistic expectation? Was my motivation altruistic or selfish?

The following meditation asks you to investigate whether you lack the patience of certainty about the Dharma and if so, what you can do about it.

THE MEDITATION

Begin as usual by settling your body and mind and then doing the practice for lamrim meditation on page 35, pausing at the right place to insert the following meditation.

See if you can recall ever feeling doubt or resistance to Dharma practice—either a specific practice like prostrations or practice in general. You might have thought, "I've been meditating for X amount of time and haven't noticed any results. Why should I keep doing this?"

If you remember having such thoughts and feelings, check if they could be due to lack of knowledge—perhaps you do not fully comprehend the purpose of the practice, or do not clearly understand the length of time needed to notice results. You may have received just a short explanation of the practice and started doing it without learning more about it or reflecting on how it relates to your spiritual development. If this is the case, resolve to broaden your knowledge about the practice and think more deeply about its purpose and benefits.

It's also useful to check whether you have unrealistic expectations about practicing Dharma—hoping to attain the experiences of past meditators like the Buddha or Milarepa quickly and easily. If so, understand that the Buddha spent many lifetimes over eons of time developing positive qualities like compassion, wisdom, generosity, and patience and accumulating the merit necessary to become enlightened. Milarepa was said to have been a *pandit*—a wise and learned person—for five hundred previous lifetimes and practiced with great intensity in his final life, during which he attained enlightenment.

The bodhisattva path is long and requires sincere dedication, but if we practice consistently, continuing to create the causes little by little each day, eventually our mind will become the mind of a buddha. In a similar way, a bucket placed beneath a dripping faucet eventually becomes full, one drop at a time. Contemplate these points to mitigate any unrealistic expectations you might have about Dharma practice.

Conclusion

To be able to continue practicing Dharma joyfully and consistently far into the future, generate the determination to increase your knowledge and understanding of the Dharma, especially the purpose and benefits of practicing it. Resolve to let go of unrealistic expectations and—with confidence in the law of cause and effect—be content to create the causes of the ultimate happiness for yourself and all other beings.

Dedication

Complete the remaining parts of the practice for lamrim meditation and dedicate the merit of your session to the peace, happiness, and enlightenment of yourself and all other beings.

The Perfection of Joyous Effort   21

Take up joyous perseverance,
which when engaged in meditation
or when working for the good of the world,
knows untiring joy alone, even should the body fall to dust.
THE SEVENTH DALAI LAMA, *Meditations to Transform the Mind*

JOYOUS EFFORT is being delighted and enthusiastic about doing what is virtuous. When practiced with bodhichitta, it is the perfection of joyous effort.

One of the tragedies of samsara is that many beings are unaware that virtue is the cause of happiness, so although that is what they dearly wish for, they avoid creating its causes. Instead, they spend much of their energy creating nonvirtue, the cause of unwanted suffering. Shantideva says:

> Although wishing to be rid of misery,
> they run toward misery itself.
> Although wishing to have happiness,
> like an enemy they ignorantly destroy it.[91]

We normally feel delighted about pleasurable activities like going on a holiday, dining in a nice restaurant, listening to our favorite music, spending time with friends, swimming, or skiing. However, the enthusiasm we have for these activities is not joyous effort unless our motivation is a virtuous one, such as bodhichitta. In contrast, those aspiring for enlightenment are joyful to do virtuous deeds like learning about and meditating on the lamrim, helping others, making offerings, and practicing the other perfections. Their enthusiasm arises from knowing that virtue is the cause of genuine happiness—in particular, the sublime state of a buddha in which one has the ability to lead all other beings out of samsara and to enlightenment as well.

Happiness is a conditioned phenomenon and does not occur without its causes, so if we want to be happy and help others experience happiness, we need to create virtue. Virtue is mainly positive mental states, such as faith, compassion, and loving-kindness, as well as the actions motivated by these states, like giving, ethical conduct, studying the Dharma, meditating, and so forth. Practicing joyous effort means doing these things happily and consistently.

The lamrim explains joyous effort by way of several points: its benefits, factors that hinder it, favorable conditions for developing it, its different types, and how to practice it. The meditation presented here covers the first two of these points: contemplating the benefits of joyous effort and learning how to counteract its chief obstacle, laziness.

The Meditation

Settle your body in a comfortable, conducive position and calm your mind. Perform the practice for lamrim meditation on page 35, pausing after the mantra recitation to do the following meditation.

Begin by contemplating the essential role joyous effort plays in Dharma practice. Just as beautiful flowers and tasty vegetables will not suddenly appear in our garden if we do not plant the seeds and tend to them regularly, spiritual qualities and attainments will not arise in our mind without effort. And that effort needs to be joyful, not reluctant; otherwise, we might quickly lose interest and give up. With joyous effort, anything is possible—we can apply ourselves continuously and unwaveringly to our practice until we achieve our goals. Reflect on these ideas to understand the importance of this quality.

We can start cultivating joyous effort by counteracting its opposite, laziness, which is a major hindrance on the spiritual path. The lamrim explains three kinds of laziness, which are presented below. Contemplate each in turn, and if you discover any of them in yourself, resolve to counteract them with the recommended antidotes.

1. The laziness of procrastination
We sometimes wake up intending to meditate but then start doing other things; before we know it, the day is over and we haven't done any practice. Or we may plan to get serious about Dharma study and practice after the kids have grown up and we've retired from our job, but we can't be sure we will live that long. As a result of this type of laziness, there is the risk that our life ends before we have been able to genuinely practice the Dharma. Consider what a great loss that would be.

Contemplating impermanence, death, and the precious human life are the best antidotes to this form of laziness. We have a priceless opportunity to create the causes for good rebirths, liberation, and enlightenment that could end at any time, even today, and there's no guarantee we will obtain such ideal conditions for practice in our next life. Therefore, we need to use our time wisely now.

2. The laziness of being attached to unwholesome
or meaningless pursuits
These pursuits refer to activities like hunting, fishing, gambling, or drug-dealing that are clearly harmful, but can also include anything done with a deluded motivation or solely for the pleasure of this life. Some people may happily stay up all night watching movies or partying, or spend the entire day skiing or surfing, but balk at the idea of meditating for an hour or listening to a Dharma talk.

Contemplating the benefits of learning and practicing the Dharma and the adverse consequences of nonvirtuous actions will dispel this type of laziness and engender enthusiasm to engage in virtue and avoid nonvirtue. It's also helpful to meditate on the precious human life, death, karma—especially the results of nonvirtue—and the unsatisfactory nature of samsara.

3. The laziness of discouragement
Examples of this third type of laziness are thinking that you are hopeless and unable to change, that Dharma practice is too difficult, or that enlightenment is impossible to attain. If such thoughts proliferate in our minds and we buy into them, we feel immobilized, unable to move forward in our practice. That is why they are considered a type of laziness.

To counteract such thoughts, reflect on buddha nature. Every sentient being is able to attain enlightenment, and this potential has always existed in us and can never be destroyed or taken away. It does take time and effort to transform our mind into an enlightened mind, but it is definitely possible if we follow the path steadily and continuously.

Another cause of discouragement is having unrealistic expectations, like attaining realizations quickly and with little effort. If you notice this in yourself, remember that the results of meditation take time and grasping for them is a hindrance, not an aid. It's far more effective to focus on creating the causes now with the confidence that the results will eventually arise. Also, go at your own pace rather than trying to imitate accomplished meditators. Start small and gradually build up your meditation practice. Treat yourself with kindness and compassion, and rejoice in your efforts, however small they may be!

Conclusion

To review, briefly contemplate the key points of this topic:

- Joyous effort—taking delight in virtue—is an essential quality while following the path to enlightenment and to be of benefit to others.
- The opposite of joyous effort is laziness, of which there are three kinds: procrastination, being attached to unwholesome activities, and discouragement.

Aware of the faults of laziness and the benefits of joyous effort, resolve to work on overcoming laziness and cultivating joyous effort to the best of your ability, for the benefit of yourself and others. Identify where laziness manifests in your life right now and make some doable plans for how you can—starting today—increase your enthusiasm for and practice of virtue.

Dedication

Complete the remaining parts of the practice for lamrim meditation and dedicate the merit of your session to the peace, happiness, and enlightenment of yourself and all other beings.

The Perfection of Concentration   22

SOME LAMRIM texts, such as Lama Tsongkhapa's *Great Treatise on the Stages of the Path to Enlightenment*, devote hundreds of pages to the last two of the six perfections, the perfections of concentration and wisdom. Although every topic in the lamrim is essential for the attainment of enlightenment, these two are particularly important. We need the ability to *concentrate* our mind on a chosen object and keep it there unwaveringly for long periods of time so we can analyze and develop the *wisdom* that clears away misconceptions about that object and realizes its true nature. In particular, the wisdom that directly realizes the ultimate nature of things—the emptiness of inherent existence—is the key that unlocks the door to freedom from samsara, so it is an indispensable aspect of the path to both liberation and enlightenment. Gaining intellectual knowledge of the last two perfections is not very difficult, but actually cultivating those realizations in our minds is challenging and requires detailed instructions.

Lamrim texts explain the perfection of concentration by giving instructions on the cultivation of calm abiding (Sanskrit: *shamatha*; Tibetan: *shiné*). Calm abiding—also translated as serenity or mental quiescence—is a special type of concentration that allows one to keep the mind single-pointedly focused on a meditation object as long as one wishes—even for hours or days—free of obstacles such as distraction, restlessness, and laxity. It is accompanied by bliss and pliancy in both body and mind. Understandably, it takes quite a bit of time and energy to reach such a high level of concentration, but any effort we make in that direction is worthwhile. Calm abiding is an essential quality on the spiritual path because we need powerful concentration to attain the realizations that enable our mind to gradually transform into enlightened mind. Cultivating concentration with the bodhichitta motivation is the perfection of concentration.

Knowing the benefits of calm abiding will inspire us to begin practicing it. These benefits include the following:

- We can more easily keep our mind focused on virtue and avoid nonvirtuous objects and activities; in this way, we can use our life skillfully to create the causes of happiness and spiritual growth and to benefit others.
- Calm abiding is vital for attaining the insight that knows the reality of emptiness, which enables us to cut the root of samsara and attain liberation and enlightenment.
- Even in our present life we will experience greater happiness because calm abiding brings mental joy and physical bliss.

A person who is serious about attaining calm abiding should receive teachings, study texts, and find a suitable environment and lifestyle in which to practice. The ideal lifestyle includes keeping pure ethical conduct, avoiding activities that interfere with meditation, reducing one's desires, and being content to live simply. Lamrim texts and other books contain detailed instructions on the obstacles to calm abiding and their antidotes, the nine stages one passes through on the way to full attainment of calm abiding, and the mental forces that enable us to attain those. Even if you are not able to dedicate yourself full-time to cultivating calm abiding, you can start practicing it on a daily basis with one or more short sessions of meditation. Doing so will bring many benefits, such as a calmer mind and improved concentration. The meditation here provides simple instructions to get you started.

You need to choose an object that you use consistently in your practice. Calm abiding will not develop if you switch objects every few sessions or days. Recommended objects include the breath, a visualized image of the Buddha, the nature of the mind, and loving-kindness. The breath is recommended for those with overly active minds, but there are many benefits to using a visualized image of the Buddha— focusing on such an image purifies our negative karma, accumulates merit, and creates the cause to attain the qualities of an enlightened being. Whichever object you choose, you need to keep your attention focused on that object as much as possible and gently but firmly bring it back whenever it wanders away.

There are some common problems, or obstacles, to look out for in your calm abiding practice:

- *Laziness.* There are different kinds of laziness, as we learned in the previous chapter on joyous effort. In the context of calm abiding, laziness refers to reluctance to meditate. When we first begin to meditate, we may be very enthusiastic, but when the practice gets difficult or the results do not happen as quickly as we wish, our energy can evaporate and we might even feel aversion for our meditation seat. If this happens, contemplate the benefits of concentration explained above. This will reinforce our aspiration to attain calm abiding and our joyous effort to practice it. With continued practice the results will start to appear.

- *Forgetting the object.* This happens when our mind gets distracted by thoughts, memories, emotions, sounds, and so on, and is no longer paying attention to our meditation object. The remedy to this problem is mindfulness. In this context, mindfulness means remembering a familiar object and keeping it in mind. So, whenever your mind forgets the meditation object you need to bring it back to this object and try to keep it there as long as possible. Don't worry if you have to do this again and again, even every few seconds. That's normal in the beginning and with regular, continued practice, you will be able to keep your mind on the object for longer periods of time before it wanders away—from a few seconds to a minute, then a few minutes, and so on.

- *Excitement* or *restlessness.* This is when your mind wanders to objects of attachment, such as pleasant experiences you had in the past, people you are attracted to, food and music you enjoy, and so forth. Remembering impermanence, death, and the unsatisfactory nature of samsara are helpful antidotes to attachment; other remedies can be found on pages 147–50. Counting your breath, as explained earlier in the meditation on the breath, is also a good way to settle your mind. You can do this even if your main object of concentration is something other than the breath, such as the image of the Buddha. Temporarily put that object aside for a while and count your breathing until your mind is more calm, then return to your meditation object.

- *Laxity* or *sinking.* This is a lack of clarity and vividness in the way the object appears to our mind. The problem is subjective rather objective—the mind has become somewhat dull and withdrawn, causing the object to appear less sharp and clear. It can be remedied by making the object clearer and brighter, or by imagining light within and around you. If that doesn't work, you can temporarily put aside your meditation object and contemplate uplifting topics such as the preciousness of human life or the qualities of the Buddha. Having tried that, if your mind continues to be sluggish, take a short break and invigorate yourself—do some stretches, splash your face with cool water, get some fresh air—then sit down and try again.

Another essential quality in calm abiding practice is introspection, or vigilance. A companion of mindfulness, this mental factor enables us to recognize faults that arise in our meditation, such as forgetfulness and excitement, and to apply the appropriate antidotes. It can be compared to a security guard in a bank whose job is to look out for trouble and deal with it as efficiently as possible.

Start with short sessions of meditation from five to fifteen minutes, depending on your ability to remain concentrated. As you progress you can lengthen the sessions. It's good to use a timer so you don't have to watch the clock.

The Meditation

As usual, start each session by sitting in a comfortable and conducive posture, and take a few minutes to settle your mind in the present. Perform the practice for lamrim meditation starting on page 35 up to the point where you pause to do the actual meditation.

Bring to mind your meditation object and focus your attention on it with the determination to stay concentrated to the best of your ability, and for as long you can.

Ignore other objects like thoughts, memories, and sounds, as you would when studying or working on a project with a deadline.

If your attention wanders and you forget the object, arouse mindfulness: remember your meditation object and refocus on it.

Do your best to keep your mind alert and energized, so that your object appears as clearly and vividly as possible. Avoid having unrealistic expectations. For instance, if you are using a visualized object, such as the Buddha, do not expect the entire image with all its details to appear, crystal clear, right from the beginning. The traditional instructions on calm abiding advise us to just do our best and be satisfied even if all we can visualize is a vague blob or a rough outline of a figure with head, arms, and legs. Even if nothing appears, feel confident that the Buddha *is* there in the space in front of you, and concentrate on that. Straining and pushing yourself to have a perfectly clear, detailed image is counterproductive.

During the session, let a corner of your mind remain vigilant, checking if any of the obstacles mentioned above have occurred. If you notice one, apply the suggested antidotes until the problem vanishes.

Conclusion

When it is time to end the meditation session, rejoice in what you have done. Even if there were obstacles—distracting thoughts, disturbing emotions, or sleepiness—don't feel discouraged or frustrated. Simply trying to concentrate our mind is highly beneficial, meaningful, and something to rejoice in, especially when our motivation is bodhichitta. We should appreciate our efforts and give ourselves encouragement, which will help ensure we will continue trying and not give up on our practice. So feel confident that what you did was beneficial, for yourself and others.

Dedication

Complete the remaining parts of the practice for lamrim meditation and dedicate the merit of your session to the peace, happiness, and enlightenment of yourself and all other beings.

The Perfection of Wisdom 23

Wisdom is the eye that sees the profound suchness,
the path destroying cyclic existence at its root.
It's a treasury of higher qualities that are praised in all scriptures,
hailed as the supreme lamp for dispelling the darkness of delusion.
Knowing this, those who aspire to liberation strive
with myriad endeavors to cultivate this path of the wise.
I, a yogi, practiced in this manner;
you who aspire to liberation should do likewise.
TSONGKHAPA, "A SONG OF SPIRITUAL EXPERIENCE,"
IN *Stages of the Path and the Oral Transmission*

WISDOM, also known as intelligence (Sanskrit: *prajna*; Tibetan: *sherab*), is a mental factor that analyzes an object to understand it and discern its characteristics, such as its merits and demerits. When practiced with the bodhichitta motivation it becomes the perfection of wisdom.

Wisdom is an important part of the spiritual path. We use it to investigate teachings and teachers to distinguish those that are reliable and those that are not; to differentiate the types of behavior we should adopt and avoid; to recognize the faults of samsara, and generate the determination to free ourselves and others from it; to understand which meditative practices to do on different occasions; and so on. It is also conducive for happiness and well-being here and now by helping us make intelligent choices regarding friends and partners, education and career, and how we spend our time and resources.

When it comes to the bodhisattva path, wisdom complements the other perfections. As explained in the introduction to the six perfections, enlightenment depends on cultivating the two wings of method—the first five perfections—and wisdom—the sixth perfection. A bodhisattva cannot attain enlightenment merely by practicing generosity, ethics, patience, joyous effort, and concentration but lacking wisdom, in particular the wisdom realizing emptiness. Buddhist scriptures compare the first five perfections to blind people who cannot see where they are going and wisdom to a person with good eyesight who can guide them to their destination—in this case, enlightenment. A verse in the *Condensed Perfection of Wisdom* says:

> Millions and billions of blind people bereft of sight,
> ignorant of the roads, how can they reach the towns?
> Without wisdom these five perfections,
> lacking sight, cannot touch awakening.[92]

How does wisdom complement the other perfections? Bodhisattvas train to reflect that the *three spheres* involved in any action—agent, action, and object—are all empty of inherent, independent existence and are merely designated by the mind. For example, when giving food to a hungry person, they recall that the three spheres of this act—the giver, the act of giving food, and the recipient of the food— do not exist inherently or independently but exist dependently. A simple way to understand this is to contemplate how they depend on each other—for someone to be a *giver*, there must be an act of giving and a recipient; being a *recipient* depends on a giver and an act of giving; and an *act of giving* only occurs when there is a giver and a recipient. Thus, none of the three aspects can stand on its own, independent of other phenomena. Such a contemplation together with the motivation of bodhichitta ensures that an action includes both wisdom and method and becomes a cause of enlightenment and not merely a cause of good results within samsara.

DIVISIONS OF WISDOM

Buddhist scriptures explain different kinds of wisdom. There is *natural wisdom* or intelligence that we possess from birth, due to past-life karma. *Acquired wisdom* is developed in this life and is of three types, corresponding to the three steps explained in the introduction: listening, contemplating, and meditating.

1. The *wisdom arising from listening* is an initial level of under-

standing acquired from listening to, reading, and studying teachings on, say, impermanence. It's like that moment of recognition: "Oh, I see. All conditioned things are impermanent and change every moment." This type of wisdom is valuable, but not very firm and clear; it could be lost if we do nothing to maintain and strengthen it.

2. Continuing to think, analyze, and discuss with teachers and friends, we arrive at the *wisdom arising from contemplation*, a correct conceptual understanding of the topic. This wisdom is stable and decisive.

3. By continuing to engage in analytical meditation and sharpening our concentration, we attain the *wisdom arising from meditation*, which focuses single-pointedly on the decisive understanding we developed in the first two steps. Buddhist scriptures say this third wisdom is the union of calm abiding and special insight (Sanskrit: *vipashyana*). Initially it is conceptual but with further practice of meditation it becomes a direct, nonconceptual realization.

Lamrim texts explain another three kinds of wisdom in the section on the perfection of wisdom. *Wisdom understanding the conventional* is knowing subjects like philosophy, medicine, arts and technology, languages and grammar, and logic—areas of knowledge that enable a bodhisattva to be adept at interacting with others and society in beneficial ways. *Wisdom knowing how to benefit sentient beings* is skillful at helping others accomplish their temporary aims—fulfilling their needs and wishes in this and future lives—as well as the long-term goals of liberation and enlightenment. The third kind of wisdom is the most important: *wisdom understanding the ultimate nature of things*, the emptiness of inherent existence.[93] This wisdom is diametrically opposed to the ignorance that is the root of samsara and its various sufferings. In fact, it is the sole antidote to all delusions—anger, attachment, jealousy, and so on. Other antidotes, like those explained in the chapter on the true origins of suffering, can only temporarily suppress delusions but not eradicate them from the root. Only the wisdom directly realizing emptiness has the power to do that.

Emptiness, also known as selflessness, is one of the most difficult

and complex subjects among all Buddhist teachings. It is often mis-
understood; some people think it means nothingness—that things do
not exist at all—but this is not correct. Buddhism does not deny the
conventional existence of sentient beings, samsara and nirvana, tables
and chairs, trees and mountains, and so on. These things *do* exist, but
the way they exist is opposite to the way we normally think and perceive. Our mind is habituated from beginningless time to see things as
if they existed from their own side, objectively, without depending on
anything else. That is the meaning of "inherent existence." Our mind
ignorantly projects this mode of existence onto phenomena, when
they are in fact empty of such existence.

Let's take ourselves as an example. Our mind instinctively believes
that somewhere within our body-mind complex there's a real "I" or
self that seems to exist on its own, independently. Most people never
doubt the existence of such a self or wonder what it is. Buddhist masters say that if such an "I" exists, we should be able to find it—we could
point to something and say, "That is me; that is my self." But when we
carefully examine the parts of our body and mind, we have a hard time
finding that self. There are only things that are *not* a self: a hand is not
a self, a heart is not a self, a stomach is not a self. Even the mind is not
a self because it consists of many different mental states that arise and
disappear every moment. You might believe your brain is your self, but
check again: the brain is made of substances like cells, nerve fibers,
arteries, and fat. Can you point to any of those components and say,
"That's me"? When you look in the mirror and think you look pretty
good or lousy, are you thinking that about your brain? When you say "I
love you" to another person, do you mean that your brain loves their
brain?

Although we have trouble identifying a real self when we search for
it, that doesn't mean there's no self or "I" at all. There *is* an "I" that
eats, sleeps, works, plays, meditates, and attains enlightenment. What
is that "I"? According to the Prasangika school of philosophy, it is simply what is imputed or designated in relation to our body and mind—a
merely designated "I." The same is true for all other phenomena, like
living beings, cars, buildings, computers, books, pizza, and so on—
they do not exist inherently, independently, from their own side, but
are merely designated by mind in relation to their parts as this or that.

When we first encounter this explanation, we might feel baffled, even shocked or frightened. That's actually a good sign—it means the ignorance that is responsible for all our suffering from beginning-less time has been thrown off balance. As Aryadeva, one of the early Madhyamaka masters, wrote:

> Those with little merit
> do not even doubt this doctrine.
> Entertaining just a doubt
> tears to tatters worldly existence.[94]

If we truly wish to become free of samsara and help all other beings do the same, we should not shy away from the topic of emptiness but rather strive to learn about it from reliable teachers, study and discuss it, and meditate on it. Proceeding in these ways, our understanding will gradually increase, like the first rays of light at dawn growing ever brighter as the sun rises and travels through the sky. It does take time and effort—students in Tibetan monastic universities study empti-ness for four years after spending around twelve years learning more fundamental subjects. Even with all that exposure to emptiness, they usually claim to not fully understand it. So do not expect to realize emptiness quickly and easily.

A useful analogy to the process of understanding the true nature of things is investigating a mirage. In a desert at midday, we see a shim-mering silver-blue appearance on the horizon that looks like a lake or river. We could swear there is a body of water over there, but if that were the case, the closer we get the more clearly the water should appear—we should be able to touch the water and dip our feet in it to cool off. What happens instead is that we do not find a drop of water, only dry sand baking under the blazing sun. Similarly, if the "I" and all other persons and phenomena did exist in the solid, objective, inde-pendent way they seem to, the more closely we investigate them, the more clearly that independent mode of existence should appear—we could put our finger on a real "I," a real car, a real friend or enemy. But as we continue to analyze and investigate, that solid appearance becomes increasingly elusive until it vanishes altogether. That is the experience of emptiness.

THE TWO TRUTHS

A full comprehension of emptiness requires understanding the two truths: ultimate truth and conventional truth. Each of the various Buddhist philosophical schools has its own way of explaining the two truths and which phenomena are included in each of these categories. According to the Prasangika, an ultimate truth is the emptiness of inherent existence—the ultimate mode of existence of all phenomena—and a conventional truth is everything other than emptiness. Whatever exists is either a conventional truth or an ultimate truth; nothing is both, and nothing is neither. However, the two truths are not completely separate things—it's not that conventional truths are down here on planet earth and ultimate truths are up in space, in another universe. They are two aspects of every phenomenon, like two sides of a coin. A car, for example, is a conventional truth and its emptiness of inherent existence—its actual mode of existence—is an ultimate truth. The two truths with respect to the car are complementary and interdependent and do not cancel each other. This is not easy to understand; in fact, it is said that to fully understand how things exist conventionally we first need to realize emptiness!

A good place to start to understand the two truths is with dependent arising. This simply means that whatever exists does so *in dependence* on other things. Nothing exists independently, or inherently. There are three principal ways things depend on other things; these will be explained in the meditation below. Contemplating and gradually understanding the truth of dependence leads to a realization of emptiness that is free of two mistakes, known as the two extremes: (1) nihilism, thinking things don't exist at all, and (2) eternalism, thinking things exist inherently, objectively, from their own side. Both have their dangers: with the first, we may deny karma and think we can do whatever we want—that there's no I and no you, so it doesn't matter if I hurt you or steal your things—and end up creating negative karma. For those following the bodhisattva path, falling into the extreme of nihilism would be particularly damaging. Thinking that sentient beings, their suffering, samsara, enlightenment, and so on do not exist would undermine one's compassion and bodhichitta. With the second extreme, eternalism, we remain imprisoned in samsara because liberation entails realizing that all phenomena do *not* exist inherently, from their own side.

Dependent arising is said to be the foremost avenue to the realization of emptiness because contemplating it enables us to avoid the two extremes. By understanding that things are dependent, not independent, we avoid the extreme of eternalism, and by understanding that although they are empty of inherent or independent existence, things *do* exist conventionally—as merely designated dependent arisings—we avoid the extreme of nihilism. Madhyamaka, the philosophical system of which Prasangika is a subschool, means *middle way*. It is the path that steers a middle way between those two perilous extreme views.

In this section you will find four meditations. The first is on dependent arising, a process of investigation and reasoning that can be used to comprehend the emptiness of any phenomenon. The remaining three meditations investigate varying levels of misconceptions we have about the self—how we think our "I" exists in relation to our physical and mental aggregates, our body and mind. These meditations will help you get started on your journey to the wisdom of emptiness. Keep in mind that this topic is highly complex. To properly comprehend and meditate on it, you need to receive teachings from qualified teachers, study reliable books, discuss what you learn with fellow practitioners, and contemplate to gain a deeper understanding. This is easily a lifetime task, one made easier with joyful effort and the other perfections.

1. MEDITATION ON DEPENDENT ARISING

Phenomena arise from causes; those causes have been taught by the Tathagata, and their cessation, too, has been proclaimed by the Great Renunciate.[95]
"Heart of Dependent Arising" dharani

Dependent arising means that things *depend* on other things for their existence. This is true for everything in the universe. Nothing stands alone, separate, or autonomous. A tree grows in dependence on a seed, water, fertilizer, and sunlight. People and animals depend on their parents, loving care, food, water, and air. A car is manufactured in a factory in dependence on people operating machines and assembling the parts.

Nonphysical things are also dependent. Mind, for instance, depends on the objects it knows and on its own previous moments that cease and give rise to subsequent ones. Even nirvana and enlightenment are dependent—their attainment depends on creating the appropriate causes and conditions while following the path. Since all phenomena are dependent, unable to exist on their own, they are all *empty* of inherent, or independent, existence. This is why becoming familiar with dependent arising helps us understand emptiness.

There are three ways things are dependent: on causes and conditions, on parts, and on concepts and names. The following meditation explains these using your own body as an example. Feel free to use other examples as well. It is particularly helpful to contemplate these points with objects of aversion or desire as a counterforce to those deluded attitudes.

The Meditation

Begin as usual by settling your body and mind, then performing the practice for lamrim meditation on page 35. After the recitation of the Buddha's mantra, meditate on the following.

First, spend a few minutes contemplating the benefits of wisdom to feel inspired to develop it:

- Wisdom understanding the conventional enables us to identify what is to be practiced—beneficial behavior like ethics and patience—and what is to be avoided—harmful behavior such as the ten nonvirtues or acting out anger and other delusions—so we can live our life wisely, creating the causes of happiness and refraining from the causes of suffering.
- Wisdom understanding the ultimate nature of things, emptiness, is the key to attaining liberation and enlightenment—it is the sole antidote to the ignorance that keeps us trapped in samsara.

- The other five perfections on their own are like blind people unable to find their way to enlightenment; the wisdom of emptiness is like a person with good eyesight who can guide them there.

Emptiness is subtle and not something we can perceive with our senses. We need to use our mental consciousness to first understand it conceptually, using reason, and eventually to realize it directly. The foremost reason for comprehending emptiness is said to be dependent arising. Think of an object, such as your body, and contemplate the following three ways it is dependent.

1. Dependent on causes and conditions
This type of dependence applies to all impermanent, conditioned phenomena, such as our bodies and all the physical phenomena in the world around us, as well as all mental states. Contemplate how your body came into existence in dependence on causes and conditions: your parents meeting, being attracted to each other, and having sex; the resulting fertilized egg gradually developing in your mother's womb, nourished by oxygen and nutrients from her body; and so on. Even now, our body depends on food, water, and air to remain alive. Reflect that without all these causes and conditions, your body would not exist.

2. Dependent on parts
All phenomena, both impermanent and permanent, have parts. Mentally separate your body into its components: skin, blood, bones, organs, cells, atoms, and so on. Those components are in turn composed of smaller, subtler parts. Spend some time contemplating these, and understand that without all those parts, your body would not exist.

3. Dependent on concepts and terms, or names
This is also known as dependent imputation, and is more subtle and difficult to understand. It also applies to everything, both impermanent and permanent phenomena. For instance, when you see or think of your body, you have the notion "body." In the language of the Prasangika system, body is the imputed object, and it is imputed in dependence on the parts of the body, which are called the basis

of imputation. Through a process involving conceptions and terms, "body" is imputed depending on its parts, such as skin, blood, bones, and so forth. That is the meaning of dependent imputation.

It might be easier to understand this by thinking of a newborn child who is named "Susan" by her parents. She isn't Susan from her own side, but is merely designated that way, either because the parents like that name, or it's the name of a beloved relative. In time they and other people who know Susan forget this naming process and relate to her as if she *is* Susan inherently, from her own side. In a similar way, all phenomena are designated in dependence on concepts and terms, or names.

We might be able to understand this intellectually, but still have a gut-level feeling that a body or a person exists inherently or independently, especially those we find attractive or repulsive. Seeing things as independent has been our dominant view from beginningless time, so it will take time to be free of it.

By contemplating these points, if you get a sense of the dependent nature of your body and other things, keep your mind focused on that experience as long as possible, even for just a few seconds.

Conclusion
Wisdom, especially the wisdom of emptiness, is an essential quality on the path to enlightenment and is also beneficial in our daily life. One of the most effective ways to develop the wisdom of emptiness is to contemplate dependent arising: how things are dependent on causes and conditions, on parts, and on the mind that designates them.

Resolve to keep dependent arising in mind and look for illustrations of it as you go through the day to expand and deepen your understanding of this important truth.

Dedication
Complete the remaining parts of the practice for lamrim meditation and dedicate the merit of your session to the peace, happiness, and enlightenment of yourself and all other beings.

2. MEDITATIONS ON THE SELFLESSNESS OF OUR "I"

Just as, with an assemblage of parts,
the word "chariot" is used,
so, when the aggregates exist,
there is the convention "a being."[96]
BHIKSHUNI VAJIRA

Emptiness is the true nature of all phenomena—everything that exists is empty of existing inherently or independently. But it's not possible to understand the emptiness of all things right from the beginning. Instead, we first realize it with respect to one object and then apply that understanding to other things. Traditional texts recommend that we start with our own self, investigating the innate sense of a real, independent "I" that seems to reside somewhere inside of us. Realizing the emptiness of such a self is highly beneficial because it targets the ignorance that is the chief cause of all our suffering, the root of samsara. Ignorance that grasps an inherently existing self leads to delusions such as anger, attachment, arrogance, and jealousy. It also lies behind our creation of contaminated karma, both virtuous and nonvirtuous, which in turn perpetuates our existence in samsara.

A word of caution: It is important to explore the topic of personal selflessness on the basis of a healthy sense of self. Many Westerners suffer from self-hatred or low self-esteem, problems that are virtually unknown in the Tibetan culture that has carried these teachings for generations. Others are afflicted with an overly inflated, narcissistic sense of self. If our sense of self is unhealthy or underdeveloped when we start learning and contemplating emptiness, we could become even more imbalanced. In a seminar on this topic, Alexander Berzin, one of the foremost Western scholars on Tibetan Buddhism, said it's recommended that emptiness not be taught to children or teenagers or to those who are seriously emotionally disturbed because they lack a healthy sense of self. He explained that we can develop a strong, healthy sense of self by learning and contemplating topics from the earlier stages of the lamrim, like the precious human life, karma, love, compassion, and so on. In the later stages of the lamrim, he says, where we encounter emptiness, we "deconstruct whatever inflation is thrown on top of the strong sense of 'me.'" Nevertheless, we will still have a healthy basis that is not lost. He says:

> First, we have to affirm that we have a conventional "me" and develop a positive attitude toward it before we start to get rid of the incorrect way of considering it.[97]

This is another reason it is important to have spiritual teachers and experienced Dharma friends who can guide us through this process and help us avoid the pitfalls.

Traditional lamrim texts ask you to plunge directly into meditation on the emptiness of an inherently existent self. However, this is quite difficult to do. Most of us have never questioned our sense of self or "I," asking, "How do I think I exist? What exactly is this self, my 'I'?" Although some people wonder who they are—and sometimes travel the world in search of their "I"—they probably assume they will discover a real self.

Buddhist philosophy explains several different misconceptions about the self. Some are coarser and easier to recognize as false; others are more subtle and difficult to dispel. Prasangika philosophers identify the following three main misconceptions of how the self exists in relation to the body and mind arranged according to subtlety:

1. The coarsest is *the conception of a permanent, unitary, and independent self.* This is the notion of an unchanging, partless self, or soul, that does not depend on causes and conditions. It seems to be distinct from our body and mind and continues to exist without changing after we die. Not everyone has such a notion; it is most commonly acquired in this life from learning non-Buddhist philosophies and religions.

2. Somewhat less coarse is *the conception of a self-sufficient, substantially existent self.* This one is innate, carried in our mind from previous lives, so we all have it from birth. This type of self or "I" appears to be somewhat separate from our body and mind and plays the role of their owner and controller. We can notice it in thoughts such as "*My* body is out of shape; *I* have to start exercising," or "He hurt *my* feelings."

3. The subtlest is *the conception of an inherently existent self.* This is

a sense that the self exists autonomously, inherently, from its own side, as if it's able to set itself up without depending on anything else. This conception is also innate; everyone has it.

Persons *do* exist. The eight or so billion people on this planet exist, as do all the other mammals, birds, fish, and insects.[98] Selflessness does not mean there is no person or self at all. It means that *certain types of self*—such as the three mentioned above—do not exist. The type of self or person that *does* exist is the self that is merely designated in dependence on a set of aggregates, a body-mind combination, as explained in the third point of the meditation on dependent arising.

The procedure for realizing selflessness involves first identifying in our experience the false sense of self—known in philosophical terms as *the object of negation*—and then contemplating reasons proving that it cannot possibly exist. The third misconception of self—that of an inherently existent self—is the one that lies at the root of all our troubles, but it's very subtle and difficult to identify. So it can be helpful to start with the more coarse misconceptions about the self, such as belief in a permanent, unitary, independent self. As mentioned above, this notion of self does not exist in everyone's mind; only people who have learned certain non-Buddhist religions have acquired it. But we might fall into that category—especially if we were raised in a Christian or Jewish family to believe in a soul—so it can be helpful to investigate whether such a self exists.

Below you will find meditations exploring each of the three misconceptions about the self explained above.

A. MEDITATION ON THE EMPTINESS OF A PERMANENT, UNITARY, INDEPENDENT "I"

THE MEDITATION

After doing the usual preparatory practices, including the practice for lamrim meditation, spend some time focusing on the breath to settle your mind—a calm mind is crucial when meditating on selflessness.

When your mind is settled, get in touch with your sense of self, such as the "I" that is meditating. Keeping your attention on that sense of "I," explore the questions that follow.

First, does this "I" seem to be *permanent* and unchanging, something that has always been there and always will be there? Do you think that the "I" of this moment is the same "I" that existed yesterday? Is it the same as the "I" that existed last year, and five years ago, and when you were a child?

When you contemplate the future, do you think the "I" that exists right now is the same "I" that will exist then, as you try to accomplish your goals and fulfill your dreams?

If you *do* have a sense of a permanent, unchanging "I," what exactly is it? Is there something in your body or mind you can point to as being that permanent "I"?

Second, does the "I" seem to be a *unitary*, partless self, as if there is some "essence" of you that can't be broken down or divided? If our self *was* unitary, we could not talk about different parts of our body—head, legs, heart, lungs, and so forth. We could not speak of different parts of our mind, such as happiness, unhappiness, love, and anger. As before, check if you can find something in your body or mind that is not made of parts but is one whole, partless thing.

Third, does the "I" seem to be *independent*, something that does not depend on causes and conditions? If that were the case, you could exist without your parents having brought you into the world. You could exist without food, water, and air. Is that possible?

All of this might seem obvious. We *know* we can't exist without parents, food, and water. And yet we can still have a contradictory belief in a self that is permanent, unitary, and independent. This is the power of ignorance—that we can hold two contradictory beliefs in our mind and not see any problem with it.

It is also helpful to ask ourselves, if a permanent, unitary, independent self *did* exist, how could it move, eat, think, talk, and meditate? To do any of these activities, changes must take place in our body and mind. A permanent "I" would be frozen, unmoving, exactly the same from one moment to the next. Is the existence of such a person feasible?

Moreover, if the "I" was permanent, unitary, and independent, it could not create karma and take rebirth. It could not practice Dharma, follow the path, and eventually attain enlightenment. It would always remain exactly the same, just as it is now—confused and stuck in samsara. In that case, it would be pointless for the Buddha to teach the paths to liberation from samsara and enlightenment because no one could transform themselves and attain those states. Fortunately, a permanent, unitary, independent self does *not* exist; it is a mere fabrication of a confused mind.

Conclusion

If you were able to recognize the unfeasibility of a permanent, unitary, and independent self, resolve to continue familiarizing yourself with that understanding. If you did not reach this understanding, resolve to continue exploring these questions.

Dedication

Conclude the practice for lamrim meditation, then dedicate the merit of your session to all beings becoming free of misconceptions about the self that bind us to samsara and swiftly attaining the sublime peace and happiness of liberation and full enlightenment.

B. MEDITATION ON THE EMPTINESS OF A SELF-SUFFICIENT, SUBSTANTIALLY EXISTENT "I"

The misconception conceiving of a self-sufficient, substantially existent self or "I" is more subtle than that of a permanent, unitary, independent one. There is an innate form of this conception that everyone has from birth, but it can also be acquired from learning certain philosophies. The self-sufficient, substantially existent self—although it does not in fact exist—appears to be different from the aggregates of body and mind, but not totally separate, as is the case with the permanent, unitary, and independent self. It also appears to be the owner and controller of the aggregates, as if their boss or ruler.

Put another way, this notion of "I" can be seen to operate within us as if it enjoys an independence from the aggregates—as if it could be identified without also having to depend on identifying the aggregates, or at least some of them. Although this type of self appears to be independent of the aggregates, the aggregates appear to be dependent on it. Khensur Jampa Tegchok gives a clear summary of what it means to grasp a self-sufficient, substantially existent self:

> *Self-sufficient* means being able to exist independently in a self-sufficient manner, without depending on anything else, such as the aggregates. [...] A self-sufficient, substantially existent person would be a person that could be seen without anything else, such as the aggregates, appearing to the mind. In fact, for us to know a person is present, the aggregates have to appear. We cannot identify a person independent of her body-mind complex.[99]

It takes a while to understand these concepts; for now, just think that this type of self appears to be something that owns and controls our body and mind, like a king ruling his subjects or an employer supervising her employees. For example, when we say, "I am gardening," there seems to be an "I" that is managing the body—making it dig, plant seeds, pull weeds, and so on. And when we say, "I am thinking," a separate "I" seems to be using the mind to solve a problem or plan a project. If there really was an "I" that existed in this way—separable from the body and mind and in control of them—the more carefully we investigate it, the clearer it should become. We should be able to locate it and point to something that is it. The following meditation will help us explore whether such a self really does exist.

The Meditation

Begin the session by sitting in a comfortable and conducive posture for meditation. Spend some time observing your breathing to settle your thoughts. When your mind is calm, do the long or abbreviated practice for lamrim meditation on page 35, pausing after the mantra recitation. Then do the following meditation.

First, get in touch with the sense of a separate, supervisory self—that "I" that seems to be in charge, controlling your body and mind. One way to do this is to think of an emotional experience—in which you could say "I feel angry" or "I feel excited"—or just an ordinary, sub-jective experience—like "I am working" or "I am thinking." Do your best to avoid getting caught up in the emotions and the stories around this situation, and instead pay attention to the sense of an "I" that lies beneath those emotions and stories.

Maintaining awareness of this sense of self, investigate it more care-fully. When the body is working, what is this seemingly supervisory "I" that tells it to do? Likewise, when the mind is thinking, what is the "I" that seems to make it think? Try to get a clearer sense of how that sepa-rate "I" seems to exist and what kind of phenomenon it is.

Then contemplate the following faulty consequences of this notion of a separate, controlling "I." If there really were a separable "I" that controlled the body, we would be able to do whatever we want with our body at will—make it healthy, attractive, forever youthful. Is that possi-ble? Also, our body would never act in ways that cause us problems—like slipping and falling on a wet sidewalk or cutting a finger chopping vegetables.

Likewise, if a separable "I" was in control of the mind, we could do whatever we want with our mind at will—make it intelligent, humor-ous, peaceful, and joyful. We could ensure that we never experience any unpleasant mental states like depression, anxiety, low self-esteem, and so on. Is that possible?

Another time we see this conception of "I" operate within us is when we yearn to exchange our body or mind for someone else's. We wish we could have the gorgeous body of a film star or have Einstein's brilliant mind. Underlying these thoughts is the belief in a self that could be separated from the body and mind and that could give away one or both of those and get new and improved ones in return.

Recall if you ever wished to trade in your body or your mind for someone else's. In these thoughts, there's a clear sense of "I" that is distinct from the body and mind. What exactly is that "I"? Can you point to it?

Do not worry if you felt confused or troubled during this meditation. Most of us never question our sense of "I"—what it is, how it exists. We just assume it exists the way it appears and get on with our life. Ques-tioning and investigating it are unconventional and bound to bring up unfamiliar thoughts and emotions. Be patient with yourself when this happens, and know that this is a positive sign. Remember, mistaken notions of the self and other phenomena lie at the root of our problems and need to be overcome to attain genuine happiness and freedom from suffering. The more you contemplate these points and investigate who or what you think you are, the clearer you will become about how the self exists and how it does not.

Conclusion

If you experienced the vanishing of this mistaken sense of self, or even if it appeared less solid than before, stay with that experience for a while to familiarize your mind with it. If you did not have such an experience, still rejoice that you made the attempt to gain a better understand of selflessness and resolve to continue exploring this crucial topic in the future.

Dedication

Complete the practice for lamrim meditation, then dedicate the merit of your session toward you and all other beings quickly gaining the realization of selflessness, which is the key to attaining complete liberation from suffering and its causes as well as the sublime peace and happiness of enlightenment.

C. Meditation on the Emptiness of an Inherently Existent "I"

An inherently existent self is the subtlest object of negation and is refuted only by the Prasangika school—the other Buddhist schools assert that such a self exists. An inherently existent self appears to exist objectively, from its own side, without depending on anything else—causes, conditions, parts, concepts, or terms. All sentient beings, including all people—regardless of their religious or philosophical education—have an innate conception that believes in an inherently existent self, or "I." This conception is the root of samsara, the principal culprit that keeps us imprisoned in this miserable situation. It needs to be eliminated from our mind in order for our mind to attain

the peaceful states of liberation and enlightenment. The wisdom realizing emptiness has the power to bring that about.

Since emptiness is a subtle object that is not perceivable by our sense
consciousnesses, we can only access it with our mental consciousness
using a process of reasoning. There are a variety of reasons that can
be used, including dependent arising (see page 275), but Lama Tsongkhapa and other authors of lamrim texts usually present the method
of the four essential points, also known as the four-point analysis: (1)
identifying the object of negation, (2) becoming certain about the
pervasion, (3) checking if the inherently existent "I" is inherently one
with the aggregates, and (4) checking if it is inherently different from
the aggregates.

1. Identifying the object of negation

In this analytical meditation, the object of negation is the inherently
existent self or "I." It is vital that we identify it in our experience for
the meditation to be successful. For instance, if we are playing darts
but are unable to see the target—the room may be too dark or we have
poor eyesight—it's unlikely that our dart will hit the bullseye. Similarly, if we do not recognize the target of the meditation—our sense
of an inherently existent "I"—contemplating reasons to prove its non-
existence will do nothing to counteract our innate grasping at this "I."

However, identifying this false self is not easy because of its subtlety
and our habitual tendency to believe in it. Even serious meditators
may need to spend a year or more working on this first point.

The object of negation, an inherently existent "I," appears most vividly when we get emotional. To catch a glimpse of it, it's helpful to
recall or imagine a situation where we are unjustly accused of some
wrongdoing and a strong sense of an "I" arises from the depths of
our heart, feeling outraged and wanting to defend itself—"*I* didn't
do that! It wasn't *my* fault!" Alternatively, we could recall experiences
of embarrassment, fear, or excitement. After thinking of such an incident, we then need to focus less on the emotions and more on the
"I" that seems to lie beneath or behind them—the "I" that is angry,
embarrassed, defensive, and so on. This should be done carefully,
otherwise it will vanish. A good analogy is photographing animals and
birds in the wild—you need to move quietly and unobtrusively so you
don't scare them away before you can snap a photo. Likewise, if we are

too intense or excited in our attempt to identify this false sense of self, we may be unable to observe it or, if it does appear momentarily, it will quickly disappear. If that happens, we can again recall the emotional situation and look for the "I."

It's likely that the "I" you initially recognize is the self-sufficient, substantially existent one rather than the inherently existent one; the latter is much more subtle and difficult to detect. You may also have difficulty noticing *any* sense of "I." If either of these occur, don't feel upset or disheartened. It's fine to continue the meditation, analyzing the remaining three points using whatever sense of self you can identify. With more practice, you will eventually be able to get a clear image of subtler objects of negation.

2. Becoming certain about the pervasion

This means that if such a self exists, it must be either inherently one with the aggregates or inherently different from them. In simple terms, the first means that the "I" is identical in all aspects to the aggregates, and the second that it exists separate from and totally unrelated to them. These are the only possibilities as to where or how an inherently existent "I" can exist; there is no third possibility.

One and different is a concept often used in Buddhist logic. Comparing two things, they must be either one with each other—exactly the same and identical in every way—or different, not identical. More precisely, being one means being the same in both name—what it's called—and meaning—what it is. For instance, car is one with car because it is the same in both name and meaning. Likewise, Dalai Lama is one with Dalai Lama.[100] However, if two things are different in name or different in meaning, they are not one but different. For instance, Dalai Lama and Tenzin Gyatso are different in name and are therefore different, even though they are two names for the same person. Dalai Lama and Pope Francis are different in meaning—they are two different people—but also different in name, so they are different, not one. One and different are a dichotomy—whatever exists must be one or the other; there's no third possibility. That is why there is a pervasion that if an inherently existent "I" exists, it must be either inherently one with the aggregates or inherently different from them.

We need to be certain about this because the last two points of the analysis involve investigating each of those possibilities to check if an inherently existent "I" can be found in either of them. To illustrate this with a simple example, let's say you are at work and your neighbor calls to tell you they saw someone trying to break into your house. You rush home and thoroughly search your house, which has just two rooms. When you do not find anyone in either room, you feel confident that there's no burglar in your house and can relax. Similarly, after identifying the inherently existent "I"—the burglar you imagined you'd find—you need to be convinced that there are only two possibilities where it could exist, namely, that it is either inherently one with the aggregates or inherently different from them—like the two rooms in your house. Once you have thoroughly investigated both possibilities and have not found this "I," you will realize its emptiness—that such an "I" does not exist. However, not finding the "I" may not be as pleasant as not finding a burglar in your house; it can be quite unsettling or frightening! Be prepared for that, but know that such reactions are temporary. For people with great merit and a deeper understanding of samsara and wish to be free from it, realizing the emptiness of an inherently existent "I" is a great relief and even blissful.

3. Checking whether the inherently existent "I" is inherently one with the aggregates

In this step you investigate the first possibility: Is this seemingly real "I" inherently one with, or identical to, the aggregates of body and mind? If it were, there would be a number of fallacies, which are listed in the meditation below.

4. Checking whether it is inherently different from the aggregates

This involves investigating the other possibility: is the inherently existent "I" different from the aggregates? This too would entail absurd consequences, as outlined below.

The ideal scenario is that after contemplating these four points, you will get an experience of emptiness of the "I"—a realization that the seemingly real, inherently existent self that you always believed in does not actually exist. But don't expect that to happen the first time, or even after a hundred times. Realistically, getting a realization of emptiness is the culmination of years of receiving teachings, studying them, thinking about them, discussing them with fellow students, and doing your best to meditate on whatever understanding you have gained. It is also important to engage in practices for purifying negative energy—karma and delusions—and accumulating merit.

This is a brief introduction to the four points.[101] More details are included in the following meditation.

THE MEDITATION

Begin by sitting comfortably in a conducive posture. Observe your breathing for a few minutes to bring your mind to a calm state. Then do the practice for lamrim meditation on page 35 and insert the following meditation after reciting the Buddha's mantra.

1. Identifying the object of negation

Although an inherently existent self doesn't actually exist, we have an innate conception that it does, so such a self appears to our mind. To identify it, your mind needs to be as calm, clear, and undistracted as possible, so focus on your breathing for a while to settle your thoughts. Then recall an emotional experience—such as feeling defensive when unjustly blamed, or feeling angry, fearful, excited, or sad—and try to catch a glimpse of the sense of "I" that lies behind the emotion, the self that seems to exist from its own side, objectively, and able to set itself up without depending on other things. Do this carefully and discreetly; don't pounce on it, thinking, "This is the false 'I' that doesn't exist!" or it will disappear. If the appearance of such an "I" does fade, recall the same emotional experience to bring it up again.

Do not immediately move on to the next point but take some time to explore this sense of "I." Use one part of your mind to stay focused on it and another part of your mind to investigate how it seems to exist. Does it seem real, solid, existing on its own and from its own side? Does it seem to exist independent of everything else—its causes and conditions, the parts that make it up, and the mind that designates it? Spend time on this point, getting a clear image in your mind of the way an inherently existent "I" appears to exist. If your understanding of this is vague or weak, the investigation of the remaining points will not be so effective.

2. Becoming certain about the pervasion

If an inherently existent self exists, it must be either inherently one with the aggregates or inherently different from them. There are only these two possibilities as to the way an inherently "I" can exist in relation to the aggregates, which are the parts that make us up. There is no third possibility.

Take some time to contemplate this concept, using ordinary things like a table and a chair or a cup and a pen. When comparing a pair of objects conventionally—in the way the concept of one and different was explained above—they must be either one—exactly the same in both name and meaning—or different, not exactly the same in name or meaning. Can you think of any other possibility besides these two?

Once you have a better understanding of this pervasion, apply it to an inherently existent "I" and the aggregates: form, feelings, discriminations, compositional factors, and consciousness. If there really is an inherently existent "I," when comparing it with the aggregates, it must be either inherently one with or inherently different from them.[102] Generate conviction that there are only these two possibilities and no third possibility.

3. Checking whether the inherently existent self is inherently one with the aggregates

As explained, *one with* means identical, exactly the same in name, meaning, and every other way. There is not the slightest difference between them. If an inherently existent self were to exist and if it were inherently one with the aggregates, there would be the following absurd consequences:

- *Just as there are five aggregates, there should be five "I"s.* If an inherently existent "I" were one with the aggregates, they would have to be exactly the same, without any difference between them, and thus they should be exactly the same in number. Since there are five aggregates, there would have to be five "I"s. Regarding this consequence, Lama Zopa Rinpoche said that it would be very expensive to travel because we would have to buy five tickets instead of just one! We would also need five passports, one for each "I."
- Alternatively, if you insist that there's only one "I," not five, then *the aggregates would have to be only one.* We could not divide

them into parts; they would be one whole, monolithic thing. Also, if the mental and physical aggregates were just one, part- less thing, we couldn't talk about our body and mind as differ- ent things.

- Being one entails being the same in name as well as in mean- ing, so if the "I" and aggregates really are one, *they should not be called by different names or terms.* Both should be suitable to be called either "I" or "aggregates." In fact, there would be no need for the word "I" because "aggregates" would refer to the person.

- Another consequence is that *whatever is true regarding the "I" should be true of the aggregates, and vice versa.* In that case, if I am a Buddhist, my body should be Buddhist. If I am thinking, my body should be thinking. If my body gets sunburned, my mind should be sunburned. Is that possible?

Recognizing the absurdity of these consequences, generate conviction that there is no inherently existent self that is inherently one with the aggregates.

4. Checking whether the inherently existent self is inherently different from the aggregates

Having explored the possibility of the inherently existent "I" being inherently one with the aggregates, now consider the other possibility: that they are inherently different. If two things are inherently existent and different, they must be totally distinct, unrelated, and indepen- dent of each other.[103] This is because inherent existence means exist- ing autonomously and not dependent on anything else. The following consequences would ensue if there was an inherently existent self that is inherently different from the aggregates:

- You could remove the aggregates one by one and still be left with the self.

- Your aggregates could be in one place—at home—and your "I" could be somewhere else—at work or in the supermarket.

- Your mind could be thinking but your "I" would not be think- ing. Your body could be sick but you could not say, "I am sick." What is happening with one would not have the slightest rela- tionship to the other.

You can also check if there is anything the "I" is capable of doing that does not depend on the body or mind. In other words, can you find an "I" that walks, talks, eats, feels, thinks, meditates, drives a car, uses a computer, and so on that does not depend on the body-mind complex?

See if you can generate conviction that there is no inherently existent self that is inherently different from the aggregates.

Conclusion

After becoming convinced about the pervasion—that there are only two possibilities as to how an inherently existent "I" could exist—and then thoroughly investigating these two possibilities, you may reach the decisive point of not finding the inherently existent "I." Then that seemingly real "I"—the "I" that is grasped by the innate misconception of self—disappears. This is the experience of emptiness. If you attain this experience, focus on it single-pointedly as long as you can.

Then, reflect on the way the self or "I" exists—the "I" that meditates, works, talks, eats, and so on. Although it is empty of inherent existence, it exists conventionally—it is merely imputed, or designated, by the mind in dependence on its basis of designation, the aggregates.

Don't worry if this experience of emptiness does not occur. It usually takes time and practice—as well as learning and study—before we are able to attain such an experience. Resolve to continue learning and reflecting on this topic as much as you can and complement that with practices for purification and accumulation of merit, which help the mind become more ripe and ready to realize emptiness.

Dedication

Return to the practice for lamrim meditation, dissolve the visualization of the Buddha, and recite the remaining verses. When dedicating the merit of your session, remember the emptiness of the three spheres: that you (the one who created the merit), the acts of creating and dedicating merit, and the objects to which you dedicate (attaining enlightenment for the benefit of all sentient beings) are all empty of existing inherently, independently, from their own side. They exist conventionally—as merely labeled dependent arisings—but do not exist ultimately.

You might also like to recite the following dedication verse from Shantideva to renew your bodhichitta motivation. This is a favorite of His Holiness the Dalai Lama.

> For as long as space endures
> And for as long as living beings remain,
> Until then may I, too, abide
> To dispel the misery of the world.[104]

APPENDICES

APPENDIX 1
Meditations on Relying on a Spiritual Teacher

Since it is due to my teacher's kindness that I have met the
Buddha's peerless teaching, I dedicate this virtue so that all beings
may be guided by sublime spiritual mentors.
TRADITIONAL DEDICATION VERSE

MANY STUDENTS are familiar with the topic of *guru devotion*, but a
more accurate rendering of the Tibetan term is *relying on a virtuous friend*—or in other words, a spiritual teacher. As mentioned in the
introduction to the book, this topic is normally placed at the beginning of the lamrim, prior to the precious human life. This is because
someone who has learned and investigated basic Buddhist teachings
in general, as well as the specific teachings on the path to enlightenment, and is intent on following that path needs to practice under
the guidance of qualified spiritual teachers. Since many readers of
this book are likely still exploring Buddhism, possibly without a personal connection to a teacher, the meditations on this topic have been
placed here, in the appendix. Feel free to meditate on them if and
when you feel they are relevant to your practice.[105]

As you are probably aware, some Buddhist teachers have been in
the news due to alleged or actual misbehavior, such as sexual abuse
and abuse of power. Such cases can cause potential students to be
skeptical of trusting any spiritual teacher and they may prefer to learn
and practice on their own. In my experience, most Buddhist teachers are reliable and ethical—they sincerely guide their students on
the path and care for them with wisdom and compassion—but sadly,
those teachers usually do not get the same press coverage as the abusive ones. If you have concerns about this issue, you can find some
practical advice from the Dalai Lama on dealing with abusive teachers

in chapter 5 of *The Foundation of Buddhist Practice.*[106] Additional advice regarding problems in the teacher-disciple relationship can be found in Alexander Berzin's *Wise Teacher, Wise Student.*[107] The meditations in this section, such as those on the need for spiritual teachers and the qualities to look for, might also help with these concerns.

This section includes five meditations: (1) why we need spiritual teachers, (2) the qualities to look for in a spiritual teacher, (3) the qualities we as disciples need to bring to the relationship, (4) the benefits we will experience by relying on a spiritual teacher, and (5) the actual way to rely on a spiritual teacher. You can spend one session meditating on each of these, or if you are doing a longer session, you might wish to combine two or more of them.

Remember to begin each session with the practice for lamrim meditation on page 35 and insert the actual meditation on the lamrim topic after the recitation of the Buddha's mantra. When you have completed that, dissolve the visualization of the Buddha and dedicate the merit of the practice.

1. The Need for a Spiritual Teacher

The Meditation

Even to learn ordinary skills—how to drive a car, use a computer, bake a cake, play a musical instrument, speak a new language, and so on—we need to rely on knowledgeable and experienced teachers. In the same way, to know how to practice Dharma and travel the path to liberation and enlightenment—states of mind we have never experienced before—we definitely need a teacher.

Although we can gain some knowledge of the Dharma from books and the internet, we need more than that to understand how to really practice it and transform ourselves in a positive way. A qualified teacher is someone who can explain the Dharma, answer our questions about it, and show through their example how to put it into practice.

Think about your own experiences in life: what you learned from your parents, teachers, music instructors, sports coaches, mentors, and so on. Would you have been able to learn these things on your own, without anyone guiding you?

See if you can understand that in order to follow the spiritual path—which mainly involves working with our mind—it's even more essential to have a teacher.

Conclusion

Whatever understanding you reach as a result of contemplating these points, focus your attention on it for a few minutes, allowing it to sink deeper and leave a powerful imprint on your mind.

If you conclude your session at this point, complete the remaining parts of the practice for lamrim meditation, then dedicate the merit.

2. THE QUALITIES OF AN IDEAL SPIRITUAL TEACHER

THE MEDITATION

When it comes to choosing a spiritual teacher, we need to be cautious. There are people who claim to have attained realizations, even enlightenment, but would it be right to blindly believe what they say and take them as our teachers? The Buddhist teachings say no. They recommend that we spend some time—at least two to three years—getting to know a person and checking to see if they have the right qualities to be a spiritual teacher for us, and only then should we take them as a teacher. While doing this, we can still learn from them, increase our knowledge of the Dharma, and experiment with the practices they teach.

What qualities should we look for? Below is a list of ten qualities of an ideal Mahayana spiritual teacher according to a scripture by Maitreya, the *Ornament for the Mahayana Sutras*.[108] Contemplate these qualities one by one, investigating why it is important for a spiritual teacher to have them, and what problems might occur if a teacher were to lack any of them.

1. A mind subdued through the higher training in ethics. This

means that a teacher should have good ethical conduct and observe whatever vows they have taken. Ethics is an essential factor in subduing the disturbing emotions in one's mind.

2. A mind pacified and undistracted through the higher training in concentration. A teacher should have trained in concentration such that their mind is pacified and they are able to keep it focused, free of distraction.

3. A mind thoroughly pacified through the higher training in wisdom. Ideally, a teacher needs to have developed the wisdom realizing selflessness of persons.

4. Having more knowledge and qualities than the disciple.

5. Having perseverance in practicing the Dharma and benefiting others.

6. Having a wealth of scriptural knowledge.

7. Having a realization of suchness. This is another term for selflessness, or emptiness, and this quality means that a teacher has attained the wisdom realizing the selflessness of phenomena—their lack of inherent existence—or at least a sound conceptual understanding of it.

8. Being skilled in teaching the Dharma. Having a wealth of knowledge alone is not enough; ideally, a teacher also needs to be skillful in imparting it to others.

9. Having love and compassion. A teacher's motivation to teach should be altruism: genuinely caring for others and wanting to benefit them by showing them the path to enlightenment.

10. Having abandoned discouragement and laziness in teaching the Dharma. For example, with students who are slow to learn, the teacher needs to be patient and try different ways of explaining complex topics until the student understands.

If we are unable to find a teacher with all ten of these, we should try to find one who has the five most important qualities:

1.–3. A mind subdued by the three higher trainings: ethics, concentration, and wisdom.

4. Having love and compassion.

5. Having a realization of suchness.

And if we cannot find a teacher with these five qualities, we should try to find one who has at least the following three:

1. More good qualities than faults.
2. More concern for others than for him- or herself.
3. More concern for future lives than this life.

Conclusion

In order to attain enlightenment, and even to obtain fortunate rebirths and liberation from samsara, we need to rely on a qualified spiritual teacher. We also need to check carefully to ensure that a person is properly qualified before making the decision to rely upon him or her as our spiritual teacher. Focus your mind on this understanding for a few minutes, to allow it to sink deeper and leave a powerful imprint on your mind.

If you conclude your session at this point, complete the remaining parts of the practice for lamrim meditation, then dedicate the merit.

3. The Qualities of a Suitable Disciple

The Meditation

For the relationship with a spiritual teacher to be beneficial and fruitful, disciples need to cultivate certain qualities in themselves. Contemplate the following five qualities, which were explained by great Indian masters of the past, and as you do, see if you can understand why they are important. Also check whether you have them and make the determination to develop those you do not have and strengthen those you do.

The five ideal qualities of a disciple are as follows:

1. Being open-minded and unbiased. This means not being attached to some people or ideas and hostile to others. We need to be open to reassessing the views and attitudes we held prior to meeting the Dharma and be willing to leave aside or modify those we recognize to be incorrect.

2. Having discriminating wisdom—the ability to know what is right and wrong, true and false.

3. Having joyous effort—a strong aspiration and enthusiasm to learn the Dharma, understand it, and practice it.

4. Having respect for the teacher and the teachings by appreciating their good qualities, rather than arrogantly focusing only on faults we might perceive.

5. Listening attentively during teachings, with mindfulness and concentration.

Conclusion

Whatever conclusion you reach as a result of contemplating these points, focus your mind on it for a few minutes to allow it to sink deeper and leave a powerful imprint on your mind. Whether or not you have a spiritual teacher, striving to develop these five qualities in yourself would benefit you and your spiritual practice. Determine to cultivate those you currently do not have and strengthen those you do.

If you conclude your session at this point, complete the remaining parts of the practice for lamrim meditation, then dedicate the merit.

4. The Benefits of Relying on a Spiritual Teacher

The Meditation

By clearly understanding the benefits we will gain by relying on a spiritual teacher, we will have enthusiasm to engage in this practice.[109] Contemplate each of the following points, using examples from your own experience or that of others you have observed.

• By following our teachers' advice and example, our thoughts and actions will gradually become more positive and virtuous. This in turn will lead to more happiness and less suffering, both for ourselves and others. For example, learning how to manage our anger will enable us to experience greater peace, and we will be less likely to harm those around us with hateful speech and behavior.

• We will begin to create the main causes of enlightenment:

merit—also called method, compassionate actions to benefit others—and wisdom—understanding the true nature of things. Under our teachers' guidance we will learn how to cultivate these causes and will thus begin our journey to enlightenment.

- We will gain more knowledge, skills, and qualities that will enable us to subdue disturbing emotions in our mind and be of greater benefit to others.

- We will learn how to purify negative karma that would otherwise cause rebirth in unfortunate realms. As a result, such karma could ripen in this life in relatively mild forms, such as having a headache or getting a flat tire while running an errand for our teacher.

- Offering service to our teachers and practicing their teachings enable us to create a vast amount of merit, bringing us closer to enlightenment.

- Correctly relying on our spiritual teachers in this life creates the cause to meet and be guided by spiritual teachers in future lives. Imagine the difficulties you would face in a lifetime in which you never encountered a spiritual teacher.

- Our good qualities and insights will increase, and by following the path to enlightenment we will be able to accomplish what is most beneficial for ourselves and others.

- Under our teachers' compassionate guidance, we will feel supported and inspired in our practice.

These benefits are the result of listening to Dharma teachings from qualified spiritual teachers with a humble and respectful attitude and putting them into practice to the best of our ability.

If, on the other hand, we develop negative attitudes toward any of our teachers and criticize them, we will not enjoy these benefits and will instead create the causes for our good qualities to degenerate and for painful experiences in this and future lives. Therefore, anytime we get angry at or behave disrespectfully toward one of our teachers, we should sincerely apologize to him or her and purify the karma with the four opponent powers.

Conclusion
Recognize how fortunate you are that you have met spiritual teachers and are able to learn from them. Let your mind rest single-pointedly in that experience for a few minutes. Finally, resolve to cherish your spiritual teachers and keep your relationships with them as pure and healthy as possible.

If you conclude your session at this point, complete the remaining parts of the practice for lamrim meditation, then dedicate the merit.

5. HOW TO RELY ON SPIRITUAL TEACHERS

THE MEDITATION

After contemplating the importance of relying on spiritual teachers and the benefits of doing so, we now come to the actual way of relying on them. There are two ways of relying on them: with our thoughts and with our actions. Contemplate the points below, recalling your experience with your own teachers—if applicable—and reflect on how you can rely on them going forward.

Relying on spiritual teachers with your thoughts
This involves cultivating two attitudes regarding your teachers, *faith* and *gratitude and respect.*

The first attitude is *faith*, or *trust*, which is cultivated by contemplating the teacher's good qualities, as well as the important role they play in your life. We do not have the karma to meet the Buddha directly, but our spiritual teachers are doing exactly what the Buddha would do if he were in the world today. They are living ethically, being compassionate toward all beings, teaching the Dharma, and helping people to follow the path to enlightenment. Bring to mind one of your teachers and contemplate his or her good qualities and how they are playing the same role as the Buddha. By reflecting on these points, cultivate trust in your teacher.[110]

The second attitude is *gratitude and respect*, which arises from contemplating their kindness. Think about the way you were and the life you were living before you met your spiritual teachers and began learning Dharma from them. Then reflect on the way you are now and how you are living your life. Can you see any positive changes? If so, understand that these are due to the kindness of your teachers who have guided you on the spiritual path. If gratitude and respect for your teachers arise in your mind, stay with these feelings for a few minutes, allowing them to sink in deeply.

Relying on spiritual teachers with our actions

This form of reliance involves three kinds of activities:

- *Making offerings.* This can be done according to your means. If you are not wealthy, you can offer a small amount of money or even a piece of fruit. The most important thing is to make the offering with genuine respect and appreciation for your teachers' kindness. Also, understand that the reason for making offerings is not because your teachers are greedy and want things from you. Instead, it is for your own benefit: to create the merit you need to progress along the spiritual path.
- *Offering service.* This means doing things to help your teacher, such as cooking a meal, cleaning his or her room, or delivering a message. It can also mean volunteering at Dharma centers founded by your teacher. Such activities are another excellent way to create merit.
- *Practicing the teachings.* This is said to be the best way of relying on your teachers and what will bring them the greatest happiness. There are many things to practice, and initially you won't be able to practice everything. A good place to start is living ethically—refraining from negative actions and doing positive actions as much as you can—and being kind and respectful to others. It's also excellent to start working on transforming your mind, reducing the negative aspects and increasing the positive ones.

Conclusion

Spend a few minutes keeping your mind focused on whatever positive feelings you gained from doing this meditation. Finally, make a resolution to rely on your spiritual teachers to the best of your ability, not only for your own benefit but for the benefit of all beings.

Dedication

Complete the remaining parts of the practice for lamrim meditation, then dedicate the merit you have created to the peace, happiness, and enlightenment of all living beings.

APPENDIX 2
Meditations on the Twelve Links

I N THE intermediate level of the lamrim we contemplate the many
varieties of samsaric suffering as well as their principal causes:
delusions and karma. You may wonder, if samsara is as horrible as a
prison, why do we continue being reborn in it, life after life? The Buddha answered this in his explanation of the twelve links of dependent
arising, the actual mechanism whereby delusions and karma lead
to repeated rebirth in samsara. The twelve links are factors that are
part of us and our life, and it is crucial to recognize them, their inter-
dependence, and the role they play in our suffering and our inability
to fulfill our highest potential. In the *Rice Seedling Sutra*, the Buddha
stressed the importance of this teaching by saying:

> Monks, he who sees dependent arising sees the Dharma; he
> who sees the Dharma sees the Buddha.[111]

In this quote, "dependent arising" refers to the twelve links, each of
which *arises* in *dependence* on the previous one. Dependent on ignorance, compositional factors arise; dependent on compositional
factors, consciousness arises; and so on through rebirth, aging, and
death.

The subject of the twelve links is complex; to fully understand it
you need to receive teachings, study texts, and contemplate the individual links and how they connect to each other. Two meditations
are presented below. One contains a brief, simplified explanation
of the twelve links that can help you identify them in your life and
experience. The second explains how they unfold over time, from
one life to another, and how each arises in dependence on the others.
Understanding this process enhances both our renunciation—the

determination to free ourselves from samsara—and our bodhichitta—
the aspiration to help all other beings become free as well.

1. THE TWELVE LINKS

THE MEDITATION

Sit in a conducive posture for meditation and take a few minutes to
settle your thoughts. Generate an altruistic motivation, then begin the
practice for lamrim meditation on page 35 and insert the following
meditation at the appropriate point. Spend time contemplating each
link to deepen your understanding of it and be able to recognize it
and the role it plays in your life.

1. Ignorance

According to the Prasangika, the ignorance that is the first of the
twelve links is that which grasps one's own self as inherently or independently existent. Although we have this wrong conception about all
phenomena—we see everyone and everything as inherently existent—
it is only the grasping at our self that is considered first-link ignorance.
Specifically, first-link ignorance includes only those moments of grasping an inherently existent "I" that motivate a complete karmic action
powerful enough to cause a rebirth—for example, killing a sentient
being or saving a life. Such an action is the second link, which we will
look at next.

Ignorance is like a tyrant. You probably would not want to live in a
country ruled by a dictator who held absolute control over every aspect
of its citizens' lives. But our existence in samsara has been controlled
by ignorance since beginningless time; it incites us to create negative
karma that leads to unfortunate rebirths and horrific suffering. Even
when we create virtue under its influence, we still find ourselves stuck
in samsara, albeit in a fortunate realm. Generate the aspiration to free
yourself from this wrong conception, the root of all suffering, by realizing emptiness, the true nature of things.

2. Compositional action

This sort of action is karma, but only throwing karma—that is, actions performed in a complete way with all four factors: object, intention, action, and completion.[112] These actions plant seeds in our mind that can cause future rebirths. Depending on the ethical nature of the action, the rebirth could be in a fortunate or unfortunate realm. This link is called *compositional actions* because these actions compose, or bring together, all the conditions for rebirth in samara.

Bring to mind some complete actions you have done, both virtuous and nonvirtuous, and contemplate that each of these has the potential to cause another samsaric rebirth if they are not opposed by other factors, such as purification practice.

3. Consciousness

Many types of consciousness arise and pass through the mind every second, but the third link includes only those moments of consciousness upon which a karmic seed has been planted by the second link. In other words, out of ignorance we do a complete action and that leaves an imprint on our consciousness. Unless it is opposed by a counterforce, this seed travels with the mind into the future until the conditions come together for it to ripen as a new rebirth in samsara.

Contemplate how your mind contains seeds of the many complete karmic actions you have done in this and previous lives. Each of these seeds or imprints has the potential to send you back to the prison of samsara for another life sentence.

4. Name and form

This refers to the physical and mental aggregates at the first moment of a new rebirth that was thrown by second-link compositional action. Being the result of karma and delusions, these aggregates are not pure but contaminated, and thus of the nature of suffering. *Form* refers to the body—or technically, embryo—of the newly conceived being and *name* refers to the other four aggregates, which are different aspects of mind: feelings, discriminations, compositional factors, and the six consciousnesses.

Contemplate that each time you perform a complete action under the influence of ignorance and other delusions, you create the cause

to take another set of aggregates—a new body-mind combination—
that will inevitably experience various types of samsaric suffering.

5. Six sources

These are the six sense powers—of the eye, ear, nose, tongue, body,
and mind—that enable us to experience six types of objects: visual
forms, sounds, odors, tastes, tangibles, and mental objects.

Having all our senses intact is generally considered fortunate,
whereas being blind or deaf is regarded as unfortunate. But there are
downsides to having good sight and hearing. For instance, our delusions can increase, since we tend to get attached to attractive objects
and feel hostile to undesirable ones.

The problem isn't with seeing and hearing; buddhas can see and
hear, but they never experience desire or hatred because they have
abandoned all delusions. In our case, we still have the seeds of delusions that can be triggered by perceiving sense objects, and these lead
us to once again create the causes to remain in samsara.

Contemplate the role that sense powers can play in causing delusions to arise in your mind, prompting you to create more suffering
for yourself. Resolve to be cautious when perceiving objects that could
arouse attachment or aversion.

6. Contact

This is a mental factor that brings together the three main conditions
for a sensory experience: object, sense power, and consciousness. For
example, it connects our eye sense power, a visual object like a rose,
and visual consciousness so that we have the experience of seeing the
rose. Contact also has the function of distinguishing objects as attractive, unattractive, or neutral and leads to the next link, feeling.

Contact may be difficult to notice, but we can get an idea of it by
reflecting that each time we have a sense perception—seeing, hearing,
smelling, tasting, or feeling a sensation in our body—it is this mental
factor that has connected the essential elements for that experience to
occur.

7. Feeling

Feeling is a mental factor that arises due to contact with an object.
There are three types of feelings: pleasant, unpleasant, and neutral.

One of these is present in every instance of our experience, with every object we perceive.

We cannot avoid having feelings—even buddhas have them. But in ordinary beings, feelings usually lead to delusions. Pleasant feelings can give rise to attachment and craving, unpleasant ones to aversion and hatred, and neutral feelings perpetuate our ignorance because we continue seeing the object incorrectly—as inherently existent.

Recall some experiences of pleasant and unpleasant feelings that occurred in your mind when you perceived various objects—a bad smell, your favorite music, a stormy sky, an attractive person. Recognize how easy it is for feelings to lead to disturbing emotions and understand the need to be careful about this.

8. Craving

This is a form of attachment generated by the previous two links, contact and feeling. There are three types of craving: craving to not be separated from pleasant feelings, craving to be separated from unpleasant feelings, and craving for neutral feelings to continue.

Using the same examples you contemplated with the previous link, see if you can recognize how pleasant feelings can lead to craving for more pleasure and unpleasant feelings can lead to craving to be free of those. The third type of craving is difficult to recognize, but this probably occurs at times when you are neither happy nor unhappy and you feel a subtle wish for that mental state to continue and not change.

9. Grasping

Grasping, or *clinging*, is a more intense form of attachment that arises from craving. Both craving and grasping occur throughout our life, but the *links* of craving and grasping refer only to the instances of those mental factors that occur at the time of death. When we realize this life is ending and we are about to die, strong craving and grasping for new aggregates arise in our mind. These activate and nourish one of our karmic seeds to take rebirth, transforming that seed into the cause our next life.

To understand grasping, it might help to recall an experience when you thought you might die—on an airplane going through strong turbulence, for instance, or almost losing your balance on the edge of a cliff. Underlying the fear that arises in such situations is intense attachment to our body and life, not wanting to lose them. We *will* lose them one day, and at that time grasping will arise for a new body and life. See if you can imagine this.

10. Existence

Also called *becoming*, existence refers to the karmic seed that was planted earlier in our consciousness by link two and was then activated and nourished by craving and grasping at the time of death. That same karmic seed in our mind at the last moment of one life has the power to project us into the next life.

Think about an ordinary seed, like an alfalfa seed. After soaking in water, it becomes thoroughly moistened and is ready to turn into a sprout. Our karmic seeds for rebirth are similar; when one of them is moistened or nourished by craving and grasping at the time of death, it becomes fully ripened and ready to bring its result: the next rebirth.

11. Birth

This refers to the aggregates of body and mind at the first moment of the new life—which, according to Buddhism, is the moment of conception. Link eleven is the result of the karmic seed that was created at link two and activated by links eight and nine at the time of death of the previous life, thus transforming into link ten.

An alfalfa seed stored in a dry container can remain dormant for a long time, but once moistened it is activated and brings its result: an alfalfa sprout. Similarly, we have within our mind countless karmic seeds with the potential to cause another samsaric life. As long as they have not been nourished, they remain dormant. But as soon as one of these seeds is activated and nourished by craving and grasping at the time of death, it becomes the tenth link, existence, and will definitely bring a new rebirth in the next moment, which is the eleventh link, birth.

12. Aging and death

Aging begins in the second moment of a new life and continues until the end of that life. We usually think that aging happens later in life, in our fifties or sixties—but according to Buddhism, it starts right after conception, as the new being gets older and travels toward death.

Death is the moment when the consciousness separates from the body at the end of one life and transfers to the next life.

Contemplate that from the second moment of your life, right after you were conceived in your mother's womb, you have been in a process of aging—your body continuously getting older, and your lifespan decreasing. At some unknown point in the future, you will encounter death—the separation of your mind and body. These are the inevitable results of taking birth in samsara under the control of karma and delusions.

Conclusion

By contemplating these twelve factors, which describe in detail the causes for repeated rebirth in samsara, you might feel anxious, realizing that you are trapped in a highly undesirable situation. Although unpleasant, this is a wholesome feeling to have; it gives rise to a powerful and genuine determination to free yourself, and you can do so by practicing the three higher trainings: ethics, concentration, and wisdom. Resolve to use your precious human life to begin working on these practices and creating the causes for enlightenment to help all other beings become free from samsara.

Dedication

Complete the remaining steps of the practice for lamrim meditation. Finally, dedicate the merit you created so that you and all other beings will correctly understand the process of the twelve links, generate renunciation, and attain the wisdom that brings liberation from samsara and the highest happiness of enlightenment.

2. HOW THE TWELVE LINKS UNFOLD

By practicing the previous meditation, you can get a basic understanding of the individual twelve links, although you may need to contemplate these several times for the information to sink in and make sense. The second meditation, below, looks at how the twelve links work together to bring about repeated rebirths in samsara. It presents a few possible scenarios of the unfolding of *a single set of twelve links*. A single set of twelve links refers to a complete karmic action (link two) that is created under the influence of ignorance (link one) and leaves a seed on the consciousness (link three). This seed is later ripened at the time of death by craving and grasping (links eight and nine), resulting in the remaining links (four through seven, ten, and eleven) and finally ending with aging and death (link twelve).

You may wonder why this order in which the links occur differs from the order explained by the Buddha in the Pali and Sanskrit sutras. This is one reason the topic of the twelve links is so complicated— different Buddhist commentators over the ages have provided diverse explanations of the way in which a single set unfolds and the number of lives it takes to do so. We won't go into all those details here but will present two versions, one in which a single set of twelve links unfolds over two lifetimes, and one in which it takes three lifetimes. The fact that multiple lives are involved confirms that the results of our karma do not necessarily ripen in this lifetime.

The two-lifetime version is as follows. In the first life (life A), links one, two, and three occur: out of ignorance, a karmic action is created, planting a seed in the consciousness. At the end of that life, links eight and nine (craving and grasping) arise, nourishing that karmic seed such that it transforms into link ten (existence). This leads to the very next life (life B), starting with link four (name and form) at the time of conception. Link eleven (birth) also occurs at that time, and links five, six, and seven (six sources, contact, and feeling) arise gradually in the womb. Link twelve (aging and death) begins in the second moment of the new life, right after conception, and continues until the end of that life. So the process that began in life A is completed in life B.

It can also happen that at the end of life A, a different karmic seed— one that was created in some previous life—is nourished and transforms into link ten, existence. That seed then causes the very next life in which its remaining links arise. In the meantime, the karmic seed created in life A remains dormant in the consciousness, possibly for many more lives, until it is nourished by craving and grasping at the time of death of one of those lives (life B) and becomes the cause for the very next life. That is life C, in which the rest of the links related to that seed unfold. In this case, the process that began in life A ends in life C, with life B occurring just prior to life C. There could be numerous lifetimes—even thousands or millions—between life A, when the initial karmic seed was created, and lives B and C, in which that seed is ripened and causes a rebirth.

The process is complicated, but the diagrams below might help to clarify it, and the following meditation provides some examples that should help you understand it better.[113]

A set of twelve links unfolding over two lives

	LIFE A		LIFE B	
BIRTH	DEATH	BIRTH		DEATH
links 1, 2, 3	8, 9, 10	4, 5, 6, 7		
		11, 12→		

A set of twelve links unfolding over three lives

	LIFE A		LIFE B		LIFE C	
BIRTH	DEATH	BIRTH	DEATH	BIRTH		DEATH
links 1, 2, 3	*		8, 9, 10	4, 5, 6, 7		
				11, 12→		

* A karmic seed that is part of another set of twelve links is activated at the time of death of life A. This becomes the cause of the very next life in which the remaining links of that other set of twelve links occur. At the end of that life—or at the end of some other life in the future (life B)—the karmic seed created in life A is activated by links 8, 9, and 10, creating the cause of life C.

THE MEDITATION

Sit comfortably and relax your body and mind. Spend some time mindfully observing your breathing to calm your thoughts.

Generate a positive motivation for doing the meditation—for example, "May this meditation help me understand the causes of suffering so I can overcome these and attain enlightenment and guide all other beings out of samsara and to enlightenment as well." Then do the practice for lamrim meditation on page 35, pausing at the appropriate point to contemplate the following.

Begin by reflecting that your mind has always been under the control of the ignorance that grasps an inherently, independently existent self. That means that from birth, without choice, you have an instinctive belief in a real, solid "I" abiding somewhere inside you that seems autonomous, as if it is independent of everything else. Such an "I" does not exist at all, but you don't realize that. You have a similar incorrect way of seeing everyone and everything else, but grasping at the "I" is the main cause of all suffering.

Due to this ignorance, your mind sometimes gets afflicted with delusions such as anger or attachment, and these can compel you to create nonvirtuous karma—killing or harming someone, stealing or lying, speaking harshly or divisively. When an action is done in a complete way with all the four aspects, the imprint it leaves on your consciousness has the power to cause a rebirth. If you do nothing to purify it, at the end of this life or at the end of another life in the future, craving and grasping arise, nourishing that karmic imprint so it becomes empowered to bring the next rebirth, like an alfalfa seed about to sprout. Since the original action was nonvirtuous, the rebirth will be in one of the unfortunate realms—as an animal, hungry ghost, or hell being. So right after death, your consciousness will leave your old body and take a new form in one of these miserable situations and the remaining links will unfold, one after another: name and form, six sources, contact, feeling, birth, aging, and death.

The same process occurs when we do virtuous actions under the influence of ignorance. Let's say that in the present life you encounter the Dharma and are inspired to take refuge and the five lay precepts. You keep your precepts well and practice purification every day to clear up any wrongdoings. When you find mosquitos and spiders in your home you refrain from killing them and instead gently catch them and remove them to a safe place. As a result, you create the virtuous karma of non-killing, and you do it in a complete way with all four factors, so it becomes a throwing karma and a compositional action, the second link. However, since your mind is under the sway of the ignorance believing yourself to be inherently existent, this karma is contaminated and will still bring another rebirth in samsara—albeit a favorable one, as a human being, asura, or deva.

At the end of this life or at the end of some other life in the future, craving and grasping arise, nourishing that karmic seed so it becomes empowered to bring the next rebirth. Right after death, your consciousness will leave your old body and take a new form in one of the fortunate realms, and the remaining links will arise: name and form, six sources, contact, feeling, birth, aging and death. In those realms you will experience less suffering and greater well-being, but it's still another samsaric rebirth, so you will encounter problems like uncertainty, being dissatisfied, having to die and take rebirth, and so on.

Also, during that life as well as every other samsaric lifetime, you continue acting under the influence of ignorance, thus creating new sets of twelve links—the causes for countless more rebirths in samsara. This is how we circle in samsara, like being stuck on a Ferris wheel that never stops. Feel that this situation is unbearable, generate a strong determination to free yourself from it, and stay focused on that experience for a few minutes or longer.

Conclusion

Remember, the situation of being imprisoned in samsara is neither hopeless nor eternal. We *can* become free, which we do by practicing the three higher trainings: living ethically, cultivating concentration, and developing the wisdom realizing emptiness. This wisdom is like a sword that cuts ignorance, the root of samsara. Conclude the meditation with the positive, optimistic determination to do whatever is necessary to free yourself from samsara and to help all other sentient beings become free as well.

Dedication

Complete the remaining steps of the practice for lamrim meditation, then dedicate the merit you created to all beings' attainment of happiness, up to the highest happiness of enlightenment.

APPENDIX 3
Meditation on the Sixteen Aspects of the Four Noble Truths

The four aspects of the four noble truths
Are always pure sublime wisdoms.
Sutra Requested by Brahma

IN ADDITION to the meditations on the details of the four noble truths in part 4, another way to meditate on the four noble truths is in terms of sixteens aspects, or attributes: four for each truth. Contemplating these counteracts sixteen mistaken conceptions, many of which are beliefs of non-Buddhist religions and philosophies that developed in India. Some of these views are also found in Western religions, philosophies, and science; we may have acquired them through our conditioning or developed them through personal speculation, so it's helpful to investigate them.

Meditating on the sixteen aspects also increases our wisdom and brings us closer to liberation and enlightenment. Understanding the aspects of the last two truths in particular leads to greater certainty about the possibility of liberating ourselves forever from suffering and its causes and then guiding other sentient beings to do the same.

This topic is not normally included in lamrim texts. Lama Tsongkhapa briefly mentions the sixteen aspects in his *Great Treatise on the Stages of the Path to Enlightenment* and says they constitute the training in wisdom, but he does not elaborate on them.[114] More details are found in classic texts such as Maitreya's *Ornament for Clear Realization* and its commentaries.[115]

The following meditation includes a simplified version of these sixteen aspects to provide an initial understanding of them. As there are many points to contemplate, it would be best to divide them among several sessions—for instance, one session on each of the four truths with its four aspects—so that you can probe them in a deeper and more extensive way. As you do so, check if you have the misconception each aspect counteracts. If you do hold any of these, be willing to reassess it: Is it true or not?

A chart at the end of the meditation shows each aspect and the misconception it overcomes.

THE MEDITATION

Begin each session by sitting comfortably in a conducive position for meditation and settling your mind with a few minutes of meditation on the breath. Do the practice for lamrim meditation on page 35, pausing after the recitation of the Buddha's mantra to meditate on however many of the sixteen aspects you choose to focus on in that session.

THE FOUR ASPECTS OF TRUE SUFFERINGS

True sufferings include not just unpleasant experiences but everything that arises from karma and delusions, including our planet and the physical things we perceive around us. However, the principal true sufferings we need to meditate on are our own five aggregates—our body-mind complex—as these are the main source of our suffering. They came into existence due to contaminated karma and delusions, and they are bound by karma and delusions throughout our life.

Using your own body and mind as the example, meditate on the following four aspects.

1. Impermanence

Contemplate the many changes your body has gone through since you were born until now. Then imagine the changes that will occur to your body as you get older. These changes don't happen all at once, but gradually, because our body is changing every single moment—even right now. Our mind is also constantly changing, not remaining the same from one moment to the next. Can you find anything within your body and mind that does not change but is fixed, stable, and permanent?

Meditating on impermanence counteracts the misconception that thinks impermanent things, like your body and mind, are permanent in the sense of being unchanging.

2. Suffering

As you go through life your body frequently experiences discomfort, pain, sickness, and injuries. It is constantly aging and will eventually die. Your mind also undergoes suffering: unsatisfactory experiences such as sadness, disappointment, grief, irritation, and so on. As long as we are in samsara, and thus not free from karma and delusions, we will never be completely free from suffering.

Meditating on this aspect counteracts seeing samsaric things like your body and mind as pure and pleasurable—a source of endless enjoyment. Did you have these notions or expectations before you encountered the Buddha's teachings?

3. Empty

In this context, *empty* refers to the lack of a permanent, unitary, and independent self.[116] We may have the notion that, within our body-mind complex, there is a self, "I," or soul that does not change, is not made of parts, and does not depend on causes and conditions. Recall the reasons given earlier, in the chapter on the perfection of wisdom (page 281), proving that this type of self is a fabrication of incorrect thinking; it doesn't really exist.

Meditating on this type of emptiness opposes the misconception that sees true sufferings as having a permanent, unitary, and independent self.[117] True sufferings are impermanent and arise from causes and conditions, so they cannot possibly be permanent, partless, and independent of causes and conditions.

4. Selfless

This aspect refers to the lack of a self-sufficient, substantially existing self—a self that seems to be somewhat independent of the aggregates and in control of them. Contemplate the reasons explained earlier, in the chapter on the perfection of wisdom (page 283), that establish such a self or "I" as false. For instance, if such a self did exist, we could control our body and mind and make them do whatever we wish. Is this feasible?

Meditating on this type of selflessness overcomes the mistaken conception that sees true sufferings as having a self-sufficient, substantially existent self, or as objects used by such a self.

Conclusion

If you noticed that you have within your mind some or all of these mistaken conceptions, resolve to work on overcoming them by continuing to learn about and contemplate these four aspects of true sufferings.

THE FOUR ASPECTS OF TRUE ORIGINS

The second noble truth, true origins, explains the causes of sufferings, which are delusions and contaminated karma. Meditation on the following four aspects of these enables us to understand them more deeply and develop the determination to overcome them.

1. Cause

Delusions—especially ignorance and craving—and contaminated karma are the main causes of our suffering. Ignorant of the true sources of happiness and suffering, we crave pleasure, wealth, success, fame, and so on and act to obtain more of these, creating contaminated karma that keeps us in samsara. Contemplate examples of this from your own experience and from the world.

Meditating on this point counteracts the idea that suffering is causeless, a view held by the Charvaka, an ancient non-Buddhist school, but one that some contemporary materialists may hold as well. Do you have this view in your mind?

2. Origins

This aspect tells us that delusions and karma produce suffering again and again. All the various forms of suffering in samsara—such as the eight, the six, and the three types of suffering—arise due to actions that sentient beings create under the control of ignorance and other delusions. Contemplate that although we do not want suffering, the delusions in our mind compel us to act in ways that bring about problems and misery repeatedly, throughout our lifetime, and in all our lives in samsara.

Meditating on this aspect counteracts the notion that suffering comes from just one single cause. We might at times think this way, for example, if we blame our parents for all our problems. However, multiple causes and conditions—not just from this life but from past lives as well—must come together to bring about suffering.

3. Strong production

Strong production means that delusions and karma produce suffering forcefully. Most, if not all, of us have had the experience of our mind being completely overwhelmed by a delusion like hatred or obsessive attachment that leads us to act uncontrollably, even destructively, only to create many problems for ourselves and others. Contemplate examples of this from your own life and from society.

Meditating on this aspect counteracts the idea that suffering is produced by others, such as a divine creator, our parents, the government, our partners, our boss, and so on. We ourselves are responsible for our experiences, both negative and positive. Understanding this point enables us to stop blaming others for our problems, to accept responsibility, and to act more skillfully.

4. Condition

In addition to being causes of suffering, delusions and karma are also conditions for it. For instance, attachment to samsara acts as a cooperative condition for producing suffering. As explained in the teaching on the twelve links, at the time of death, strong craving for a new body-mind complex arises in our mind, activating and nourishing one of our karmic seeds and throwing us into another rebirth in samsara—another life of suffering and dissatisfaction.

Meditating on this aspect counteracts the idea that suffering is permanent but its states are changeable. For example, some people think that although problems and difficulties come and go, we will never become completely free of suffering. Have you ever thought this way?

Knowing that suffering depends on causes and conditions leads to the understanding that by eliminating those, we can become free of suffering—just as an epidemic disease can be eradicated by eliminating the causes and conditions that give rise to it.

Conclusion

After contemplating these aspects of true origins, generate the determination to free yourself from the causes of suffering, not only for your own peace and well-being, but in order to help all other beings become free as well.

THE FOUR ASPECTS OF TRUE CESSATIONS

A true cessation is the elimination of at least a portion of a delusion such that it will never arise again. A person following the path attains various true cessations from the time they directly realize emptiness and become an arya. The final, ultimate true cessation is attained with nirvana, or liberation—the complete abandonment of all delusions and their seeds, forever.

To get an idea of cessation, think of a time when you were caught up in some delusion—strong hatred, desire, or jealousy—and remember how painful and disturbing that experience was. Later, as a result of applying antidotes, the delusion subsided and your mind became free of those painful experiences. Recall how peaceful and liberating that felt. Although such an experience is not an actual true cessation because it is only temporary, it can help us appreciate the value and desirability of true cessations.

Contemplating the following four aspects of true cessations will enhance that appreciation and inspire you to want to attain them.

1. Cessation

Nirvana is the complete cessation of suffering because its causes—ignorance and the other delusions—have been eliminated, so suffering will never again occur. The Buddha said that delusions are adventitious, temporary, and not in the nature of the mind. They can be eliminated by applying the right antidote, which is the wisdom directly realizing emptiness.

Meditating on this point counteracts the idea that there is no liberation from samsara—that is, no way to overcome suffering and its causes, delusions. This is a view of the Charvaka, as well as some present-day materialists who believe that we are hardwired to experience anger, greed, jealousy, fear, and so on, and that we can never be free of these emotions. Is this a view you have learned and believe?

2. Peace

Nirvana is peace, or pacification, because it is a state in which delusions have been abandoned. Imagine having a mind in which anger, craving, jealousy, ignorance, and so on—the principal causes of all your suffering—never arise again. You would feel peaceful all the time, no matter what circumstances you encounter.

Meditating on this point counteracts notions that nirvana is some other state that is not completely free of delusions but is still within samsara, such as the meditative absorptions of the form and formless realms.[118] People sometimes attain these states and mistake them for nirvana because they are so peaceful. However, in these states, delusions have only been temporarily suppressed, not abandoned from the root. Therefore, it is important to develop a correct understanding of nirvana and be able to distinguish it from other peaceful, blissful states of mind.

3. Sublimeness

Nirvana is sublime in the sense that there is nothing more blissful and beneficial; this is because delusions have been abandoned forever. States of temporary suppression of delusions do not last; when they come to an end, delusions again arise, disturbing the mind and even impelling one to create nonvirtuous karma.

Meditating on this point opposes any belief that a state of temporary or partial elimination of suffering—such as a meditative absorption or zoning out in a thoughtless state—is liberation. If delusions and problems arise after being in such a state, it's clear that it is not the nirvana spoken of in Buddhism.

4. Definite emergence

Nirvana is a state of liberation that is irreversible; once attained, it will never be lost. A person who has attained nirvana has utterly abandoned all the causes of suffering—ignorance, craving, and the other delusions—and no longer creates karma to take rebirth. Therefore, they will never again be born in samsara, nor experience any of its sufferings.

Meditating on this point counteracts the idea that nirvana, once attained, is reversible—that you could fall back from it. Have you ever entertained such a notion?

Conclusion

After meditating on these four aspects, feel the wish to attain true cessations and resolve to develop their causes: the three higher trainings, especially the wisdom directly realizing emptiness. Generate the determination to increase your knowledge and understanding of true cessations and nirvana so you can clearly differentiate these from other states that may appear similar.

FOUR ASPECTS OF TRUE PATHS

True paths are the realizations that enable us to attain true cessations. The principal true path is the wisdom directly realizing selflessness; it is the ultimate antidote to ignorance and the other delusions that cause suffering. According to the Prasangika school, true paths are either the wisdom directly realizing the emptiness of inherent existence of all phenomena, or another realization conjoined with that wisdom. That wisdom is the opposite state of mind to the ignorance grasping things as inherently existent and is thus able to eliminate it.

To better understand true paths, contemplate its four aspects.

1. Path

The wisdom directly realizing selflessness is a path because it leads out of samsara and to the state of liberation, nirvana. Although we might be far from this realization, contemplate that many others—the Buddha and great masters of the past and present—have attained it and have been able to attest to its efficacy. If we continue learning, contemplating, and meditating on selflessness, we can gain that experience as well.

Meditating on this aspect counteracts the idea that there are no paths that lead out of samsara—in simple terms, thinking there is nothing we can do to free ourselves from suffering and its causes. If you have this notion, check your reasons. Since many others have been able to achieve liberation, can you prove that it is not true?

2. Suitable

This wisdom is suitable for us to learn about and meditate on because it is the antidote to ignorance, the root cause of suffering. It may be difficult to appreciate this now, but many people have found that even an initial exploration of emptiness helps them see things in a more realistic and beneficial way. As Lama Yeshe would say, it softens the "concrete view" we normally have of things. We are less likely to get caught up in our delusions and unrealistic projections and will experience a lessening of our suffering. See if you can recall any such experience.

Meditating on this point counteracts the notion that meditating on selflessness is not a path to liberation. Recall if this is an idea you have ever held, and consider how this aspect could have counteracted that notion.

3. Achievement

This wisdom realizing emptiness is also an achievement because it realizes the true nature of the mind directly and unmistakably. The true nature of the mind is its emptiness of inherent existence, according to the Prasangika. As long as we do not realize this, we will continue to hold mistaken notions about our mind, such as grasping it as independently and objectively existent. These views obstruct our attainment of liberation and enlightenment. What are your ideas about your mind? Do you think you understand it correctly?

Meditating on this point counteracts the idea that some mundane path—such as ascetic practices, taking hallucinogenic substances, or the meditative absorptions of the form and formless realms—is the path to liberation. Although concentration is an essential element of the paths to liberation and enlightenment, it can only temporarily suppress the delusions but not eradicate them from the root. Only the wisdom directly realizing selflessness has the power to do that.

4. Deliverance

The wisdom directly realizing selflessness is a way of deliverance because it completely eradicates suffering and its causes such that they will never occur again, and thus enables us to attain the state of irreversible liberation. Contemplate that this is possible because ignorance, the root of all suffering, is a misapprehension of things—seeing phenomena as inherently, independently existent—while the wisdom of selflessness sees things correctly—as empty of inherent existence and dependent on other factors for their existence. If we familiarize ourselves with dependent arising and other reasonings that prove emptiness, we too can gain this wisdom and free our minds from ignorance and all other factors that cause suffering.

Meditating on this point counteracts the notion that there is no path that can totally eradicate suffering. Have you ever come across such a view, and if so, did you accept it as true?

Conclusion

After contemplating these four aspects, generate the aspiration to attain true paths, recognizing that they are the antidote to the principal cause of suffering: the ignorance that does not see things as they are. Realistically, it can take many years or even lifetimes to attain the wisdom directly realizing selflessness, but we can begin taking small steps in that direction by listening to teachings on this topic, studying and discussing it with Dharma friends, and thinking about it. Slowly, gradually, our understanding will grow and start to exert a positive influence on our way of thinking and living our life, bringing benefit to ourselves and those around us.

Dedication

Return to the practice of lamrim meditation, dissolve the visualization, and finally dedicate the merits of your meditation to the happiness, well-being, and enlightenment of all sentient beings.

The sixteen aspects of the four noble truths and the misconceptions they dispel

Truth	Aspect	Misconception dispelled
True sufferings, such as our body and mind	*Impermanence:* Our body and mind change each moment.	Seeing what is impermanent as permanent, in the sense of being unchanging.
	Suffering/ unsatisfactoriness: Our body and mind experience discomfort, pain, sickness, aging, and eventual death.	Seeing samsaric things like our body and mind as pure and pleasurable.
	Empty: Our body-mind complex lacks a permanent, unitary, and independent self.	Seeing our body-mind complex as having a self, "I," or soul that does not change, is not made of parts, and does not depend on causes and conditions.
	Selfless: Our body-mind complex lacks a self-sufficient, substantially existent self.	Seeing true sufferings as having a self-sufficient, substantially existent self, or as objects used by such a self.
True origins— delusions and karma	*Cause:* Delusions and karma are the main cause of suffering.	Thinking that suffering is causeless.
	Origins: Delusions and karma produce suffering again and again.	Thinking that suffering has only one cause.
	Strong production: Delusions and karma produce suffering forcefully.	Thinking that suffering is produced by others, such as a creator.
	Condition: Delusions and karma are also conditions for suffering.	Thinking that suffering is permanent but its states are changeable.

Truth	Aspect	Misconception dispelled
True cessations—principally, nirvana	*Cessation:* Nirvana is the complete cessation of suffering because its main causes (ignorance and the other delusions) have been eliminated.	Thinking there is no liberation from samsara.
	Peace: Nirvana is peace because it is a state in which delusions have been abandoned.	Thinking that nirvana is a state that is still in samsara.
	Sublimeness: There is nothing more sublime, blissful, and beneficial than nirvana.	Thinking that a state of temporary or partial elimination of suffering is nirvana.
	Definite emergence: Nirvana is irreversible.	Thinking that nirvana is reversible, that you could fall back from it.
True paths—principally, the wisdom directly realizing selflessness	*Path:* The wisdom directly realizing selflessness is a path that leads out of samsara and to nirvana.	Thinking there are no paths leading out of samsara.
	Suitable: This path is suitable for us to learn and meditate on because it is the antidote to ignorance.	Thinking that meditating on selflessness is not a path to liberation.
	Achievement: This wisdom is an achievement because it realizes the true nature of the mind directly and unmistakably.	Thinking that a mundane path (such as the *dhyanas*) is the path to liberation.
	Deliverance. This wisdom is a way of deliverance because it utterly eradicates suffering and its causes and leads to liberation.	Thinking there is no path that can totally eradicate suffering.

APPENDIX 4
Results of Nonvirtuous Karma

THE CHAPTER on karma in part 3 included a meditation on the results of karma, explaining three types of results of an action that is complete with all four factors:

1. *Ripened result.* This is the rebirth we will experience in a future life as a result of that karma.

2. *Results similar to the cause.* These are of two types:
    i. *Experiences similar to the cause.* These are experiences we will have in a later life that are similar to our past behavior toward others.
    ii. *Actions similar to the cause.* This is the instinctive tendency to commit that same action again.

3. *Environmental results.* Living in an environment with certain types of pleasant or unpleasant conditions, depending on the nature of the original action.

In that chapter, the nonvirtuous action of harsh speech was used to illustrate the three types of results. The chart below shows the results of all ten nonvirtuous actions, with the exception of two types of results:

- their *ripened results*, given that the ripened result of a complete nonvirtuous action is always rebirth in an unfortunate realm; and

- their *results similar to the cause in terms of actions*, since these are always the tendency to commit the same action again.

Thus only the remaining two types of results—*results similar to the cause in terms of experience* and the *environmental results*—are shown in the chart.

Results of Nonvirtuous Karma

ACTION	RESULTS SIMILAR TO THE CAUSE IN TERMS OF EXPERIENCE	ENVIRONMENTAL RESULTS
Killing	In a later human life, you will have a short life, poor health, and little or no success in your activities.	Living in a place with violence, war, and many problems. Food, drink, and medicine are not potent.
Stealing	Lack of wealth and resources; your things are stolen or lost.	Living in a barren place where there are many natural disasters, shortages of food, and business ventures fail.
Unwise and unkind sexual conduct	Relationship problems; having to separate from relatives, friends, and so on.	Living in an unclean, foul-smelling place.
Lying	Others do not believe you even when you tell the truth.	Living among people who lie and cheat, and your efforts to support yourself constantly fail.
Divisive speech	Loneliness; having difficulty making friends; being divided from friends.	Living in a rugged, uneven, inhospitable place where travel and communication are difficult.
Harsh speech	You are verbally abused and criticized; when you speak pleasantly, others interpret your words negatively.	Living in a dry, barren place filled with thorns, sharp rocks, many broken things, and dangerous creatures.
Idle talk	Others will not listen to you or take you seriously.	Living in place where crops do not grow properly, rain falls at the wrong time, and activities are not successful.
Covetousness	You will be unable to achieve your aims and obtain what you wish for.	Living in a place with poor crops and material resources are easily destroyed or lost.

Action	Results similar to the cause in terms of experience	Environmental results
Harmful intent	You will be a person who is easily frightened and anxious for no reason.	Living in a place where there is much violence, war, and contagious disease.
Wrong views	You will be ignorant of what is correct and will find it difficult to develop understanding and realizations of the Dharma.	Living in a place where food and water are scarce and there are no precious things such as religious works of art, scriptures, and spiritual teachers.

APPENDIX 5
Mental Factors

A MENTAL FACTOR is an aspect of mind that always accompanies a main mind and apprehends specific features of its object. Main minds are also called primary minds or consciousnesses, and are of six types, related to our six senses: eye consciousness, ear consciousness, nose consciousness, tongue consciousness, body consciousness, and mental consciousness. Main minds can never occur on their own without mental factors that accompany them. For example, when we see or hear something, together with the main mind that perceives the mere presence of the object, there are various mental factors that discern its unique characteristics, experience it as pleasant or unpleasant, and so on. When we look at a flower, for instance, there is an eye consciousness—a main mind—and a number of mental factors accompanying it. The eye consciousness knows the mere presence of the object, the flower, and the mental factors engage with it in different ways: *feeling* experiences it as pleasant, unpleasant, or neutral; *discrimination* distinguishes the flower from other types of objects, like birds; and if *attachment* is present, it sees the flower as a source of happiness and wants to possess it. In Tibetan Buddhism fifty-one mental factors are studied, although this is not an exhaustive list.

The fifty-one mental factors are divided into six categories: (1) five ever-present mental factors, (2) five object-ascertaining mental factors, (3) eleven virtuous mental factors, (4) six root delusions, (5) twenty secondary delusions, and (6) four changeable mental factors. Below you will find a brief description of these categories and the mental factors included in them, with the exception of the six root delusions—ignorance, attachment, anger, arrogance, deluded doubt, and deluded views, which were explained in the chapter on true origins of suffering (page 138).

You may find it helpful to see if you can identify the eleven virtuous mental factors and the twenty secondary delusions in your own experience. Can you also identify the causes and conditions that lead to their arising? What is their effect on your actions of body, speech, and mind? Are they mental states you wish to strengthen or to abandon?

Five Ever-Present Mental Factors

Five mental factors accompany all main minds and are needed to fully cognize or apprehend an object. They are ethically neutral but become virtuous or nonvirtuous when accompanied by another mental factor that is either virtuous or nonvirtuous.

1. *Feeling* experiences the object as pleasant, unpleasant, or neutral. It experiences the ripened results of our past actions and can lead to attachment, anger, and confusion.
2. *Discrimination* apprehends the characteristics of an object and can distinguish it from other objects—for instance, distinguishing blue from yellow, or a cat from a cow.
3. *Intention* moves the mind to an object and causes the mind to get involved with it. Intention is action, karma.
4. *Attention* directs the mind to an object and focuses the mind on that object without allowing it to move elsewhere. It differs from intention in that intention moves the mind to general objects, such as a garden, while attention directs the mind to particular objects, a flower or leaf.
5. *Contact* brings together the three main conditions for a sensory experience: object, sense power, and consciousness. It distinguishes objects as attractive, unattractive, or neutral and leads to feelings.

Five Object-Ascertaining Mental Factors

Five other mental factors apprehend the individual features of an object. Some scholars say they are ethically neutral and can become virtuous or nonvirtuous when they are accompanied and influenced by other mental factors that are virtuous or nonvirtuous. Other scholars say they accompany only virtuous mental states; they are not virtuous themselves but become so when associated with a virtuous state of mind.

1. *Aspiration* focuses on a desired object and takes a strong interest in it. It is the basis for joyous effort.
2. *Appreciation* firmly holds a previously ascertained object and does not let the mind be distracted elsewhere.
3. *Mindfulness* does not forget a familiar object and repeatedly brings it to mind. It is the basis for concentration.
4. *Concentration* remains one-pointedly on its object. It is the basis for developing calm abiding and for increasing wisdom.
5. *Wisdom* thoroughly discerns the positive and negative qualities of an object. Different types of wisdom were explained in the chapter on the perfection of wisdom; see page 270.

Eleven Virtuous Mental Factors

When any of the eleven virtuous mental factors arise in the mind, they cause the main mind and other mental factors in that same mental state to likewise become virtuous. Being virtuous means they are the cause of happiness and peace, for oneself and others. They are also antidotes to particular delusions.

1. *Faith* is confidence in such things as karma and the Three Jewels; it is the antidote to non-faith. It makes the mind joyful and free from disturbing emotions. There are three kinds of faith: (1) *faith of conviction,* which knows the qualities of the object and has confidence in it; (2) *admiring faith,* which knows the qualities of the object and rejoices in them; and (3) *aspiring faith,* which knows the qualities of the object and aspires to attain them.
2. *Integrity*—sometimes translated as *sense of shame*—refrains from nonvirtue out of self-respect or for the sake of one's spiritual tradition.
3. *Consideration for others*—sometimes translated as *sense of embarrassment*—refrains from nonvirtue out of consideration for others, such as one's parents, teachers, and so on.
4. *Nonattachment* is the opposite of attachment and the antidote to it. For example, regarding an object in cyclic existence, such as chocolate, nonattachment prevents and counteracts attachment to it by understanding its true nature.
5. *Nonhatred* is the opposite of anger and hatred. It is love and

benevolence. For instance, regarding a person who harms oneself or others, nonhatred prevents hatred and increases love and patience.

6. *Nonconfusion*, or *nonignorance*, is the opposite of confusion and ignorance. It can arise from an inborn disposition, study, reflection, or meditation, and acts as a remedy for confusion and ignorance.

7. *Joyous effort* delights in virtue and counteracts laziness.

8. *Pliancy* is mental suppleness or flexibility that enables the mind to focus on a constructive object for an extended period of time, free of mental or physical rigidity.

9. *Conscientiousness* cherishes virtue, familiarizes the mind with virtue, and guards the mind against nonvirtue. It prevents the mind from being overwhelmed by delusions such as anger, attachment, jealousy, and so on.

10. *Equanimity* is the antidote to restlessness and laxity. It enables the mind to settle on a virtuous object and is essential for the development of calm abiding.

11. *Nonharmfulness* is compassion: wishing sentient beings to be free from suffering. It prevents disrespecting or harming others and increases the wish to benefit them.

Six Root Delusions

The six root delusions were explained in the chapter on true origins of suffering in part 4; see pages 139–41.

Twenty Secondary Delusions

Twenty secondary delusions are branches of the root delusions—in particular, the three poisons of anger, attachment, and ignorance—and arise in dependence on them. Like the root delusions, they disturb the mind and can lead to nonvirtuous karma. Below they are grouped according to which root delusion they derive from.

Five secondary delusions derived from anger

1. *Wrath*—or belligerence, aggression—is due to an increase in anger; this mental factor wishes to cause immediate harm to others.

2. *Vengeance*—or resentment, grudge-holding—firmly holds on to past harm done by another, does not forget it, and wishes to retaliate.

3. *Spite* is preceded by wrath or vengeance and wants to speak harsh words in response to unpleasant words said by others.

4. *Jealousy,* or envy, is a type of anger that, out of attachment to respect or material gain, cannot bear others' good things and accomplishments and feels resentful about them.

5. *Harmfulness,* or cruelty, is a type of anger that, with a malicious intention devoid of any compassion or kindness, desires to inflict harm on others.

Three secondary delusions derived from attachment

1. *Miserliness* is a mental factor that, out of attachment to respect or material gain, firmly holds onto one's possessions with no wish to give them away.

2. *Complacency*—or haughtiness, self-satisfaction—is a type of attachment that, being attentive to our accomplishments and good qualities, generates a deluded sense of confidence.

3. *Excitement*—or agitation, restlessness—is a type of attachment that does not allow the mind to remain focused on a virtuous object but scatters it here and there to many other objects.

Six secondary delusions derived from ignorance

1. *Concealment* is a type of ignorance that wants to hide one's faults when another person talks about them with a beneficial motivation.

2. *Dullness*—or lethargy, foggy mindedness—is a type of ignorance that makes the mind lethargic and dark so it cannot comprehend its object clearly.

3. *Laziness* is a type of ignorance that, having firmly grasped an object offering temporary happiness, either does not wish to do anything virtuous, or although wishing to, is weak-hearted.

4. *Lack of faith* is a type of ignorance that does not believe, does not have admiration for, and does not aspire to the qualities of virtuous objects. It is the opposite of faith.

5. *Forgetfulness* is a mental factor that, having caused the apprehension of a virtuous object to be lost, induces memory of and distraction toward nonvirtuous objects.

6. *Non-introspective awareness* is a type of deluded intelligence that is not fully alert to one's actions of body, speech, and mind, and thus causes one to become carelessly indifferent.

Two secondary delusions derived from both attachment and ignorance

1. *Pretension* is a type of ignorance or attachment that, motivated by attachment to respect or material gain, wants to pretend to have qualities one does not have.
2. *Dishonesty*—or dissimulation—is a type of ignorance or attachment that, motivated by attachment to respect or material gain, does not want others to know one's shortcomings.

Four secondary delusions derived from all three poisons

1. *Lack of integrity* is a type of ignorance, anger, or attachment that is devoid of shame; it does not avoid nonvirtue out of self-respect or for the sake of one's spiritual tradition.
2. *Inconsideration for others* is a type of ignorance, anger, or attachment that is devoid of consideration for other sentient beings, lacking embarrassment; it does not avoid nonvirtue out of consideration for others.
3. *Nonconscientiousness,* also known as heedlessness or recklessness, manifests along with one of the three poisons and with laziness and wishes to act in an unrestrained manner without cultivating virtue or guarding the mind against contaminated phenomena.
4. *Distraction* is a type of anger, attachment, or ignorance that, being unable to direct the mind to a virtuous object, disperses it to a variety of other objects.

FOUR CHANGEABLE MENTAL FACTORS

Four mental factors are called "changeable" because on their own, they are neither virtuous, nonvirtuous, or neutral but become so in dependence on our motivation and the other mental factors that accompany the same mental state.

1. *Sleep* is a mental factor that withdraws the five sense consciousnesses inward and makes the mind unclear and unable to apprehend the body.

2. *Regret* feels remorse for actions of body, speech, or mind we did in the past. Regretting misdeeds is virtuous but regretting virtuous actions, such as an act of generosity, is nonvirtuous.

3. *Investigation* roughly examines the general nature of an object.

4. *Analysis* thoroughly examines the detailed nature of an object.

Appendix 6
Verses from Shantideva on the Disadvantages of Delusions

THE FOLLOWING collection of verses from chapter 4 of Shanti-deva's *A Guide to the Bodhisattva's Way of Life* can be used to supplement the meditation on the disadvantages of delusions in part 4 of this book.[119]

> 28
> Although enemies such as hatred and craving
> have neither any arms nor legs,
> and are neither courageous nor wise,
> how have I been used like a slave by them?

> 29
> For while they dwell within my mind
> at their pleasure they cause me harm,
> yet I patiently endure them without any anger;
> but this is an inappropriate and shameful time for patience.

> 32
> All other enemies are incapable
> of remaining for such a length of time
> as can my disturbing conceptions,
> the long-time enemy with neither beginning nor end.

> 33
> If I agreeably honor and entrust myself (to others)
> they will bring me benefit and happiness,
> but if I entrust myself to these disturbing conceptions
> in future they will bring only misery and harm.

44

It would be better for me to be burned,
to have my head cut off and to be killed,
rather than ever bowing down
to those ever-present disturbing conceptions.

46

Deluded disturbing conceptions! When forsaken by the eye
    of wisdom
and dispelled from my mind, where will you go?
Where will you dwell in order to be able to injure me again?
But, weak-minded, I have been reduced to making no effort.

47

If these disturbing conceptions do not exist within the
objects, the sense organs, between the two nor elsewhere,
then where do they exist and how do they harm the world?
They are like an illusion—thus I should dispel the fear
within my heart and strive resolutely for wisdom.
For no real reason, why should I suffer so much in hell?

APPENDIX 7
Using the Lamrim to Work with Problems

IN ADDITION to bringing us closer to enlightenment, lamrim meditations can also be used to manage our everyday problems—both personal ones as well as difficult emotions we might feel in response to societal and global issues. They help us develop more realistic and constructive ways of thinking that are counterforces to anger, fear, depression, jealousy, and so on. Below are some suggested ways you could use meditations in this book to deal with such difficulties.

1. *Meditation on the breath* (page 31). When we face problems, our mind can get lost in a flurry of thoughts and feelings, many of which are not helpful and may even make things worse. Sitting down and focusing on the breath for a while can bring calmness and clarity to the mind so we can look at things more rationally and explore genuine solutions.

2. *The nature of mind* (page 45). This meditation helps us see that thoughts and emotions are not permanent parts of us but rather things that come and go in the mind, like clouds in the sky. The nature of the mind is always clear, pure, and rich in potential. Those qualities can never be lost or damaged, no matter how confused or negative we may sometimes feel.

3. *Precious human life* (page 51). Problems can overwhelm us and make us lose sight of the positive aspects of our life and our potential, so contemplating these can restore mental balance and optimism.

4. *Impermanence* (page 80). Disturbing thoughts, emotions, and problems are transient; they do not last forever. Recognizing this bestows inner peace and patience.

5. *Refuge* (page 89). The buddhas and other objects of refuge are always compassionately aware of us and our suffering and are ready to help. Asking for their guidance can help us discover solutions. Just

thinking of them can bring comfort. Lama Zopa Rinpoche has said, "You are never alone: everywhere, all the time there are numberless buddhas and bodhisattvas surrounding you, loving you, guiding you—after all, that is what they do."[120]

6. *Karma* (page 101). Problems are the result of our past unwholesome behavior. Accepting this prevents us from blaming others and enables us to take responsibility. If we don't want more problems in the future, we need to avoid nonvirtuous karma and engage in virtuous karma as much as possible.

7. *Sufferings of samsara* (page 125). The nature of samsara, the situation we are trapped in, is *duhkha*—suffering and unsatisfactoriness—so why be surprised when problems happen? Although it's normal to feel upset when they occur, it is more skillful to put our energy into freeing ourselves and others from suffering and its causes.

8. *The origins of suffering* (page 137). Suffering and problems are the results of causes and conditions, mainly delusions. Investigate your mind to identify which delusions lie behind your current problem and apply antidotes to these.

9. *Cultivating bodhichitta* (page 171). Contemplating the suffering of others helps us view our problems more constructively; we see that we are not the only person who has them, that some have greater problems than ours, and that it's important to not despair but arouse courage, compassion, and altruism to do what we can to relieve others' misery and bring them genuine happiness. It's also helpful to recognize the role self-centeredness plays in our problems and work on decreasing that attitude and increasing its opposite: cherishing others.

10. *Taking and giving (tonglen)* (page 221). The meditation on tonglen for one's own suffering is a quick solution to any problem you might encounter. Tonglen for others' suffering is a particularly effective meditation for the problems and difficulties of other people we know or hear about, such as victims of war and natural disasters.

11. *The perfection of giving* (page 231). Giving material aid and doing volunteer work are beneficial to ourselves as well as others—we feel happier, more useful, and less likely to be caught in depression and despair.

12. *The perfection of ethics* (page 237). Living ethically, which starts with refraining from nonvirtue and engaging in virtue, is a wonderful contribution we can make to peace in society and the world.

13. *The patience of disregarding harm* (page 246). Here you will find numerous methods for working with anger, one of the most harmful delusions, both for oneself and others.

14. *The patience of voluntarily accepting suffering* (page 250). Problems don't have to cause us misery; they can even be brought into the path to enlightenment, helping us grow spiritually. Various methods for doing this are presented under this topic.

15. *The patience of certainty about the Dharma* (page 254). This is an effective remedy to problems related to our spiritual practice such as discouragement, boredom, and thoughts of giving it up.

16. *The perfection of wisdom* (page 269). Although more difficult to comprehend than other remedies, meditations on dependent arising, selflessness, and emptiness are the most powerful as they target the root of all problems: ignorance about the way things exist. You can use these meditations in regard to the object of the problem—another person, for example—or yourself, the one experiencing the problem.

17. *The meditations on the breath* (page 31) and *nature of mind* (page 45). Both these meditations are effective for fear and anxiety. Taking refuge provides relief for some people as well. For an analytical approach to facing and dealing with fear, see the section on "Feeling Safer" in chapter 5 of Rick Hanson's book *Buddha's Brain*.

Notes

1. See, for example, *Relative Truth, Ultimate Truth* by Geshe Tashi Tsering (Somerville, MA: Wisdom Publications, 2008), *Appearance and Reality* by Guy Newland (Ithaca, NY: Snow Lion Publications, 1999), and *Appearing and Empty* by the Dalai Lama and Thubten Chodron (Somerville, MA: Wisdom Publications, 2023).

2. In Buddhist scriptures, the term "enlightenment" is sometimes used for both nirvana, liberation from samsara, and the fully enlightened state of a buddha. In this book, this term is used for the latter state, and "liberation" is used for the former, as in "liberation and enlightenment."

3. Geshe Jampa Tegchok, *Transforming Adversity into Joy and Courage* (Ithaca, NY: Snow Lion Publications, 1999), 50. Tegchok received the title Khensur, "abbot emeritus," after serving as abbot of Sera Jey Monastery in India from 1993 to 2000, and this title was included in his later books.

4. Tegchok, *Transforming Adversity*, 50. His comment "that is not necessary" probably means that we should do our best to concentrate, even if it's not always single-pointed, as mentioned on p. 11: "if our ability to concentrate is still limited, we do our best to keep our mind focused on the topic and bring it back when it wanders away."

5. Rick Hanson, *Buddha's Brain* (Oakland, CA: New Harbinger Publications, 2009), 67–77.

6. Kathleen McDonald, *How to Meditate*, 2nd ed. (Somerville, MA: Wisdom Publications, 2005).

7. An e-booklet with instructions on how to set up an altar and make waterbowl offerings is available from FPMT: https://shop.fpmt.org/The-Preliminary-Practice-of-Altar-Set-up-Water-Bowl-Offerings-eBook-PDF_p_2577.html.

8. Further information about purification can be found in the chapter on karma in part 3.

9. The order of the two—requesting the buddhas to not pass away and requesting them to teach the Dharma—is sometimes reversed.

10. This point is related to emptiness, explained in chapter 23.

11. Pabongka Rinpoche, *Liberation in the Palm of Your Hand* (Somerville, MA: Wisdom Publications, 2006).

12. The Dalai Lama and Thubten Chodron, *The Foundation of Buddhist Practice* (Somerville, MA: Wisdom Publications, 2018), 173–74.

13. Bhikkhu Anālayo, *Rebirth in Early Buddhism and Current Research* (Somerville, MA: Wisdom Publications, 2018), 5–35.

14. As this advice may not be sufficient for those experiencing severe or chronic pain, additional tips on dealing with pain can be found in Bhante Gunaratana *Mindfulness in Plain English* (Somerville, MA: Wisdom Publications, 2002), 97–103.

15. The Buddha's mantra can be explained as follows:
    tadyatha: Thus
    om: the enlightened state; the positive qualities of the buddhas' body, speech, and mind
    muni: control—over unfortunate rebirths and self-grasping ignorance
    muni: control—over the sufferings of cyclic existence and the self-cherishing attitude
    maha muniye: great control—over the sufferings of subtle illusions and dualistic thinking
    svaha: may my mind receive, absorb, and keep the blessings of the mantra, and may they take root in my mind

16. Extracted with permission from Geshe Sonam Rinchen, *The Three Principal Aspects of the Path: An Oral Teaching*, translated and edited by Ruth Sonam (Ithaca, NY: Snow Lion Publications, 1999).

17. See, for example, the work of Pim van Lommel, Jeffrey Long, Ian Stevenson, and Jim Tucker.

18. Hanson, *Buddha's Brain*, 10–11.

19. See the Dalai Lama and Thubten Chodron, *The Foundation of Buddhist Practice*, chapter 7, for a discussion about the differing views of mind in Buddhism and science.

20. *Pabhassara Sutta*, Anguttara Nikaya (AN) 1.49–50, as translated by Bhikkhu Bodhi in *The Numerical Discourses of the Buddha* (Somerville, MA: Wisdom Publications, 2012), 97.

21. See the Dalai Lama and Thubten Chodron, *Saṃsāra, Nirvāṇa, and Buddha Nature* (Somerville, MA: Wisdom Publications, 2018), chapters 12–14.

22. Various Buddhist scriptures explain this freedom in different ways, as mentioned in Tsong-Kha-pa's *The Great Treatise on the Stages of the Path to Enlightenment*, vol. 1 (Ithaca, NY: Snow Lion Publications, 2000), 118–19. For example, it sometimes refers to freedom from rebirth in the formless realm. Also, within the various god realms are aryas, beings who have directly realized emptiness. They take birth in these realms to continue practicing the path to enlightenment, so they are not included in this unfree state.

23. According to data from the mathematician and animal rights advocate Brian Tomasik, the total number of individual animals on the earth is approximately 20,000,121,091,000,000,000; see https://animals.mom.com/number-animals-earth-3994.html.

24. Majjhima Nikaya (MN) 129, as translated by Bhikkhu Bodhi in *The Middle-Length Discourses of the Buddha* (Somerville, MA: Wisdom Publications, 1995), 1021.

25. Pabongka Rinpoche, *Liberation in the Palm of Your Hand* (Somerville, MA: Wisdom Publications, 2006), 282.

26. The Dalai Lama and Thubten Chodron, *The Foundation of Buddhist Practice*, 199.

27. AN 8.5, in Bodhi, *The Numerical Discourses of the Buddha*, 1116.

28. See Lama Zopa Rinpoche, *How to Practice Dharma* (Lincoln, MA: Lama Yeshe Wisdom Archives, 2012), for extensive teachings on the eight worldly concerns.

29. Translation by Brian Beresford in Geshe Rabten and Geshe Dhargyey's *Advice from a Spiritual Friend* (Somerville, MA: Wisdom Publications, 1996), 3.

30. Tibetan: *bardo*. This is the period between the end of one life and birth in the next life. It can last anywhere from one second to forty-nine days.

31. Devas, also known as suras or gods, live in various celestial realms and have less suffering and greater happiness than do human beings. Asuras, also known as demigods, have less opportune circumstances than devas and frequently start wars with them due to jealousy.

32. Shantideva, *A Guide to the Bodhisattva's Way of Life*, translated by Stephen Batchelor (Dharamsala, India: Library of Tibetan Works and Archives, 1979), verses 5.7–8, 35.

33. Details about virtue and nonvirtue and methods for purification are explained in chapter 10.

34. Note that *preta* is Sanskrit for hungry ghost.

35. Quoted in the Dalai Lama and Thubten Chodron, *Approaching the Buddhist Path* (Somerville, MA: Wisdom Publications, 2017), 202.

36. The second and third levels of concern or fear will become clearer as you learn about and practice the meditations included in the intermediate and advanced levels of the lamrim.

37. When you feel confident about committing yourself to the Buddhist path you can do so in a refuge ceremony with a qualified teacher. However, it is also fine to make such a commitment on your own in front of an image of the Buddha, actual or imagined.

38. In the context of karma, the ignorance that makes an action nonvirtuous is ignorance of the workings of karma, rather than the ignorance that grasps things as inherently existent. The latter type of ignorance is not necessarily nonvirtuous because it can motivate virtuous actions, such as prostrating to the Buddha while viewing him as inherently existent.

39. Gareth Sparham, trans., *The Tibetan Dhammapada* (London: Wisdom Publications, 1986), verses 25–6, 140. This book is a translation of the *Compilations of Indicative Verse* (*Udānavarga*).

40. Sparham, *The Tibetan Dhammapada*, verse 7, 68.

41. An explanation of purification practice can be found at the end of this chapter.

42. See the Dalai Lama and Thubten Chodron, *The Foundation of Buddhist Practice*, 254–58, for details about the weight of karma.

43. Traditional lamrim texts mention only speaking, not writing. I asked Geshe Dadul Namgyal about creating nonvirtuous karma through writing (letters, emails, books, articles, social media posts, and so on), and he agreed that all the four nonvirtues of speech can also be created by writing.

44. A chart showing the results of all ten nonvirtuous actions can be found in appendix 4.

45. *Four noble truths* is the best-known translation for these, but a more accurate

rendering of the Sanskrit and Tibetan terms is *four truths of aryas*, or noble beings.

46. In addition to the meditations in this section, appendix 3 contains a meditation on sixteen aspects of the four noble truths, which further enhances our understanding of those truths.

47. Methods for alleviating problems and using them in the spiritual path can be found in the chapter on the perfection of patience, in part 5.

48. *Dhammacakkappavattana Sutta*, or *Setting in Motion the Wheel of the Dhamma*, Samyutta Nikaya (SN) 56.11, as translated by Bhikkhu Bodhi in *The Connected Discourses of the Buddha* (Somerville, MA: Wisdom Publications, 2000), 1844.

49. The meditation on the twelve links, in appendix 2, explains the process whereby contaminated aggregates arise from karma and delusions.

50. A translation of this text by Alexander Berzin is available online at http://studybuddhism.com/en/tibetan-buddhism/original-texts/sutra-texts/letter-to-a-friend.

51. SN 45.165, in Bodhi, *The Connected Discourses of the Buddha*, 156.

52. See the Dalai Lama and Thubten Chodron, *The Foundation of Buddhist Practice*, 59–68, and Geshe Rabten, *Mind and Its Functions* (Le Mont-Pélerin, Switzerland: Editions Rabten Choeling, 1992).

53. Additional antidotes for anger, attachment, and other disturbing emotions can be found in my book *How to Meditate* and in the Dalai Lama and Thubten Chodron's *Saṃsāra, Nirvāṇa, and Buddha Nature*, 112–19.

54. Appendix 2 contains a meditation on the twelve links, a detailed explanation of the process whereby we take repeated rebirth in samsara.

55. This explanation of the ignorance that is the root of samsara is according to the Prasangika school of Buddhist philosophy, which most Tibetans follow. Other schools of Buddhist philosophy explain ignorance and the root of samsara in different ways. See the Dalai Lama and Thubten Chodron, *Saṃsāra, Nirvāṇa, and Buddha Nature*, 73–76.

56. For the Prasangikas, this is also a type of the ignorance that is the root of samsara.

57. The twenty secondary delusions are explained in appendix 5.

58. Shantideva, *A Guide*, translated by Stephen Batchelor, verses 4.28, 29.

59. Methods for cultivating these constructive mental states are explained in part 5.

60. See the chapter on the perfection of patience in part 5 for further information about the meaning of patience and how to cultivate it.

61. More information on the eight stages can be found in Lati Rinpochay and Jeffrey Hopkins, *Death, Intermediate State, and Rebirth in Tibetan Buddhism* (Ithaca, NY: Snow Lion Publications, 1985) and the Dalai Lama and Jeffrey Hopkins, *Advice on Dying and Living a Better Life* (New York: Atria Books, 2002). A more extensive meditation on these stages composed by Roshi Joan Halifax can be found at https://www.upaya.org/dox/dissolution.pdf.

62. The four elements are not particles of earth, water, and so on as we normally perceive them. They are properties of all physical phenomena: the

earth element is the property of solidity; the water element is the property of cohesion; the fire element is the property of heat; and the air element is the property of expansion.

63. The Pali tradition explains true paths in terms of the noble eightfold path. Taught by the Buddha in his first discourse, these eight are an elaboration of the three higher trainings.

64. MN 135.20, in Bodhi, *The Middle-Length Discourses of the Buddha*, 1057.

65. The Dalai Lama and Thubten Chodron, *In Praise of Great Compassion* (Somerville, MA: Wisdom Publications, 2020), 62–63. Recent studies on compassion confirm some of these benefits; see Thubten Jinpa, *A Fearless Heart* (New York: Avery, 2016), 11–23.

66. An alternative explanation given by some masters is that the first six steps are causes and the seventh, bodhichitta, is their result.

67. *Mata Sutta*, SN 15.14–19, in Bodhi, *The Connected Discourses of the Buddha*, 659.

68. Some Mahayana teachings say that those who strive for nirvana—that is, self-liberation—have self-cherishing because they do not wish to attain full enlightenment to benefit all beings. The Dalai Lama explains that this is a subtle form of self-centeredness that should be distinguished from the coarse form of selfishness that ordinary beings are afflicted with (*In Praise of Great Compassion*, 124).

69. The points in this book have been slightly modified to use contemporary examples. A more traditional explanation can be found in the Dalai Lama and Thubten Chodron, *In Praise of Great Compassion*, 119–22.

70. Shantideva, *A Guide*, translated by Stephen Batchelor, verse 8.129, 110.

71. See the Dalai Lama and Thubten Chodron, *The Foundation of Buddhist Practice*, chapter 11, for a detailed explanation on the results of karma, and appendix 4 in this book.

72. Shantideva, *A Guide*, translated by Stephen Batchelor, verse 8.129, 110.

73. Acharya Geshe Thubten Loden, *The Path to Enlightenment in Tibetan Buddhism* (Melbourne: Tushita Publications, 1993), 369–71, 561.

74. Shantideva, *A Guide*, translated by Stephen Batchelor, verse 6.14, 55.

75. See Shantideva, *A Guide*, translated by Stephen Batchelor, verses 8.90–100, 104–5, for additional reasons as to why we should be concerned about others' suffering.

76. Buddhist scriptures also list ten perfections, although there are variations in these lists. See the Dalai Lama and Thubten Chodron, *Courageous Compassion* (Somerville, MA: Wisdom Publications, 2021), chapters 1–3 and 5. In the Tibetan tradition, the four additional perfections—skillful means, prayer, power, and transcendental wisdom (Tibetan: *yeshe*)—are subsumed in the sixth, the perfection of wisdom.

77. Some teachers and texts say that to be a perfection, a practice also needs to be accompanied by the understanding of emptiness. More will be said about this in the chapter on the perfection of wisdom.

78. These are briefly explained in the meditation on the qualities of the Buddha, in the chapter on refuge, p. 89.

79. As translated in Batchelor 1979, verses 5.9–10, 35.

80. These include the five precepts taken by lay people—to avoid killing, stealing, lying, unwise and unkind sexual behavior, and taking intoxicants—and several levels of monastic precepts taken by monks and nuns.

81. Tsongkhapa, in his *Middle-Length Treatise on the Lamrim*, says: "The nature of patience is the mind abiding at ease without being overwhelmed by harm and suffering, as well as a very staunch belief in the Dharma." *The Middle-Length Treatise on the Stages of the Path to Enlightenment*, translated by Philip Quarcoo (Somerville, MA: Wisdom Publications, 2021), 254.

82. Verse 3.4. Quoted in *Compassion in Tibetan Buddhism*, translated and edited by Jeffrey Hopkins (Ithaca, NY: Snow Lion Publications, 1980), 207.

83. Feeling, the second of the five aggregates, is an ever-present mental factor. One of the three types of feeling—pleasant, unpleasant, and neutral—accompanies each of our experiences, whether sensory or mental. Feelings play a role in the arising of delusions: pleasant feeling usually leads to attachment and unpleasant feeling to aversion, while neutral feeling perpetuates ignorance.

84. *Sallatha Sutta*, SN 36.6.

85. Tsong-Kha-pa, *The Great Treatise on the Stages of the Path to Enlightenment*, vol. 2, translated by the Lamrim Chenmo Translation Committee (Boston: Snow Lion Publications, 2004), 172.

86. Shantideva, *A Guide*, translated by Stephen Batchelor, verse 6.10, 54.

87. The Happiness Blog, November 16, 2023, https://happyproject.in/non-religious-serenity-prayer/.

88. Geshe Lhundub Sopa, *Steps on the Path to Enlightenment*, vol. 3 (Somerville, MA: Wisdom Publications, 2008), 412.

89. Sopa, *Steps*, vol. 3, 412.

90. Sopa, *Steps*, vol. 3, 413–14.

91. Shantideva, *A Guide*, translated by Stephen Batchelor, verse 1.28, 5.

92. Quoted in Tsongkhapa, *Illuminating the Intent*, translated by Thupten Jinpa (Somerville, MA: Wisdom Publications, 2021), 159.

93. There are various Buddhist philosophical systems with different explanations of topics like selflessness and ultimate truth; the explanation here is according to Prasangika Madhyamaka, the system favored by most Tibetan traditions. For a clear survey of these Buddhist systems and their explanations of the two truths, see *Appearance and Reality* by Guy Newland (Ithaca, NY: Snow Lion Publications, 1999).

94. *Aryadeva's Four Hundred Stanzas on the Middle Way* with additional commentary by Geshe Sonam Rinchen, translated by Ruth Sonam (Ithaca, NY: Snow Lion Publications, 2008), verse 180, 188.

95. Quoted in *Pearl of Wisdom, Book 2* (Newport, WA: Sravasti Abbey, 2014), 85. Translation of the Sanskrit dharani: *om ye dharma hetu prabhava hetun teshan tathagato hy avadat / teshan ca yo nirodha evam vadi mahashramanah svaha*. Before he met the Buddha, Shariputra heard this recited by Ashvajit, a disciple of the Buddha. It enabled him to attain the direct realization of emptiness and become a stream-enterer; a short time later, he attained nirvana.

96. SN 5.10.544, quoted in the Dalai Lama and Thubten Chodron, *Realizing*

the Profound View (Somerville, MA: Wisdom Publications, 2022), 15. This is the response given by the bhikshuni (fully ordained nun) Vajira to Mara when he tried to interrupt her practice. This verse was used by Chandrakirti when he presented his sevenfold reasoning refuting inherent existence; for more, see *Realizing the Profound View*, 15–31.

97. Alexander Berzin, "Healthy Development of One's Self through Lam Rim," *Study Buddhism by Berzin Archives*. Recordings and a transcript of this seminar can be accessed at https://studybuddhism .com/en/advanced-studies/lam-rim/the-three-scopes/healthy-develop ment-of-one-s-self-through-lam-rim.

98. In Buddhist philosophy, the terms *person, self, being,* and *I* are synonymous and can be used to refer to all types of living beings, not only human beings. Pet owners will probably agree that their pets have personhood!

99. Khensur Jampa Tegchok, *Insight into Emptiness* (Somerville, MA: Wisdom Publications, 2012), 69.

100. Daniel Perdue writes: "Whatever is one with something must be one with that thing in both name and meaning; thus, what is one with something must be *exactly the same* as that phenomenon. This means that they are identical, not just the same in some way." Perdue, *The Course in Buddhist Reasoning and Debate* (Boston: Snow Lion Publications, 2014), 321.

101. Further explanations of the reasoning of the four essential points are found in Tegchok, *Insight into Emptiness*, 155–73; the Dalai Lama and Thubten Chodron, *Realizing the Profound View*, 104–13; and Paṇchen Losang Yeshé, *The Swift Path* (Somerville, MA: Wisdom Publications, 2023), 236–45.

102. The term "inherently" is added here because we are searching for an inherently existent "I," and if such a self does exist, it would have to be either inherently one with (absolutely the same in every way) or inherently different (completely separate from and unrelated to) the aggregates.

103. This is the case with two things that are *inherently existent* and different, but not with two things that are just different in a conventional sense. For example, a mother and her child are different conventionally but are still related and mutually dependent—the child would not exist without the mother, and the mother is only a mother because she gave birth to the child.

104. Shantideva, *A Guide*, translated by Stephen Batchelor, verse 10.55, 167.

105. For instance, based on advice from the Dalai Lama, Dagyab Rinpoche, founder of Tibethaus in Frankfurt, Germany, composed a lamrim text of sixty verses in which the topic of relying on spiritual teachers is placed at the end of the intermediate level of the lamrim.

106. The Dalai Lama and Thubten Chodron, *The Foundation of Buddhist Practice*, 118–26.

107. Alexander Berzin, *Wise Teacher, Wise Student* (Ithaca, NY: Snow Lion Publications, 2010). This book was originally published in 2000 as *Relating to a Spiritual Teacher*.

108. For more information on these ten, see the Dalai Lama and Thubten Chodron, *Foundation of Buddhist Practice*, 88–90.

109. This list, which differs somewhat from those mentioned in traditional

lamrim texts, is based on the list of benefits explained in the Dalai Lama and Thubten Chodron, *The Foundation of Buddhist Practice*, 102–3.

110. Many lamrim texts and commentaries explain this point of cultivating faith in the spiritual teacher to mean seeing him or her as a buddha. The Dalai Lama clarifies that this is the way of viewing spiritual teachers in tantra and that it should not be taught to beginners. He says there are three ways of relating to teachers according to three levels of practice: (1) at the initial level, students learn the four noble truths and the faults of samsara, and take refuge and the five lay precepts. At this level they regard their teachers as representatives of the Buddha. (2) Later, when learning and practicing the bodhisattva path, students should regard those who teach this path as emanations of the Buddha or high bodhisattvas. (3) Students who have a stable understanding and practice of the previous two levels and who wish to take an empowerment and engage in tantric practice should view their tantric master as a buddha. Tantric practice involves imagining oneself and all other beings as buddhas, so it would be strange not to see one's teachers as buddhas. See *The Foundation of Buddhist Practice*, 83–85. In a recent book, he further explains how this tantric practice became incorporated into lamrim commentaries and says that "the practice of lamrim from a purely sutric perspective and the practice of it combined with tantra should be separated." See *The Fourteenth Dalai Lama's Stages of the Path*, vol. 2, compiled and edited by H. E. Dagyab Kyabgön Rinpoche, translated by Sophie McGrath (New York: Wisdom Publications, 2023), 140–45.

111. For this sutra and a commentary to it, see Geshe Yeshe Thabkye, *The Rice Seedling Sutra*, translated by Joshua and Diana Cutler (Somerville, MA: Wisdom Publications, 2020); quote from a translation of the sutra by Jeffrey D. Schoening on p. 1.

112. These four factors were explained in the meditation on the results of karma, p. 108.

113. More details about the twelve links and the various ways they are explained can be found in the Dalai Lama and Thubten Chodron, *Saṃsāra, Nirvāṇa, and Buddha Nature*, chapters 7 and 8.

114. Tsong-Kha-pa, *The Great Treatise on the Stages of the Path to Enlightenment*, vol. 1, 341–42.

115. For more information about the sixteen aspects, see Jeffrey Hopkins, *Meditation on Emptiness* (Somerville, MA: Wisdom Publications, 1996), 292–96, and the Dalai Lama and Thubten Chodron, *Saṃsāra, Nirvāṇa, and Buddha Nature*, 19–37. Note that there are variations in the way the sixteen aspects are paired with the mistaken conceptions.

116. In the explanation of the sixteen aspects that is common to all Buddhist schools, the third aspect of true sufferings—that they are empty—refers to the emptiness of a permanent, unitary, and independent self, and the fourth aspect—that they are selfless—refers to the emptiness of a self-sufficient, substantially existent self. But according to the unique explanation of the Prasangika school, both aspects—empty and selfless—refer to the absence of inherent existence.

117. An alternative explanation is that meditating on the aspect of being empty

counteracts seeing the aggregates as pure and clean. See the Dalai Lama and Thubten Chodron, *Saṃsāra, Nirvāṇa, and Buddha Nature*, 23–25.

118. For more information about these meditative absorptions, see Lati Rinbochay and Denma Lochö Rinbochay, *Meditative States in Tibetan Buddhism* (Boston: Wisdom Publications, 1983).

119. Shantideva, *A Guide*, translated by Stephen Batchelor, 29–33.

120. Lama Zopa Rinpoche, *How to Be Happy* (Somerville, MA: Wisdom Publications, 2008), 76.

Glossary

A

absorption. See meditative absorption.

afflictions. See delusions.

aggregates. The body-mind complex that makes up a living being, composed mainly of five factors: form, feelings, discriminations, compositional factors, and consciousness. Beings in the formless realm have only the latter four aggregates.

altar. An arrangement, on a table or shelf, of representations of the body, speech, and mind of the Buddha, along with the offerings that a practitioner makes to them.

arhat. Foe destroyer; a person who has attained liberation.

arya. Noble one; superior being; a person who has attained the wisdom directly realizing emptiness.

asura. A being in one of the fortunate realms; also known as demigods or jealous gods, they frequently wage war on the devas.

Atisha. Eleventh-century Indian scholar and meditator who spent the last seventeen years of his life in Tibet; author of many works, including *A Lamp for the Path to Enlightenment*, the first lamrim text.

B

bardo. Literally, *intermediate state* in Tibetan; the state between the end of one life and the beginning of the next, during which beings have a subtle body that can travel to another place as soon as they think of it.

beginningless lives/mind/time. According to the Buddha, the various worlds and their inhabitants arise due to karma, not a creator, and there is no ultimate beginning to everything. Individual worlds come into existence and go out of existence in a cyclic manner; beings are born, die, and then are reborn.

bodhichitta. The aspiration to become a buddha in order to benefit all beings, stemming from genuine, universal love and compassion.

bodhisattva. A person who has developed spontaneous bodhichitta and is completely dedicated to helping others and to becoming a buddha for the benefit of all beings.

buddha. An awakened one; a fully enlightened being; one who has completely abandoned all obscurations and is fully developed in wisdom and compassion and thus capable of perfectly benefiting every being. The buddha of this age is known as Shakyamuni.

buddha nature. The innate potential of every being to become fully enlightened.

buddhafield. Buddha land; pure land; a place manifested by a buddha where sentient beings can take birth and have favorable conditions for becoming enlightened. The best-known example is Sukhavati, the pure land of Buddha Amitabha.

buddhahood. See enlightenment.

C

calm abiding (Sanskrit: *shamatha*). Also translated as *tranquility* or *serenity*; an advanced state of concentration in which the mind can remain on its chosen object as long as desired, free of restlessness and laxity.

cause and effect. See karma.

Chenrezig (Sanskrit: *Avalokiteshvara*). The Buddha of compassion.

compassion. The wish for beings to be free of suffering and its causes; one of the principal causes of bodhichitta.

compositional action. The second of the twelve links of dependent arising; actions done under the influence of ignorance and in a complete way, such that they have the power to cause another rebirth.

compositional factors. The fourth aggregate; includes all mental factors other than feelings and discriminations.

concentration. A mental factor enabling the mind to remain one-pointedly on its object.

consciousness. Another term for mind; the fifth aggregate. There are six types: eye, ear, nose, tongue, body, and mental consciousnesses.

contaminated. Under the influence of delusions, especially the ignorance that grasps things as inherently existent.

conventional existence/reality. The way things exist conventionally or relatively. According to the Prasangika school, it is the only way things can exist because nothing exists ultimately—ultimate existence is a synonym of inherent existence.

conventional truth. According to the Prasangika school, this is anything that exists other than emptiness.

cyclic existence. See samsara.

D

Dalai Lama, His Holiness the. Spiritual leader of the Tibetan people, recognized as the human manifestation of Avalokiteshvara, the buddha of compassion. The current Dalai Lama, fourteenth in the lineage, was born in 1935 and lives in Dharamsala, India.

delusions. Disturbing mental states; mental afflictions; six root and twenty secondary delusions are studied in Tibetan Buddhism. See appendix 5.

dependent arising/dependent origination. Arising or existing in dependence on other things; applies to all phenomena and is the foremost reason for proving that things are empty of inherent, independent existence.

desire realm. One of three principal realms in samsara—the other two being the form and formless realms—in which the beings are preoccupied with desire for objects of the five senses.

deva. A being, sometimes translated as god, born in a fortunate realm due to virtuous karma. There are various deva realms within the desire, form, and formless realms.

Dharma. That which protects from suffering; one of the Three Jewels Buddhists take refuge in; spiritual teachings and practices. The actual Dharma consists of true cessations and true paths.

dhyana (Pali: *jhana*). One of the four levels of meditative absorption of the form realm.

discriminations. The third aggregate; a mental factor that apprehends the characteristics of objects and distinguishes one object from another.

duhkha. Suffering; unsatisfactoriness.

E

eight types of suffering. Birth, aging, illness, death, separation from what is pleasant, meeting with what is unpleasant, not getting what we want, and having contaminated aggregates.

eight worldly concerns. Also known as eight worldly dharmas; the eight are concern about material gain and loss, pleasure and pain, praise and blame, and fame and lack of fame.

empowerment. Also known as initiation; the entrance to tantric practice; a ritual conducted by a Vajrayana master that allows disciples to engage in tantric meditation practices.

emptiness. The absence of a false mode of existence superimposed by ignorance. According to Madhyamaka Prasangika, it is the absence of inherent existence, objective existence, independent existence, and so on—terms that are synonymous—and is the ultimate truth, the actual way everything exists.

enlightenment. Also known as awakening or buddhahood; can also refer to liberation (Sanskrit: *nirvana*). Enlightenment in the sense of buddhahood is the state of being free of all defilements and obscurations and perfected in all positive qualities.

F

faith. Also known as confidence or trust; a virtuous mental factor that has confidence in someone or something endowed with excellent qualities and abilities. See appendix 5 for the three types of faith.

foe destroyer. See arhat.

form realm. A realm in samsara with four main levels that are subdivided for a total of seventeen levels; beings are born there as a result of training in certain practices, such as the *dhyanas,* on the basis of calm abiding; its inhabitants are devas with subtle bodies, long lives, and little suffering.

formless realm. The highest realm in samsara, which has four levels; birth there is due to training in special practices on the basis of calm abiding; its inhabitants are devas who possess only four of the five aggregates—they do not have a physical body.

four elements. Earth, water, fire, and air. According to Buddhism, these are four properties of all physical phenomena: the earth element is the property of solidity, the water element is the property of cohesion, the fire element is the property of heat, and the air element is the property of expansion.

four noble truths. The four truths of aryas: true suffering, true causes or origins of suffering, true cessation of suffering and its causes, and true paths that lead to that cessation.

four opponent powers. Four attitudes and practices used to purify nonvirtuous karma: regret, reliance, remedy, and resolve.

FPMT. Acronym for the Foundation of the Preservation of the Mahayana Tradition, founded in 1975 by Lama Thubten Yeshe, and under the spiritual guidance of Lama Zopa Rinpoche for thirty-nine years until his passing in 2023.

G

geshe. Literally, *virtuous friend* in Tibetan; a title conferred on those who have completed an extensive course of study in Gelug monastic universities.

graduated path to enlightenment (Tibetan: *lamrim*). Buddhist teachings outlining the progressive stages of development on the path to buddhahood, originally articulated by the eleventh-century Indian master Atisha.

great compassion. The type of compassion cultivated by a bodhisattva in which they not only wish all beings to be free of suffering but feel committed to bring this about.

great love. The type of love developed by a bodhisattva in which they wish all beings without exception to have happiness and its causes and are dedicated to bringing this about.

guru (Tibetan: *lama,* meaning "heavy with qualities"). Spiritual teacher.

H

Heart Sutra. A short Perfection of Wisdom (Sanskrit: Prajnaparamita) Sutra that is commonly recited in Mahayana Buddhist monasteries and temples and explains the emptiness of inherent existence of all phenomena.

hungry ghost (Sanskrit: *preta*). A being born in one of the three unfortunate realms as a result of nonvirtuous karma and subject to prolonged and intense hunger and thirst.

I

ignorance. A mental factor that is a state of unknowing brought about by lack of clarity about things such as the four noble truths, karma, and the Three Jewels. It is of various types, including ignorance of karma and ignorance that is the conception grasping things to exist inherently—the latter of which is the principal cause of suffering and cycling in samsara.

impermanence. The changing nature of all things arising from causes and conditions. It has two aspects: (1) coarse impermanence is the death or destruction of something, and (2) subtle impermanence refers to the imperceptible changes that occur each moment and cause coarse impermanence.

inherent existence. According to the Prasangika school, a false mode of existence projected by ignorance onto the self and all other phenomena. Synonymous with independent existence, true existence, objective existence, existence from its own side, and so on.

K

karma. Literally, *action* in Sanskrit. The law of cause and effect; the natural process whereby virtuous actions of body, speech, and mind lead to happiness and nonvirtuous ones to suffering.

karmic seeds. Imprints left on the mind or consciousness after doing an action; they have the potency to cause future experiences.

kaya. One of four types of "bodies" of a buddha: wisdom truth body, nature truth body, enjoyment body, and emanation body.

L

lama. See guru.

lamrim. See graduated path to enlightenment.

liberation. Nirvana; the state of being free from samsara—that is, free of suffering and its causes.

lojong. See thought transformation.

lorig. Mind and awareness; a subject of study comprising the various types of minds and mental factors.

love. Loving-kindness; the heartfelt wish for sentient beings to have happiness and its causes.

M

Madhyamaka. Literally, *middle way* in Sanskrit. A school of Buddhist philosophy founded by Nagarjuna that rejects true existence; it has two subschools, Prasangika and Svatantrika.

Mahayana. Literally, *Great Vehicle* in Sanskrit. A division of Buddhism in which the ultimate goal is the attainment of full enlightenment, buddhahood, for the benefit of all beings.

main mind. Also known as primary mind; one of the six types of consciousness; cognizes the mere presence of its object and is always accompanied by mental factors.

Maitreya. A being who is regarded as a buddha or a high bodhisattva predicted to be the next buddha who will teach the Dharma in our world; purported author of five classic texts of the Nalanda tradition.

mandala. Literally, *circle* in Sanskrit. A circular diagram depicting the universe; a practice of mentally offering the entire universe to the objects of refuge; in tantra, the pure environment of a tantric deity.

mantra. Literally, *protection for the mind* in Sanskrit. Syllables, usually Sanskrit, recited during certain meditation practices, such as the visualization of Shakyamuni Buddha on p. 35.

meditation (Tibetan: *gom*). Literally, *familiarization* in Tibetan. The process of becoming deeply acquainted with positive states of mind.

meditative absorption (Sanskrit: *samapatti*; Tibetan: *nyomjuk*). An advanced state of single-pointed meditation, such as those of the form and formless realms.

mental factor. An aspect of the mind that accompanies a main mind and apprehends specific characteristics of the object. See appendix 5.

merit. Virtuous karma created by avoiding nonvirtue and acting virtuously; the cause of happiness and fortunate rebirths. It nourishes the attainment of realizations needed to progress on the path to liberation and enlightenment.

method. One of the two principal aspects of practice on the path, the other being wisdom; for bodhisattvas, method includes cultivating bodhichitta and practicing the first five perfections.

mind. That which is clear and knowing; synonymous with consciousness; a nonphysical part of us that perceives, thinks, remembers, feels emotions, and so on.

mindfulness. A mental factor that remembers a familiar object, such as an object of meditation, virtue and nonvirtue, advice given by our teacher, and so on, and prevents the mind being distracted from it; essential in the practice of meditation.

monastic. A monk or nun; a person who has taken lifelong precepts established by the Buddha, including celibacy, and wears robes.

Mount Meru. According to ancient Indian cosmology, the center of the universe.

N

Nagarjuna. Second-century Indian master who wrote numerous texts and founded the Madhyamaka school.

Nalanda. A Buddhist monastic university that flourished in northern India from the fifth through twelfth centuries.

negative state of mind. See delusions.

nirvana. See liberation.

nonvirtue. States of mind and actions that cause unfortunate rebirths and suffering.

O

object of negation. Something to be negated or eliminated in, for example, meditation on selflessness. There are different objects of negation according to the assertions of the various Buddhist schools of philosophy. In the Prasangika school, the main object of negation is inherent existence, which does not exist and is negated by reasoning, but Tsongkhapa says there are objects of negation that do exist—such as the two types of obscurations—and are negated by the path.

obscurations. Also known as obstructions or stains. These are of two types: (1) obscurations that prevent liberation, known as deluded obscurations or afflictive obscurations, which consist of delusions and their seeds; and (2) obscurations that prevent full enlightenment, known as obscurations to knowledge or cognitive obscurations. According to the Prasangika, these consist of the subtle imprints or latencies of delusions, especially ignorance.

omniscience. Directly perceiving all phenomena—conventional truths and ultimate truths—simultaneously, in each moment. A quality of a buddha's mind.

P

Pali. A language of ancient India. The Pali canon consists of the Buddha's teachings preserved in the Pali language and mainly used by Theravada Buddhists.

path. A realization in the mind of a practitioner who has at least attained uncontrived renunciation—the determination to be free of samsara.

perfection (Sanskrit: *paramita*). One of six or ten practices of a bodhisattva performed for the attainment of enlightenment.

pliancy. One of the eleven virtuous mental factors; mental suppleness or flexibility that enables the mind to focus on a constructive object for an extended period of time, free of mental or physical rigidity.

Prasangika. Literally, *consequentialist* in Sanskrit. One of two subschools of Madhyamaka or its followers; unlike the followers of the other Madhyamaka subschool, Svatantrika, the Prasangika reject inherent existence, even conventionally.

Pratimoksha. Literally, *individual liberation* in Sanskrit. Various sets of precepts taken by both monastics and laypeople to guard their ethical behavior and create the cause for liberation.

precepts. Also known as vows; commitments undertaken by those who seriously wish to follow the Buddhist path—for example, promising to refrain from killing, stealing, lying and so on. There are three main types of precepts taken within three levels of practice: Pratimoksha precepts for the attainment of liberation; bodhisattva precepts for the attainment of full enlightenment; and tantric precepts, taken at the time of receiving empowerment in the two higher classes of tantra, and also kept for the attainment of full enlightenment.

pure land. See buddhafield.

R

refuge. The attitude of relying upon someone or something for guidance and help; in Buddhism one takes refuge in the Three Jewels: Buddha, Dharma, and Sangha.

renunciation. Also known as the determination to be free. The attitude aspiring to be free of samsara, recognizing that it is in the nature of suffering and devoid of genuine happiness or satisfaction.

S

samsara. Cyclic existence; the cycle of death and rebirth, fraught with suffering and dissatisfaction, that arises from ignorance of the true nature of reality. It is divided into either six realms—three unfortunate realms (hell, hungry ghost, and animal) and three fortunate realms (human, asura, and deva)—or into three realms (desire, form, and formless).

Sangha. One of the Three Jewels of refuge; the actual Sangha are arya beings, those who have attained true paths and true cessations, but the term *Sangha* is also used for a community of four or more fully ordained monastics. Both serve as objects of refuge.

selflessness. The absence of a type of self mistakenly conceived to exist by ignorance; used interchangeably with *emptiness.*

sentient being. Any being with a mind who has not yet attained full enlightenment.

seven limbs. A sevenfold practice for accumulating merit and purifying negativities: prostrating, offering, confessing, rejoicing, requesting the buddhas to not pass away, requesting the buddhas to teach the Dharma, and dedicating merit.

Shakyamuni Buddha. Born as a prince in the Shakya family in India approximately 2,500 years ago, the "Sage of the Shakyas" renounced his kingdom and achieved enlightenment, teaching the path until he passed away at age eighty.

Shantideva. Eighth-century Indian master; author of *A Guide to the Bodhisattva's Way of Life* (*Bodhicarayavatara*).

six types of suffering. Uncertainty, dissatisfaction, having to die again and again, being born again and again, going from high to low again and again, and being alone.

T

taking and giving (Tibetan: *tonglen*). A meditation practice for cultivating love, compassion, and bodhichitta in which one visualizes *taking* on the suffering of others and using it to overcome self-centeredness, then *giving* to others one's happiness and fortunate circumstances.

tantra. Vajrayana; Mantrayana; an advanced form of Mahayana Buddhism with special techniques, such as working with subtle energy-winds in the body, used for the swift attainment of enlightenment.

Tara. A buddha in female form representing all enlightened beings' skillful activities. She appears in various forms, such as Green Tara and White Tara.

Theravada. Tradition of Buddhism followed in Southeast Asian countries such as Sri Lanka, Thailand, and Burma.

thought transformation (Tibetan: *lojong*). A genre of Mahayana teachings and practices for transforming one's thoughts, attitudes, and behavior from selfishness to bodhichitta.

three higher trainings. Ethics, concentration, and wisdom practiced with renunciation of samsara.

Three Jewels. The objects of Buddhist refuge: Buddha, Dharma, and Sangha.

three poisons. The three main delusions: attachment, anger, and ignorance of karma.

three principal aspects of the path. A way of summarizing the main points of the lamrim into three: renunciation, bodhichitta, and the right view of emptiness.

three types of suffering. Experienced throughout samsara, they are the suffering of suffering, the suffering of change, and the pervasive suffering of conditionality.

throwing karma. Also called projecting karma; the karmic imprint left by a complete action that has the power to propel us into another rebirth.

tonglen. See taking and giving.

true existence. For the Prasangika, a synonym of inherent existence and existence from its own side.

Tsongkhapa. Fourteenth-century Tibetan scholar, teacher, meditator, and author; founder of the Gelug school of Tibetan Buddhism.

twelve links of dependent arising. A system of twelve factors involved in our continued rebirth in samsara.

two truths. A system outlining two levels of reality: the conventional, or relative, and the ultimate. *See also* conventional truth; ultimate truth.

U

ultimate truth. According to the Prasangika, the emptiness of inherent existence; the actual way all things exist. *See also* conventional truth; two truths.

V

Vajrayana. The path of tantra; one of two divisions of Mahayana, the other being Sutrayana. Both are practiced to attain enlightenment for the benefit of all beings. *See also* Mahayana; tantra.

virtue. Mental states and actions that are the cause of fortunate rebirths and positive experiences.

vows. See precepts.

W

wheel of Dharma. An ancient symbol in India with various meanings and numbers of spokes; used as a symbol for the Buddha's teachings. The Buddha is said to have "turned the wheel of Dharma" when he gave his first discourse, the *Dhammacakkappavattana Sutta,* or *Setting in Motion the Wheel of the Dhamma.*

wisdom. A mental factor, also known as intelligence, that analyzes things to understand their various characteristics; insight into the reality, or truth, of things; for the Prasangika, the principal wisdom is the realization of emptiness of inherent existence; this wisdom is the antidote to ignorance.

Suggested Further Reading

Introductory Books

Chodron, Thubten. *Open Heart, Clear Mind*. Snow Lion.

The Dalai Lama and Thubten Chodron. *Approaching the Buddhist Path*. Wisdom.

Khema, Ayya. *Being Nobody, Going Nowhere*. Wisdom.

Kornfield, Jack. *A Path with Heart*. Bantam.

McDonald, Kathleen. *How to Meditate*. Wisdom.

Rahula, Walpola. *What the Buddha Taught*. Grove Press.

Wallace, Alan. *Tibetan Buddhism from the Ground Up*. Wisdom.

Yeshe, Lama Thubten, and Lama Thubten Zopa Rinpoche. *Wisdom Energy*. Wisdom.

Books on Lamrim

Short

The Dalai Lama. *Becoming Enlightened*. Atria.

The Dalai Lama. *How to See Yourself as You Really Are*. Atria.

The Dalai Lama. *The Way to Freedom*. Harper.

Rinchen, Geshe Sonam. *The Thirty-Seven Practices of Bodhisattvas*. Snow Lion.

Rinchen, Geshe Sonam. *The Three Principal Aspects of the Path*. Snow Lion.

Yeshe, Lama Thubten. *The Essence of Tibetan Buddhism*. Lama Yeshe Wisdom Archives.

Medium-Length

The Dalai Lama. *The Path to Enlightenment*. Snow Lion.

Jampa, Gyumed Khensur Lobsang. *The Easy Path*. Wisdom.

Rinchen, Geshe Sonam. *Atisha's Lamp for the Path to Enlightenment*. Snow Lion.

Tsondru, Yeshe. *The Essential Nectar.* Commentary by Geshe Rabten. Wisdom.

Tsongkhapa. *The Middle-Length Treatise on the Stages of the Path to Enlightenment.* Wisdom.

Yeshé, Panchen Losang. *The Swift Path.* Wisdom.

Long

The Dalai Lama and Thubten Chodron: The Library of Wisdom and Compassion Series. Wisdom.

    Vol. 1: *Approaching the Buddhist Path*
    Vol. 2: *The Foundation of Buddhist Practice*
    Vol. 3: *Saṃsāra, Nirvāṇa, and Buddha Nature*
    Vol. 4: *Following in the Buddha's Footsteps*
    Vol. 5: *In Praise of Great Compassion*
    Vol. 6: *Courageous Compassion*
    Vol. 7: *Searching for the Self*
    Vol. 8: *Realizing the Profound View*
    Vol. 9: *Appearing and Empty*
    Vol. 10: *Vajrayāna and the Culmination of the Path*

Jinpa, Thupten, translator. *The Stages of the Path and the Oral Transmission.* Wisdom.

Loden, Acharya Geshe Thubten. *The Path to Enlightenment in Tibetan Buddhism.* Tushita.

Pabongka Rinpoche. *Liberation in the Palm of Your Hand.* Wisdom.

Sopa, Geshe Lhundrup. *Steps on the Path to Enlightenment.* 5 volumes. Wisdom.

Tsong-kha-pa. *The Great Treatise on the Stages of the Path to Enlightenment.* 3 volumes. Snow Lion.

Index

of spiritual teachers, 297–98,
299–300
ethics, higher training in, 162,
166–68
ethics, perfection of, 237, 346
benefits and disadvantages, contemplating, 238–39
three ways of practicing, 239–41
excitement, 265, 266, 339
existence (becoming), link of, 312

F
faith, 89, 260
lack of, 339
mental factor of (three kinds), 337
of non-Buddhists, 113
refuge and, 94, 96–97
in spiritual teachers, 304
fear, 214, 324
of death, 128–29, 153
in everyday life, 345, 347
during meditation, 126, 223
refuge and, 89, 94, 95–96
and self, sense of, 173, 232, 287, 290
at time of death, 71, 73, 75, 312
feelings
link of, 310–11
mental factor of, 335, 336
three types, 310–11, 354n83
five extreme negative actions, 58
forgetfulness, 266, 339
forgiveness, 113, 144, 181, 189, 191,
249
form body (rupakaya), 230
form realm, 325, 327
formless realm, 325, 327, 350n22
fortunate rebirth
aspiring for, 65
creating causes of, 59, 64, 75, 77
ethics and, 165, 238

ripened result of, 111
Foundation for the Preservation of
the Mahayana Tradition, 21
Foundation of Buddhist Practice (Dalai
Lama and Thubten Chodron),
298
four elements, 155, 352n62
four great rivers of suffering, 40
four immeasurables, 19, 24, 37–38
four noble truths, 6, 92, 319
contemplating, 125–26
distinctions between, 159
sixteen aspects of (chart), 329–30
translations of, 351n45
See also true cessations; true origins; true paths; true sufferings
four opponent powers, 25, 105,
112–15, 303

G
generosity, 62, 231, 260
generosity, perfection of, 231, 346
benefits of, 231–34
three kinds of giving, 234–35
"Glance Meditation on All the
Important Points of Lamrim"
(Losang Jinpa), 43, 117, 169
god realms, 135, 350n22
gods, long-life, 56, 350n22
graduated path to enlightenment
(lamrim), 21
benefits, 3–4
intended audience, 21–22
meaning of term, xii
meditations, general outline for,
35–39, 41–42
motivation for, 35
order of, 19–20, 21–22
recitation, optional, 39–41
resources of, xiii

virtuous actions
damaging, 104, 105
ignorance and, 173–74
twelve links and, 316–17
See also ten virtuous actions
visualizations, 17–18, 19, 35–37, 39,
41–42
vows. *See* precepts and vows

W
wealth and material possessions, 19,
63, 322, 332
attachment to, 40, 67, 339, 340
generosity of, 234, 346
as motivation, 65
at time of death, 53–54, 71, 72, 78,
233
wisdom, 62
benefits of, 276–78
discriminating, 302
higher training in, 162, 300, 319
hindrances to, 143
mental factor of, 337
natural, 270
qualities that supplement, 159
role of, 269
See also acquired wisdom, three
types

wisdom, perfection of, 263, 347
other perfections and, 269–70
three kinds of wisdom in, 271
See also selflessness
wisdom directly realizing emptiness,
137–38, 166, 263
developing, 317
perfections and, 270
time in attaining, 328
as true path, 162, 326
as ultimate antidote, 159, 161, 271,
324
wisdom truth body (*jnana dharmakaya*), 92, 230
wrong views, 41, 57, 105, 107, 333

Y
Yeshe, Lama Thubten, 21, 101, 256,
327

Z
Zopa Rinpoche, Lama
on aggregates and self, 291
on bodhisattvas, 253
on buddhas and bodhisattvas, love
of, 346
on eight freedoms, 55
Power of Meditation, 29

About the Author

Originally from California, Kathleen McDonald (Sangye Khadro) began studying Buddhism with Tibetan lamas in Dharamsala, India, in 1973. She became a nun in Nepal the following year, and received full (*bhikshuni*) ordination in 1988. At the request of her teachers, she began teaching in 1980, and since then has been teaching Buddhism and meditation in various countries around the world, occasionally taking time off for personal retreats. She served as resident teacher in Buddha House, Australia, for two years and in Amitabha Buddhist Centre in Singapore for eleven years. From 2008 to 2013 she followed the Masters Program at Lama Tsong Khapa Institute in Italy. Since then she served for seven years as a faculty member of the Human Spirit Psychoanalytic-Buddhist Training Program in Israel, and for a year and a half as the resident teacher at the Center for Wisdom and Compassion in Copenhagen, Denmark. She currently resides at Sravasti Abbey in Washington State, USA, and teaches online.

What to Read Next
from Wisdom Publications

How to Meditate
A Practical Guide
Kathleen McDonald

"Jewels of wisdom and practical experience to inspire you."
—Richard Gere

Awakening the Kind Heart
How to Meditate on Compassion
Kathleen McDonald

"Through clear explanations, straightforward practices, and basic
goodheartedness, this book explains how to navigate the path to love,
even under very trying circumstances. Truly, there is nothing more
needed at this time—our very future may depend upon it."
—Susan Piver, author of *The Wisdom of a Broken Heart*

Buddhism
One Teacher, Many Traditions
His Holiness the Dalai Lama and Thubten Chodron

Winner of an IndieFab Award from *Foreword Reviews*

Introduction to Tantra
The Transformation of Desire
Lama Thubten Yeshe

"The best introductory work on Tibetan Buddhist tantra available
today."
—Janet Gyatso, Harvard University

The Library of Wisdom and Compassion series (10 volumes)
The Dalai Lama with Thubten Chodron

In this series, His Holiness the Dalai Lama shares the Buddha's teachings on the complete path to full awakening that he himself has practiced his entire life. The topics are arranged especially for people seeking practical spiritual advice and are peppered with the Dalai Lama's own unique outlook. Assisted by his long-term disciple, the American nun Thubten Chodron, the Dalai Lama sets the context for practicing the Buddha's teachings in modern times and then unveils the path of wisdom and compassion that leads to a meaningful life and sense of personal fulfillment. This series is an important bridge from introductory to profound topics for those seeking an in-depth explanation from a contemporary perspective.

Steps on the Path to Enlightenment series (5 volumes)
A Commentary on Tsongkhapa's Lamrim Chenmo
Geshe Lhundub Sopa

"An indispensable companion to Tsongkhapa's elegant and elaborate Great Exposition on the Stages of the Path."—*Buddhadharma*

About Wisdom Publications

Wisdom Publications is the leading publisher of classic and contemporary Buddhist books and practical works on mindfulness. To learn more about us or to explore our other books, please visit our website at wisdom.org or contact us at the address below.

Wisdom Publications
132 Perry Street
New York, NY 10014 USA

We are a 501(c)(3) organization, and donations in support of our mission are tax deductible.

Wisdom Publications is affiliated with the Foundation for the Preservation of the Mahayana Tradition (FPMT).